IN MY
GRANDFATHER'S
SHADOW

IN MY GRANDFATHER'S SHADOW

A story of war, trauma
and the legacy of silence

ANGELA FINDLAY

BANTAM PRESS

TRANSWORLD PUBLISHERS
Penguin Random House, One Embassy Gardens,
8 Viaduct Gardens, London SW11 7BW
www.penguin.co.uk

Transworld is part of the Penguin Random House group of companies
whose addresses can be found at global.penguinrandomhouse.com

Penguin
Random House
UK

First published in Great Britain in 2022 by Bantam Press
an imprint of Transworld Publishers

A CIP catalogue record for this book
is available from the British Library.

ISBNs 9781787634060 (cased)
9781787634077 (tpb)

Typeset in 12/15 pt by Granjon LT Std by Jouve (UK), Milton Keynes.
Printed and bound in Great Britain by Clays Ltd, Elcograf S.p.A.

The authorized representative in the EEA is Penguin Random House Ireland,
Morrison Chambers, 32 Nassau Street, Dublin D02 YH68.

Penguin Random House is committed to a sustainable
future for our business, our readers and our planet. This book
is made from Forest Stewardship Council® certified paper.

MIX
Paper from
responsible sources
FSC® C018179

1

The past is never dead. It's not even past.
William Faulkner, *Requiem for a Nun*

For my mother, with love

This book is dedicated to all those whose lives
are affected by discrimination, oppression or war

Contents

Contents

Author's Note

There have been many times in the course of writing this book when I have felt as if a rip tide has sucked me out of my depth into an ocean of infinite darkness. Navigating the unfathomable horrors and sensibilities of this most heinous of episodes in history, I have focused on the aspects that intimately touched my family in the sincere hope of finding a way to comprehend this epoch and to contribute something of worth to the huge efforts made by others before me.

Although there are things in my experience of the world that I find regrettable, looking back over the totality of my life, I have few regrets. On the contrary, I feel deep gratitude for the challenges and broader perspectives my dual heritage has afforded me. And a strange sense of triumph for having stayed true to my soul through the noisy battles. I am thankful to have been granted such valuable opportunities for growth and transformation. For the rich odyssey I had to undertake to dive down through the layers of my humanness to reach my genes. For the amazing people and beautiful places I have encountered along the way. And for the lightness and freedom I now feel.

No, I love my life, even though at times it nearly killed me.

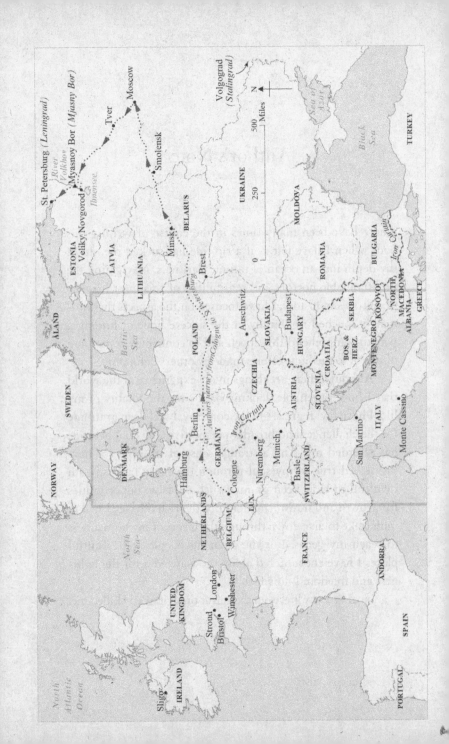

Prologue

To be ignorant of what occurred before you were born is to remain always a child. For what is the worth of human life unless it is woven into the life of our ancestors by the records of history?

Marcus Tullius Cicero, *Orator ad M. Brutum*

1 February 1945

I N THE SMALL GERMAN town of Jüterbog, a mother shakes awake her ten-year-old daughter. It's 4 a.m. The little girl, barely conscious, is told to get dressed quickly. They must leave now. She may choose one doll to bring with her. She hesitates. Should she take her old, love-worn doll or the new one her father sent from Italy? In a snap decision she will come to regret, she grabs the new doll before being bundled into the car with her eight-year-old sister and driven north to Berlin. Large parts of the city are already smouldering.

It is still dark when they reach the railway station several hours later. The mother looks round, scanning the bustling mass of coated strangers for one particular person: a man carrying a rucksack with six pockets. He will escort her children to the safety of their relatives in the north.

The younger child is hungry and complains that her shoes hurt. The woman is looking for somewhere to buy bread when she sees the man. He urges them towards the platform. The mother, clutching a small suitcase in one hand and her younger daughter's hand in the other, tells the elder girl to hold on tight to the hem of her coat, so that she doesn't get lost. As the trio inches forward amid the jostling crowd scrambling to board the train out of the city, the child hangs for dear life on to this extension of her mother.

2 May 1945

In the guesthouse of the sleepy Italian hamlet of La Stanga, on the edge of the Dolomites, a fifty-two-year-old Wehrmacht general stares into the embers of last night's fire and drags tobacco smoke into his lungs. He holds it there longer than usual before throwing his cigarette butt into the ashes and stepping out into the cool May morning. Straightening his belted overcoat, he pulls down the peak of his officer's hat to cast his eyes in shadow. Hitler has been dead for three days and representatives of the German command in Italy have signed an unconditional surrender. Today, at 2 p.m., it will come into effect. His war is finally over, but he knows that he and his men will not be going home.

First he will negotiate the handover of arms, horses and soldiers with the American infantry located a little to the west. He will ask that his men – some eight divisions and 30,000 troops – are allowed to keep their rifles to defend themselves against the Italian bandits still firing in the mountains. And then he will organize transport, petrol and rations.

The mountain air feels fresh but it will be much warmer further south. His latest billet has been comfortable but, as prisoners of war, he and his troops will be housed outside regardless of the heat. Placing one leather-booted foot in front of the other, just as he has done for thousands of miles across Russia, he walks towards his new commanders.

3 August 1987

Outside Long Bay Gaol in Sydney, Australia, a twenty-two-year-old woman bangs on the heavy door. She is carrying a portfolio containing photographs of murals, and the black fabric sticks to the bare skin of her arm. A small shutter flicks open and an eye quickly looks her up and down before blinking closed again. The door opens, just enough to allow her small frame to slip through. Inside, a guard escorts her across the cobbled courtyard and through a series of locked gates. It is then that she can smell them, the men: old socks, rancid stubble, stifled testosterone. As the guard leads the way into another courtyard, overlooked by more barred windows, she begins to relax. Four prisoners stand in front of a huge blank wall, squinting in the harsh sunlight. Any rising trepidation is quashed by a far greater sense of relief; the relief of kicking off uncomfortable walking boots at the end of a long trek.

For years she has been searching for a solution to her inexplicable sense of her own badness. 'This is it!' the cells of her body seem to sing in unison. 'This is it!'

Less than a minute after 'Little Boy' was released above Hiroshima, the world's first atomic bomb detonated. 'My God, what have we done?' one of the co-pilots of the plane that dropped it scribbled into his logbook as a lethal cloud instantly annihilated 80,000 Japanese people. Three days later, 'Fat Man' made its deadly descent on to Nagasaki to deal a final blow to the enemy. Within five weeks, the Second World War was officially over.

Except it wasn't.

Like the atomic fallout, the war persisted, invisibly

poisoning bodies and minds for generations. Like all armed conflicts, it left trauma in its wake. But in this, the deadliest war in history, civilian casualties far outweighed those of the military, and it was non-combatants who experienced the unequalled levels of destruction and depravity: men, women and children, many of whom, along with front-line veterans, found it impossible to speak about the horrors they had endured.

As the chaos of battle subsided, survivors accustomed to the threat of imminent death brushed themselves down and attempted to build a new normality from the ruined homes and flattened cities. In the Allied countries across Europe, the sting of personal loss and devastation was partially anaesthetized by the jubilation of victory. People found meaning in the sacrifices made by family and friends, and governments started the process of etching their narrative into the history books. It would be one of triumph over unprecedented evil, evoking national pride as the antidote to hardship. It would be a vindication of the tactical decisions that had left hundreds of thousands of civilians dead. It had all been worth it.

There was no such balm for the losses of the German people, just deeper shades of hatred as the world discovered the monstrous truth of Hitler's vision. Soldiers were rounded into barbed-wire encampments; Nazis, stripped of their telltale uniforms, blended into the moving mass of exhausted humanity fleeing westwards; civilians scavenged the wreckage of their cities for food and debris to burn to keep themselves warm. With the death of their Führer, the Nazi ideology and its promise of a thousand-year kingdom collapsed. Now the occupying enemy was throwing accusations of complicity rather than grenades. A fog of defiant silence descended over communities and families. With few on the victorious side interested in the suffering of their enemy, German men, women and children learned to wrap their experiences into bundles, seal them tightly and hide them away.

Decades later, children and grandchildren would find those bundles buried in the backs of family closets and begin to unpack them.

This is the story of three generations of one family, knotted together and woven into an episode of history that continues to appal and fascinate. The ten-year-old German girl fleeing the Soviet troops was my mother, Jutta. The German general was my grandfather, Karl. And I was the young woman who finally felt at home in a prison.

I never met my grandfather.

A week after I took my first breath, he took his last. But I always felt we connected during those few days when our lives overlapped. As he departed the world and I entered it, our paths crossed. And, like a relay racer passing on a baton, he handed me something. It would take me over four decades to discover that, just as we might inherit the physical or character traits of our forebears, we can inherit their unresolved emotions, traumas or crimes, too; that these do not simply disappear, but may remain festering among our roots ready to erupt into our present, seeking resolution.

My story is one of many emerging from the long shadows cast by violent conflict that wasn't personally experienced but none the less retains the power to shape a life.

In Germany, as the grandchildren of the war generation reached their forties around the turn of the new millennium, the full impact of their ancestors' guilty or traumatized silence began to surface. It was at this age that, I, too, a woman born and brought up in England, turned to my German origins to uncover the source of similar inexplicable feelings and symptoms that had plagued me since my teens.

My quest to understand these feelings took me into the dark terrain of Germany's Second World War. It led me into society's barred and locked institutions of crime and punishment and to the art and cultures of national remembrance. It also immersed me in the emotion that lurks in some of the most avoided or forgotten corners of the human psyche and experience: shame.

I found my way into history and into my mother's and grandfather's experiences, all of which had long been housed in straightforward black-and-white narratives of good and bad, perpetrator and victim, winner and loser, but which inevitably became more complex, challenging and nuanced the more I explored them. I learned that, to varying degrees, we all carry unprocessed traumas and wrongdoing from the past – whether familial, societal or historical. They sit in our unconscious, these untold stories, wanting to be heard and resolved.

In recent years, psychologists, geneticists and neurobiologists have begun to uncover mechanisms for the potential transmission of such apparently metaphysical baggage from one generation to another and to explore how it may contribute to contemporary epidemics of addiction, depression, ill health and division. Can inherited guilt or trauma trigger the rage of unacknowledged suffering that flares up on our streets in protests or conflicts? Do they perpetuate the systemic injustices born of slavery and colonialism? Do they shape attitudes and policies towards everything from the environment to wealth distribution to education? Perhaps, is the answer from all academic corners.

And then the burning question. Can we as individuals untangle ourselves from a past that binds us to the suffering and deeds of our predecessors? *In my Grandfather's Shadow* is the story of a woman who was determined to try.

1

A Perfect Childhood

Every war is a war against children.

Eglantyne Jebb, founder of Save the Children

Jutta von Graffen, my mother, 1936.

I NEVER DETECTED ANY DISTRESS in my mother when she told us stories about her childhood. She'd share them intermittently, punctuating our sunlit days with faded images from an altogether unfamiliar world. Time would stand still as she talked, and I'd follow each word, creating vivid pictures in

9

my mind, *feeling* my way deeper into this other time and place. Sometimes I'd look at her, trying to shrink her back into that little blonde girl. Or I'd slip into her stories, lining up the vignettes of her early life on the empty shelves of my memory, like souvenirs from a far-off land.

I remember standing by the back door to our house and hearing her describe being shot at from a plane.

'I saw the whites of the pilot's eyes,' she said, widening her own for effect, yet offering no sense of the fear she must once have felt. 'He flew over me, very low, as I was walking to school on my own. Then he aimed at me. And I had to jump into a ditch.'

I gasped, thinking of my own journey to school, always in a car, dropped off and picked up safely at the gate.

'But luckily he missed,' she concluded coolly, 'and hit my aunt's greenhouse instead.'

On another occasion she remembered the night-time bombings and how she and her siblings would watch the dark sky light up with the green and red flares of the target indicators – the 'Christmas trees', they called them. She often talked about food, too: the single weekly boiled egg shared by the family and the broad beans, grown huge but powdery, so that there were more to go round. She loved to recall the time she came home from school starving – just like we always seemed to do – and found a meatball in the larder. She knew it was naughty to help herself, but she couldn't resist the temptation. To her horror, as she bit into it, her mouth closed on a writhing mass of maggots.

Back then, her stories were simply that – stories; adventures like those in the books we read. It was only decades later, when the tragedy and trauma began to feel real, that I was struck by the lack of emotion my mother showed while telling them. There was no sense of self-pity or anguish as she described going with my grandmother to the local railway station to give water and coffee to wounded and dying soldiers returning from the Eastern Front. Even the moans of the men were recounted with strange detachment. I imagined her as little eight-year-old Jutta, stepping from row to row, bending over bandaged, bloodied bodies, holding a cup to their lips. When I asked her about it, she would shrug and say, 'That's just how it was back then.'

Her most dramatic story was the sudden departure from the family home in Jüterbog, just south of Berlin. We didn't know the context, just that when she was ten years old, she and her younger sister Dorothee, our Tante Dörli, were woken at four in the morning by their mother to be sent by train to their grandparents' farm, Wildenhorst, in Schleswig-Holstein in the north of Germany. The Russians were advancing rapidly from the east and everybody was trying to flee. Her mother and older sister, our Tante Marlen, followed a month or two later, abandoning their home and all they owned. Her fifteen-year-old brother, Adolf, had to stay behind to fight the Allies somewhere near Berlin.

In Schleswig-Holstein, the female members of the family resumed their lives as best they could. A tutor was hired, but fired soon afterwards for inappropriate behaviour. In a display of uncharacteristic and bold defiance, the usually shy eleven-year-old Jutta climbed on to the window ledge and threatened to jump if he laid a finger on her. She then attended a private school in Preetz, a five-mile walk away – the same route on which she was shot at from that plane – until a year later, when she moved with her mother and sisters to Grödersby, a house

11

on an inlet of the Baltic that had been in the family for 300 years. This house, like my great-grandparents', had been requisitioned to accommodate those displaced from their homes by the war and was full of refugees. But the family was allotted three rooms and a veranda. Most importantly, the girls were able to go to the local school.

In the years after the war, life revolved around survival: foraging for herbs and firewood and trying to keep the family fed. The winters were particularly bitter but, with a roof over their heads, they were among the luckiest ones. My mother finished her schooling and, chasing her dream of travelling the world as a glamorous Pan Am air stewardess, moved to Hamburg to study languages, eventually becoming fluent in five. She did not in the end join Pan Am, but set off on her own to live and work in Spain. A heady life of sun, sea and romance in Barcelona was curtailed by the offer of a job at the headquarters of the brand-new North Atlantic Treaty Organization – NATO – in the Château de Fontainebleau near Paris. By her mid-twenties, she was occupying one of the most prestigious secretarial positions in one of the hot spots of postwar Europe.

It was here, in a multicultural social whirl, that my parents met in 1961. Jutta had blossomed into a beautiful, gregarious, elegant, young woman, confident in her role as personal assistant to General Hans Speidel, the commander-in-chief of the Allied NATO ground forces. She was at ease with her responsibilities in this international society and pursued by many hopeful admirers. My father, Jonathan, a dashing British naval officer recently returned from service on Prince Philip's world tour aboard *HMS Britannia*, had a broad smile and a dark blue Jaguar. He was a little cocky but kind, and soon won my mother over with his sense of humour, fun and his impeccable manners.

My parents married in 1962 in a small church in north Germany near the family home. It was only later in my life that their marriage struck me as unusual. In the 1960s, a second series of Auschwitz trials was once again placing Germany's recent past in the spotlight as more details emerged of atrocities on a monumental scale. Europe had been sliced into East and West territories of opposing ideologies by an 'Iron Curtain' and irreconcilable tensions between the wartime Allies were escalating. Meanwhile, my parents were falling in love, inadvertently building bridges across the divides.

For their own parents, the marriage was initially challenging. Here was the daughter of a former Wehrmacht general and prisoner of war, whose wife had been forced to

My parents at their wedding in Germany, 1962.

flee the Allied bombings and advancing Soviet troops, being joined in matrimony to the son of a former naval officer turned organic farmer, who had fought the Germans in both world wars, and an aristocrat whose only brother, and heir to the family title, had been killed by Rommel's troops in North Africa. And yet they all put their personal feelings aside and embraced the union, overcoming language barriers with wild, gesticulating hand movements that sent crystal glasses flying off the dining table during their first meeting. My grandmothers would go on to develop a genuine friendship and fondness for each other that continued until their deaths, both at the age of ninety-six.

After my parents' honeymoon in Sicily, my father received an appointment to command the minesweeper *HMS Puncheston* in south-east Asia. The newlyweds relocated to Singapore. My mother, soon pregnant with my older sister, Caroline, gave up her secretarial role at NATO, although she would remain in close contact with her boss until his death. There was a huge community of British expats in Singapore and, with the luxury of domestic help to look after the children, my parents enjoyed an active social life. Many of the young couples became lifelong friends and settled with their families in the same area of southern England when their husbands finished serving at sea.

I was born in Kent two years later, a fat-faced baby with red cheeks, and my brother, Christopher, arrived two and half years after that. Our first years were nomadic, spent between a flat in London and with various relatives across England, Germany and Canada while my father served on ships on the other side of the world. In 1969, on his return to shore, we set up home in a small village in Hampshire.

The first ten years of my life were idyllic. My lasting memories are of seemingly endless summers passed clambering in the shady branches of the old yew tree in our garden or collecting shards of untypically flowery 'Roman' pottery buried among its roots; of practising handstands on the lawn and picking beans and lettuces from the neat rows of my father's vegetable patch.

With my mother at the helm, occasions were marked by a unique blend of traditional English and German customs. Birthdays were memorable not just for cake and games of Pass the Parcel, but for the crowns of seasonal flowers arranged around the celebrant's breakfast plate. Christmas, often spent with relatives in Germany, began in Hampshire with Advent. Each Sunday, lights were extinguished and candles lit, transforming the living room into a heavenly gallery of hand-painted wooden angels from my mother's childhood collection. We feasted by the fire on Stollen, *Lebkuchen* and *Spekulatius* cinnamon biscuits sent to us from Germany in brown packages.

Easter was usually celebrated at my English grandparents' farm, surrounded by lambs, cows and daffodils. My grandfather, a tall, white-haired gentleman with huge hands, had a garden shed that smelled of freshly cut grass and a wooden box filled with pink and white sugared almonds. Gran, considerably smaller, pottered around in tweed skirts with a handkerchief tucked into her waistband. We'd feed the chickens and walk through fields of sheep with her two spaniels, laughing and bleating at the gambolling lambs.

At the age of eleven, during the long hot summer of 1976, I was excited to be taken out of school early to spend six weeks on my own with my other grandmother in Hamburg in order to improve my German. She lived in a high-ceilinged, one-bedroom flat on the first floor of a three-storey house in a leafy suburb. It was painted charcoal grey and had balconies overlooking a quiet cobbled street at the front and an exotic garden filled with birdsong at the back.

There was a rhythmic routine to her day. Mummygroß (the correct word for grandma would be Großmami, but my sister mixed up her English and German words when she was tiny and the pet name stuck) woke early and, sitting at a beautifully laid breakfast table bedecked with a white cloth, drank several cups of strong black coffee and read the newspaper. While I was there, I joined her for bread rolls sprinkled with black poppy seeds, fresh from the bakery. In the mornings, we shopped for strawberries and white asparagus at the market under the railway bridge and in the afternoons, we walked beside the Alster, a tributary of the River Elbe, admiring the affluent white houses and sprinkled lawns that lined the residential streets.

I was fascinated by the incongruous, blackened spire that rose above the rooftops of the city centre in stark contrast to the modern cleanliness of the buildings below.

'That's the St Nicolai Church,' Mummygroß told me. 'It was badly bombed in the war.'

Then she gently turned my attention elsewhere.

I could talk to Mummygroß about anything – except the war. Whenever I asked about it, she would subtly change the subject, tucking my question into the folds of her starched linen napkin and placing it, neatly rolled in its silver ring, in a drawer. Her past was shielded by a veil of silence. It wasn't aggressively out of bounds, nor did it seep conspicuously into her present. It just existed behind the books that lined the pristine white shelves in her living room; under the foot pedal of her electric sewing machine; in the fridge where sugared raspberries would appear overnight.

I recall a family road trip through Germany the following year when the past broke momentarily into our present. Between sightseeing and visiting relatives, we stopped in a huge forest where a bare strip of land, flanked by a barbed-wire fence, stretched as far as we could see in both directions, punctuated only by watchtowers occupied by East German guards with guns. My grandmother and mother got out of the car and stood in a sad silence. Christopher and I – bored and unaware of the significance of our location – started mucking around, daring each other to jump in and out of no-man's-land, taunting the guards to notice us while giggling at our remarkable bravery. Then one of them raised his gun towards us and both adults, snapping out of their sorrowful reverie, scolded us for our stupidity.

It was Mummygroß who introduced us to German culture. She recited poems by Rilke and Goethe and took us to theatre productions and art exhibitions, activities she had enjoyed in Berlin with her husband before the war. She had moved to Hamburg after she was widowed and the family farm was sold in order to re-embrace the city life she had loved.

Very occasionally, my mother would give us glimpses of her late father. He had been a phenomenal athlete, winning numerous prizes – high jump, long jump, swimming, tennis, horse-riding, diving – and had nearly qualified for the 1936 Berlin Olympic Games. He was also a quality craftsman. It was he who had carved and painted the old wooden pictures of Hansel and Gretel and other fairytale characters that now hung on the walls of our bedrooms. He had an enviable talent for finding four-leafed clovers and had done a handstand on his sixtieth birthday. I knew that he had fought in the war and had spent much of the last twenty years of his life a 'broken man,' growing tomatoes and sitting in his chair overlooking the garden smoking seventy cigarettes a day, lighting one from the stub of the last.

For me, my grandfather existed only as the face of a man in uniform in a framed black-and-white photograph that stood on my mother's writing desk. It never struck me as strange that a German soldier presided over my mother's typewriter, envelopes and stamps. Until the evening of one of my parents' many dinner parties. My siblings and I were dressed in our best clothes, standing excitedly in the hallway, jumping at each strike of the brass knocker. It was

My mother's writing desk with her photo of my grandfather, taken in 1942.

Christopher's job to open the front door, I would take the guests' coats and Caroline would hand them a glass of sparkling wine. It was a well-oiled drill. But on this particular evening a woman followed me into my mother's study, where we were storing the coats. She saw my grandfather and her face paled.

'A bit tactless of Jutta to have a Nazi sitting on her writing desk!' she muttered to her husband before stretching a smile across her face and joining the other guests.

I knew the Nazis as the baddies in *The Sound of Music*, but I also knew from my parents that not all Germans were Nazis. And that my grandfather wasn't one. He was just a German soldier. But thereafter I began to notice the slightly panicked glances exchanged between certain people when they discovered our family's dual nationality.

For many children growing up in England in the sixties and seventies, it seemed that the Second World War felt an age away. But around families that included former enemies, the rumblings of conflict could still be heard. They were communicated in discreet elbow digs or resentments that leached out of the older generation. But they were definitely there, small incidents that sowed little question-marks in my mind.

My mother, who spoke English beautifully and with almost no accent, told me how a man with whom she had been in conversation at a social event had simply turned on his heel and walked off when she'd mentioned that she was German. On another occasion, after she returned home upset, my father quietly explained how someone had announced that 'the only good German is a dead German'. A boy in my brother's class taunted him by jeering 'Your mother is Mrs Hitler.' The grandmother of one of my friends refused to sit at their lunch table with me because of my nationality. And, when my mother set up a language school during the spring and summer holidays, attracting scores of young German students, employing countless locals as hosts and providing us children with full-time holiday jobs teaching English and co-ordinating leisure activities, it was the 'bloody Germans' that the village shop assistant complained about, regardless of the roaring trade in crisps and chocolate bars they brought her in the breaks between classes.

All of this concerned me. But one moment in particular crystallized in my mind as the first time I felt the chill of shame associated with my identity. The first time I felt different, excluded, othered.

I must have been ten or eleven. I had contracted impetigo and my mother had covered the affected red parts with pink, chalky calamine lotion – round the base of my nostrils, my top lip and chin – until my face resembled a badly decorated cupcake. I looked ridiculous. I was relieved when nobody commented on these unsightly blotches as I congregated with my friends outside the village shop. I almost convinced myself they hadn't noticed. But then someone made me laugh and the pink crust above my lip split. One of the older boys, spotting the red blood oozing through it, pointed at me: 'Oh look,' he exclaimed. 'She's bleeding!' And, with a loud guffaw, he added: 'Bloody Kraut!'

The others turned and laughed, and I did, too, dabbing at my mouth with the back of my hand, trying to stem the rising sense of mortification. I didn't fully understand the insult: I had only ever heard 'Kraut' used to describe a kind of pickled cabbage. But I knew that it had something to do with my heritage.

A quiet confusion began to take root. In my first year at boarding school – a perk paid for largely by the Navy but one that was anathema to my mother, who couldn't understand why parents should send away their children at such a young age – I was seen as bright, hard-working, popular and 'trendy'. By the second, however, my school reports painted me as aggressive, argumentative and failing to achieve my academic potential. I rejected the unfair advantage and privilege that were used by the school like sticks to beat an undeserved sense of superiority into us. I conspicuously flouted rules and vociferously challenged the teacher's demands for respect and obedience. And I arrogantly dismissed most subjects as irrelevant to any life beyond school. It was as if a stranger had broken into my childhood idyll and was wreaking havoc there. It began to dog me, instilling in me an encroaching sense of not belonging: not to my beloved family, not to the ethos of the school, not to the people around me, not even to myself. It was around this time that I had the nightmare for the first time, a dream that would recur again and again over the next three decades. It was always the same.

The sun is shining. I am part of a team of schoolgirls playing lacrosse when an energetic pass sends the ball soaring over our heads into the strictly out-of-bounds rhododendron woods. I run headlong into the bushes with several other girls to retrieve the ball, using my stick to thrash a path through the leaves. I am drawn deeper and deeper into the gloomy undergrowth. A distant voice calls, 'Found it!' and I try to retrace my steps, but I can't find my way. I can see the bright green grass, bathed in sunlight, through a web of branches and stems; I can hear the chatter and laughter of my classmates. But I can't reach them. Suddenly, I stumble into a pit with steep banks, full of decomposing autumn leaves. Every time I attempt to scramble up the sides, a fox appears and forces me to the bottom again. I try for years and years to outwit the fox, but I never succeed. And nobody ever notices I am missing.

During my teenage years, I grew more and more aware of the anti-German sentiment around me and how it pushed me out on to the margins. Not so much from the school history lessons that seemed to reduce Hitler and the Second World War to a series of military bombardments won by the British, which paled in impact as we dodged books intermittently hurled across the classroom by our ill-tempered history teacher, who had no tolerance of inattentiveness. The antipathy stemmed more from the steady stream of war films on television and at the cinema. And then, in 1975, came the *Fawlty Towers* episode 'The Germans' that made it permissible, perhaps unintentionally, to relentlessly mock the Germans in the guise of quoting Basil's famous line 'Don't mention the war'.

Germans were ridiculed for being disciplined, punctual, formal, stiff and so overly law-abiding that they would wait unnecessarily at the red lights of pedestrian crossings. They were characterized as lacking any sense of humour and wholly unable to indulge in small talk to the point of rudeness or conceit. And of course, they all loved beer and sausages. It appeared that efficiency, precision and order – qualities my mother both possessed and strove for – had been turned into negative stereotypes. The jokes saddened me as I thought of my mother and her family and their infinite kindness. But simultaneously I longed not to be part of this seemingly unacceptable group.

The jocular mood sobered in 1979, when the American miniseries *Holocaust* landed in European living rooms. Starring a young Meryl Streep, it graphically depicted the fate of a fictitious German Jewish doctor and his family living in Berlin. As renewed shockwaves rippled around the globe, leaving a sense of inexcusable horror in their wake, it became normal for my classmates to fervently and loudly declare that they loathed the Germans. German schoolchildren spending their holidays at my mother's language school quietly asked her if their host families would now hate them. Defending Germans, as I had always done, by firmly declaring that not all of them were Nazis, became impossible.

I, too, felt disgust. But despising the Germans wasn't as straightforward for me. It required me to hate part of my family.

And a part of myself.

2

A Kind of Knowing

Later . . . I kept feeling as if someone else were walking beside me,
or as if something had brushed against me.

W.G. Sebald, *Austerlitz*

AS A CHILD, I felt my mother as part of myself. A separation,
even for a night, would trigger intense homesickness
that could only be remedied by returning to the dry land she
represented. For her it was the same. We were intricately
bound by invisible threads.

For all of us, she was a devoted and engaged parent who
imbued her children with a love of British culture, gardens,
music and beauty. She was good-hearted and thoughtful and
deeply interested in people. She was daring, too, a fast driver
with a disregard for authority that amused us and made our
friends think her cool.

But, as teenagers, it was through the lens of my mother's
high standards that we children began to see ourselves. There
was a hidden template that outlined the right way to be:
strong, successful and compliant. It offered little room for
mistakes and ample scope to disappoint. Her own father
had, we knew, been a stern disciplinarian, but her strictness
seemed fuelled by a need for control. In spite of her own non-
compliance with conventions, she desperately wanted us not

only to adhere to the norms of the society in which our family was embedded, but to embrace them.

When we began to shed the family swaddling to take our first steps in the world as individual characters, we first had to negotiate a series of portcullises, each of which provoked a battle. There was an unhealthy power to our mother's opinions, A concerned glance from her to our father could spark doubts that gnawed at any conviction like woodworm at the leg of a chair. At first, the skirmishes revolved around minor things – mild disapproval of silly behaviour, our choice of clothing or our school grades – but gradually they progressed to more complex issues.

I had always been slim as a child and the first signs of pubescent puppy fat went unnoticed, by me, at least. But the German side of the family, while excellent cooks, were deeply critical of weight gain. Caroline and I came to dread the quick visual assessment in the school car park when our mother collected us for a long-awaited weekend at home. A congratulatory 'You've lost weight,' would send a wave of joy coursing through us, while a rhetorical, accusatory 'Have you put on weight?' would crumple our self-esteem. Driven by our mother's fattist gaze, we became obsessed with diets, see-sawing between feeling starved and stuffed, guilt-ridden for succumbing to such a base need as appetite or triumphant for rising above it.

Growing up with dual nationality was inevitably going to present us with some conflicting cultural messages. My mother advocated the benefits of the straight line: setting a goal and going for it like an arrow to a target. This involved speaking the truth in an uncluttered way, which made it impossible for her *not* to tell you if your bum did indeed 'look big in this'. My father, on the other hand, was the archetype of British diplomacy. He taught us the benefits of the circle, of tiptoeing round and round an uncomfortable issue before eventually getting to the point – or not, as the case would often be – of saying, yes when you meant no, or vice versa.

Trips to restaurants would frequently see us sliding down our chairs in embarrassment as my mother answered a waiter's mandatory 'Was everything all right?' with her fatal combination of high standards and honesty. My father, meanwhile, would smile apologetically and say yes, thank you, even if his coffee had been tea and the fish pie still frozen. For us children, it was a matter of learning how to navigate different situations and choose the most appropriate response.

I never doubted that my mother loved us, but as a family we had to tread warily around a part of herself that threatened to unravel her. We all colluded in protecting this inner vulnerability. Around the dinner table, if I tried to take issue with her, the eyes of my siblings warned me to shut up. We must not upset Mummy. She could be forceful one moment, and the next she would melt into defenceless tears. My sister and brother developed coping strategies. Caroline clashed with my mother and would then defiantly go her own way. She was born with a thicker skin and a tougher constitution. Christopher would appear to be listening to her but his ears would be firmly closed. He would diplomatically agree and then withdraw. I, on the other hand, feeling constantly silenced, absorbed the tension until I was full, at which point it either exploded in a pointless confrontation or sunk me into depression.

Occasionally, I'd catch glimpses of a listlessness in my

mother. At other times, she seemed discontent and lost. She had a beautiful home, a large circle of friends and was running a thriving language school she had built from scratch. But something was missing. Incessant activity served as a distraction from an emptiness she could neither articulate nor fill. Achievement was evidence of self-worth. Moments of relaxation were viewed as laziness and the sweet sense of a job done well was quickly replaced by another job. It was a cycle. And we were all caught up in it.

I couldn't work it out. Was she, like any other proud parent, keen for her children to reach the top positions in class for their own sakes, or did she need to bask in the glow of our academic attainment to make up for a lack of her own? With her promising early career brought to a premature end, did she feel straitjacketed in the traditional roles of wife and mother in a quintessentially English village, with muddy dogs and sticky children in tow, in spite of her flourishing business? And behind her reluctance to let us grow up, might there have been a secret longing for the freedom and opportunities she had been denied as a child? Or was she just afraid she would be left alone?

Her French and Italian friends – with their adorable accents and national idiosyncrasies – were considered charming. But there wasn't the same tolerance of exoticism in a German woman. Like many who have felt the chill of public loathing and rejection, she needed to hold tightly to the norms of acceptable English behaviour, becoming more English than the English.

As a teenager, I would stare at the large black-and-white portrait of my mother, in a red leather frame, that stood on one of my bedroom shelves. The photograph had been taken

My mother on her engagement to my father, 1961.

on her engagement. She must have been twenty-six or twenty-seven. She looked so beautiful, so happy, so carefree. So different from the woman I knew.

I longed to see more of her younger self, of the free-spirited, multicultural woman breaking with convention and trailblazing independence for subsequent generations. I felt strangely protective of that person. But when I encouraged my mother to reconnect to this version of herself, to pursue her former dreams of travelling and leave us to look after ourselves, we just argued, which left us both feeling wretched.

Caught in a tension of deeply loving my mother but feeling

oppressed and debilitated by her anxious conformity and criticism, I tried in vain to please her. I wanted to break free but a sense of responsibility for her emotional pain, whatever it was, led me to either suppress my will or fight hard against hers.

Guilt – or was it shame? – slipped into my soul discreetly. Its presence was initially little more than an occasional flicker, a brief tonal dimming of the colourful world around me. But it would soon become master of my internal world, switching off the lights for increasing periods of time and leaving me fumbling in the dark. I felt guilty that I had so many advantages over others. Guilty about rejecting the well-meant opportunities my parents and comfortable upbringing created for me. And guilty about the distance that was growing between me and my mother.

Guilt, it transpires, is one of a number of potential by-products of trauma. I couldn't link my guilt to any trauma of my own, but it was none the less there, driving my actions, forming, or possibly deforming, my emerging character.

The word 'trauma' comes from the Greek *traumatikos*, meaning 'wound', which originally referred to external violence that inflicted injury. It's still used in this way in medicine and surgery. But today it also describes any event or ongoing situation that triggers significant levels of fear, confusion, loss of control, pain, humiliation, and/or helplessness. Something that is so overwhelming, you don't know how to deal with it. Causes can range from divorce, violent crime or bereavement to natural disasters, rape and war. It is not, however, the event or the level of threat that define the extent of the traumatic impact but the subjective response of the individual. Not so much what happens *to* you as what happens *inside* you as a consequence.

Since the early 1990s, brain-imaging tools have been able to show what occurs in the brains of traumatized people. They reveal how certain key brain circuits become limited by trauma, resulting in a fundamental reorganization of the way the person thinks – not just how they think, but their very capacity to think. The prefrontal cortex, which is responsible for a wide variety of functions – including complex thinking, emotion- and stress-regulation, decision-making and appropriate behaviour – can become dysfunctional. The process of memory creation in the hippocampus can be compromised by flashbacks. The event doesn't recede, but still resides in the present, ready to intrude at any time. The amygdala, which activates the fight-flight-freeze response to danger, now reacts to memories and thoughts as if they are situations occurring currently, leaving the traumatized individual with a continuing sense of imminent threat. The hypothalamus becomes overactive, creating imbalances in hormone levels and increasing stress and anxiety.

In my forties, while researching trauma, I recognized that, unlike those of her siblings, my mother's memories of the past weren't linear. They were more dreamlike: islands of disjointed incidents, emotionally muffled by a blanket that left no sharp edges, no strong colours, no real shape. I wondered how the war might have affected her.

Could it be that my mother, a sensitive child, was impacted more than her siblings by the dramatic backdrop to their childhood? Or did she experience something that the others hadn't? Of all her stories, it was the one about her flight from the family home that left the deepest impression on me. I would revisit it from many angles, slipping myself into the shoes of my mother at ten years old, feeling each moment.

I imagined the Russian troops approaching from the southeast. They are in Cottbus, only 100 kilometres, some sixty miles, from Jüterbog. Heralding their inevitable arrival are such terrifying stories of indiscriminate rape and brutality that my grandmother decides it is time to send her two youngest daughters to her parents.

Jutta has to leave her beloved canary, Hansi, with her best friend and neighbour. She will later wonder at her mother's decision to allow her to take a doll rather than giving her silver, or some other useful object with trading value, to carry. That she has chosen the ugly new doll recently sent by her father rather than her favourite older one seems to be what bothers her most of all. At Berlin station, in the midst of the burning city, the two girls are ushered through the heaving crowds, too small to see where they are going. Dorothee will clearly remember them being lifted up and pushed through the window of the train. They don't know when, or even if, they will see their mother again.

Decades later, while going through cupboards with my mother and sorting clothes to take to a charity shop, I asked her, out of curiosity: 'What has been the most terrifying moment of your life?'

Without hesitation she named this experience and expanded on the story, as though it was still dancing in the front of her mind. At the station, my grandmother – who was holding Dorothee's hand and carrying their bags – told my mother to hang on to one of the small lead weights in the hem of her coat, sewn in to help the coat sit properly. My mother gripped the button-like object and shuffled through the throng behind her in the direction of the train. Then the button slipped from her little fingers.

Her voice wobbled.

The contact with her mother was severed and she was cast into the current of a human sea; a drowning child. In that moment, she felt terrifyingly alone, possibly lost for ever.

As if in a trance, she put down the dresses she was folding and went out of the room and downstairs. I followed, in awe of the tininess of that moment and its huge implications. Rummaging at the back of a panelled cupboard, she produced a small hardback book. Its pages were ochre with age. On the cover was a hand-painted green woodpecker perching on a wild pink rose and the word '*Tagebuch*', written in black letters.

My mother handed me the diary without so much as glancing inside. I opened it and instantly recognized her handwriting in the neat, girlish script. The first entry was from 1945, when she was nearly eleven – the same age at which I had started keeping my diary. I stared at her, rendered speechless by both the sudden appearance of this unexpected treasure and her apparent total absence of nostalgia. What *was* that? Was it simply a lack of interest? Or had she become detached from her eleven-year-old self?

The first pages were recollections of events from the year before: a trip into the Harz mountains, gathering cherries and strawberries and visiting relatives; the death of her much-loved grandfather, how his coffin had been placed on a cart and how the twenty-five Russian prisoners of war working his land had lined up and saluted him; the presents her father sent from Italy for the Christmas of 1944, when he was refused leave. And then the day her world changed: 1 February 1945.

My mother's diary, 1945.

*As the Russians were getting closer and closer . . . Mami
thought it would be better that we should head for
Wildenhorst after all. Suddenly everything happened
really fast. Mami quickly went into town because we still
didn't have a travel permit. On the grounds of being 'sick
children' we then got the permits and at 4 a.m. the
following morning, we drove out of Jüterbog. It was
really hard for us, Dorothee and me, as we would never
see Jüterbog and our lovely home and our toys and all the
other beautiful things again . . . Dorothee couldn't walk
in her shoes so she waited on the platform with Alexa
[their maid] and the luggage while Mami and I went to
the office of Herr Kroebel – that was the man we were
meant to travel with. Unfortunately, he had already left
for the station. His secretary said he was wearing a*

> *rucksack with six pockets . . . Mami asked a station guard*
> *if he would call out for him. The man said no and turned*
> *to a man with a rucksack and asked if he was Herr*
> *Kroebel. He said 'yes' and that's how we found him!*
> *Then at 7 a.m. we got on to the train, as it was high*
> *time. We said goodbye to Mami but couldn't get to a*
> *window to wave any more because the train was*
> *overfull.*

There was no mention of the hem weight. Nor of the terror of separation from her mother that she could now recall with such ease.

One of the primary impacts of trauma is speechlessness: an inability to give voice to what you have experienced. This is caused by the left-hand side of the brain – the linguistic, sequential and analytical side – being deactivated during a traumatic event, which is why people may become mute, scream, whimper, hurl obscenities or howl in fear. This inability to articulate can continue indefinitely.

Because the traumatic situation is often one in which the individual has had no choice or agency, the sense of self can become impaired. A loss of ability to be autonomous can make it hard for the person to make decisions or take charge of their life, so they seek the approval of others. The fight-flight-freeze response, once a healthy reaction to threat, may keep the body in a state of ongoing alertness or cause it to shut down, preventing relaxation and connection with emotions and sensations. Angry outbursts, loss of control, trust issues and low self-esteem may develop, leaving sufferers feeling vulnerable and doubtful of gut feelings. A fear of relationships and intimacy may then force them to withdraw into unhappy isolation.

I could recognize some of these symptoms of trauma in my mother. Low self-esteem and a lack of self-confidence lay behind some of her behaviour. A reluctance to stop and to relax. And there were occasions when she sought approval. Yet at other times, her directness and spirited rejection of officialdom took assertiveness to astonishing and amusing levels, and she taught us all how to stand up to authority and perceived injustice by imagining the person in the position of power without their clothes on. Her approach was also highly effective. The time I was expelled from boarding school was a case in point.

My deteriorating attitudes and behaviour had become unacceptable to the new headmistress, a feminist academic powerhouse. After an incident involving a pair of forbidden court shoes and a defiant bout of swearing at a teacher, she phoned while I was home for the weekend and informed my parents that I was not to return. My mother, who couldn't reconcile this troublesome school version of me with the daughter she knew, responded with an unequivocal 'That's ridiculous!' and declared that she would bring me back to school a week later without further discussion. She was as good as her word.

Even she, however, couldn't save me from subsequent expulsion from sixth-form college. I had opted to leave boarding school to do my A-Levels but, although the college was refreshingly liberal, my frequent truancy and blatant disinterest in my chosen subjects left my long-suffering tutors with no alternative. I was expelled and banned from setting foot on the premises except to sit my exams. I didn't care. By this time, I had discovered that only art, with its mad sanity, made any sense to me. Whenever I stepped into the paint-splattered studio, with its rickety easels and smell of oils, all self-doubt vanished. There, thoughts were encouraged to roam, horizons were expanded and feelings found shape in line and colour. The art teachers saw something in me that nobody else had noticed and, motivated by their inspiration and support, I worked boldly and large and discovered my strength.

Beyond the art room, however, I felt like an outsider. Misunderstood and critical of the values around me, I was increasingly drawn to the rebels and cultural anti-heroes who fell foul of the law. A darkness descended as the happy little girl of my childhood disappeared and, at sixteen, in the soli-tude of my bedroom at home, I plunged into my first full-blown depression.

The world dulled to tones of grey as my feelings numbed. Nothing had meaning or worth. I had a strong sense of the person I could be, but something was in my way, holding me back, pulling me down. I could feel part of myself solidifying into an impenetrable block that repelled the amorous advances of the boys around me and the concern of those I loved. Behind that stony façade, I was struggling.

It was much more than hormones or teenage angst. Unbe-knownst to me, I was showing symptoms typical of trauma but, with no obvious cause, I did what many teenagers do. I blamed my mother.

3

A Heart Behind Bars

If you want to build a ship, don't drum up the men to
gather wood, don't divide the work and give orders.
Instead, teach them to yearn for the vast and endless sea.

Antoine de Saint-Exupéry, *Citadelle*

I EMERGED FROM SIXTH-FORM COLLEGE in 1982 with a handful
of unimpressive grades and an unhelpful attitude to virtually everything. What I did have was a longing to explore the
world and I was ready to embark on the next chapter of my
life.

Art was the obvious subject to pursue and my parents,
recognizing that it was where both my passion and my talent
lay, agreed to fund a three-month history of art course in
Florence. Along with two college friends, I stayed at a ram-
bling old villa weighed down by heavy furniture and huge
embroidered lampshades. We wandered the streets, intoxicated by the candlelit churches and late-summer bustle of
colourful markets and piazzas. I lapped up *cappuccini* and
haloed Madonnas with equal gusto, but I was also drawn to
the darkly exotic, olive-skinned young people in the Piazza
della Signoria. They were – for the most part – drug addicts
but, with their long, curly hair, silver jewellery and low-
slung black jeans, they encapsulated the spirit of rebellious
bohemianism that so beguiled me. And their lives, free of

convention, embodied the kind of thrill I had found riding on the back of a fast motorbike in a miniskirt. When it came to danger, I was up for it.

So when one of them invited me for a coffee two weeks after my arrival, I agreed without hesitation. His name was Ivano. He was a student, apparently. We chatted over an excessively sweet – and, as it turned out, spiked – espresso, and then he escorted me to my class where, over the course of two hours, I became vaguely aware of my head nodding uncontrollably and my handwriting disintegrating into a diagonal scrawl.

The teacher asked if I was tired.

I said I was fine.

Ivano was waiting for me when I re-emerged. And that's all I remember.

My friends say that I appeared six hours later, propped up against the gate of our villa by a drunk stranger who'd found me in a bad way at the bottom of the road. I didn't seem to be injured, but my purse had been emptied of money. They undressed me and put me to bed as I rambled on about the amazing time I'd had.

I slept for twelve hours, waking to a haze of amnesia that was gradually punctuated by a series of flashbacks: a street corner littered with used syringes; Ivano holding a knife to my throat, assuring me that he'd do this to anybody who tried to hurt me; my mind working but my body failing; my T-shirt being lifted; sitting among a large circle of people around a fire; stumbling, falling, pushing off a man who was drunk. And then nothing.

To this day, I watch this sequence of images like a movie, detached from the lead role. I never felt traumatized, only intrigued, a little excited, even, by my initiation into the underworld. This would, however, become the traumatic event on to which I, and others, would try to hang my worsening symptoms. But they always slipped off. Because, while the drama of being drugged and robbed and sexually assaulted provided reasons enough for my problems, deep down, I knew they had started long before.

At the end of my course, I returned from Italy with my head full of impressions of the frescoes that adorned the walls of basilicas, monasteries and monks' cells. I arranged an apprenticeship in colour-mixing and in the fashionable paint effects of the eighties and then, with premature confidence, set up on my own in London, practising mural painting and ragging, dragging and stippling my way through clients' houses with varying degrees of success. To top up my income, I organized my first solo exhibition of photographs, framing them myself in evening classes and hand-delivering invitations to galleries and journalists on my moped. I wanted to earn enough money to buy a round-the-world airline ticket and travel the globe.

Rejecting my mother's vision for her daughters – a sensible job with a vibrant social life, puffed up like a meringue in silk taffeta dresses, charming husband in tow – I thought that travelling to far-off continents would offer escape, not only from the outer constraints of parents, class, nationality and gender expectations, but also from the inhibiting presence growing inside me. It had no name or shape. It just wafted through me like an echo, insidiously instilling a sense that something was wrong. In my head, there was a stern voice repeatedly telling me that I was bad, that happiness was only for the deserving, and that I was not among them. It insisted on atonement, but never told me what I needed to atone for. If I ignored it, I was punished with a debilitating sense of worthlessness, ingratitude and guilt.

Eventually, equipped with my air ticket, a new ruck-sack, sleeping bag and a spending budget of two dollars a day, I set off with a friend for South America. I couldn't have known then that the next three years of travelling – sometimes with my sister or friends, other times alone – would provide me with the tools and experience of the world I needed to uncover the mystery of what was wrong with me.

As a natural risk-taker, I was drawn to off-the-beaten track experiences. I followed a silent guide, a benign instructor in bravery who would lead me into dangerous situations and then, like a scout leader, abandon me to find my own way out. I quickly learned how to fine-tune my survival instincts. I learned that listening and acting calmly could disarm and engage macho men more effectively than becoming defensive. Once, trapped in the back of a Jeep while two men who clearly thought I couldn't understand their conversation plotted my rape and the subsequent disposal of my body, I resisted the natural urge to scream and flee. Instead I heard myself exuding childlike wonder at the beautiful scenery and gushing excitement for the (invented) birthday party and friends awaiting me later that afternoon. I saw how my apparent innocence unnerved them and gradually dismantled their plans. But I only knew I had succeeded when, a tense hour later, we reached their village. They told me to wait in the vehicle. After a short while they returned with a group of villagers who seemed to be chanting. It became clear that they were singing 'Happy Birthday' to me. I had no idea what had happened, or where that protective bubble of stillness and clarity had come from, but I knew I had discovered a psychological strength to overcome adversity.

After a year on the road, I needed to replenish my dwindling finances. I travelled to Sydney, a city humming with tanned bodies and endless possibilities, and found full-time work painting theatre backdrops and murals. I was outwardly confident and landed good jobs with my gung-ho optimism as I continued to learn my trade, often ending up in sticky situations with curtains and cars covered in pimples of paint, or artworks crumbling off finished canvases in big chunks as they were rolled up for transport.

To my frustration, settling in a house with three new friends gave my internal tormentor a chance to catch up with me. I was again overwhelmed by crippling self-criticism and guilt and a driving need to earn my right to exist. I felt worldly injustices with disproportionate rage and I was desperate to do something about them. I ranted about the plight of the South American Indians and the trampled rights of native Aboriginals; involved myself in petitions against McDonald's and its bony cows in Mexico; redistributed surplus food to the homeless. I kept myself on the go by working all hours, adding evening jobs as a waitress or a backstage dresser to my already full schedule.

My new friends advised me to lighten up, to be less hard on myself. I did try. I hitch-hiked up the east coast, disappearing into the northern outback with five 'ockers' – wild, uncultivated men with guns and knives and four-wheel-drives as strong as tanks. We bumped our way across rough terrain in terrifying heat, slaloming the lines of the law, to occupy caravans filled with flies beside a turquoise estuary.

They had jobs building a bridge. In their free time, they lobbed stolen sticks of dynamite into crocodile-infested rivers to blast stunned fish out of water. They shot at kangaroos and barbecued their haunches. They screeched off into the pitch blackness with headlights doused, the police in hot pursuit. I learned how to chisel out the chinks in their misogynist views and get them to soften their muscled bravado and confide surprisingly tender sides. I was twenty-two and felt strangely at home among the masculine aura of these badass boys: a Bonnie in a posse of Clydes, traversing the wilderness in pursuit of adventure.

It wasn't long, however, before I was smoking and drinking too heavily. I hitched several thousand miles back to the city and resumed my jobs and emancipated lifestyle there. But, caught up in a cycle of weed-induced inspiration and clarity followed by paranoia and apathetic emptiness, I passed negative judgement on my every move. Then, torn between pursuing the thrills of a life on the edge or surrendering to my inner need to do good, I froze in a state of indecision. My engine was running but there was no driver at the wheel.

After a book on reincarnation and karma fell off a shop shelf and landed at my feet, I discovered a vocabulary for concepts and possibilities that resonated with me but for which I had never had the words to describe. Looking for answers, I enrolled on a ten-day silent Vipassana meditation retreat in the mountains outside Sydney.

It was excruciating.

For the first four days, I went through intense physical withdrawal. To make things worse, we were required to sit still, observing our own extreme discomfort, from morning until night, with no distractions. I didn't experience waves of blissful bubbles rippling through my torso, nor did I receive any dramatic insights. Instead I frequently nodded off. It was only when I emerged that I noticed the benefits. I was ready to give up the substances that had enabled me to escape my inner unrest and I knew what I wanted to do next. I had a plan that would build on all my experiences, interests and skills to date, uniting the twin desires to address my internal conflict and to help others. With the lightning speed of conviction, I set my scheme in motion.

I don't remember exactly how I ended up banging on the door of Sydney's largest jail with my portfolio, having volunteered to run a mural-painting course for the convicts. But it wasn't my first encounter with a foreign prison. That had been in the Bolivian capital of La Paz. A notice pinned to a board in the foyer of the hostel where I was staying, a crumbling colonial building with a large, faded courtyard, asked guests to visit three Europeans residing in San Pedro jail on cocaine charges. Long fascinated by the tales of *Papillon* and *Midnight Express,* by the mindset of 'bad boys', by questions of outer confinement versus inner freedom, I responded without hesitation.

The prison in La Paz was like a small shantytown, bustling with inmates and their families, who were permitted daytime entry to set up stalls, as if it were a local marketplace. One of the three Europeans, a Dane with white powder dribbling from his nose, met me and took me on a tour. Each prisoner, he explained, had to buy whatever tiny patch of floor space he could find and build his own cell from scraps of cardboard and sacking.

A rounded pool in the middle of the main courtyard

served as a washing-up bowl, launderette and bath. Steps led into water black with filth, colourful laundry fluttering like bunting from its handrails. The worst part by far was the punishment area: a narrow space between the two outer walls with a thin shaft of sky above. In summer, midday might offer brief moments of warm sunshine. In winter, no sunlight reached the bottom, leaving the penalized prisoners to huddle like penguins against the freezing temperatures.

The second prison I visited was in Quito, Ecuador. The atmosphere of San Pedro had left a deep impression on me, which, far from putting me off, had only intensified the inexplicable pull I felt to explore the nature of punishment and imprisonment, and gaining entry to Latin American jails seemed relatively and surprisingly straightforward. This was another overcrowded, grey-walled hub of extreme violence and drugs with tiers of tiny barred windows set deep into walls; men with cold and empty eyes pacing, going nowhere; corridors disfigured by scribbled words and blue peeling paint. Rats tightroped the water pipes. Behind locked metal cell doors, prisoners lay on concrete bunks, waiting for nothing. There was no comfort to be had, just a perpetual sense of imminent danger.

Long Bay Gaol, one of Australia's most notorious prisons, would, then, be my third. I felt no nervousness as I waited outside for the guard, absorbing my surroundings: the large front door, embedded in a mustard brick wall, and the watchtowers with roofs pitched like visors against the bright sun. Inside, across a courtyard, another heavy door severed our connection to the outside world with a heavy clunk and nudged us into a dark corridor painted in thick green gloss. The eyes of the residents, unrestrained by social etiquette, followed us with the same hunger I'd seen in the eyes of the prisoners in Latin America. I smiled, but my instinctive friendliness was not returned.

We paused briefly in an art room cluttered with paint-daubed sheets of paper, which offered a moment of familiarity. But soon we were on the move again, now accompanied by the art teacher. We crossed another yard, this one occupied by clusters of tattooed men who stopped talking to monitor our movements, foreheads locked in frowns. I halted suddenly, catching sight of an array of beautifully painted murals soaring high above them on the gable ends of the buildings: a dense jungle, a palm-lined beach, naked figures, even God reaching out his hand to Adam in a reproduction of Michelangelo's famous rendition of the Creation. I was told that the artist responsible for the murals would be in the group of prisoners selected to participate in my project.

Eventually we stood at the foot of my canvas, a white wall dotted with floating, unfinished and badly painted depictions of sporting activities like windsurfing and running. It was my job to help the prisoners bring the abandoned enterprise to completion. I was used to climbing ladders to dizzying heights and painting large. This wall, though, took high and large to a new level. I noticed a small group of prisoners shuffling towards me with a different guard. This was my team: two Brazilian coke-smugglers, a murderer and a bank robber. I instantly felt at ease.

Over the following weeks, it became clear that the meagre selection of dried paints and small brushes was as inadequate for the task as the team and their leader. But, under the hot sun, the sessions provided valuable talking time, both for the men and for me. I was given a crash course in criminality by the mural artist, whose well-read, philosophical and curious mind had explored the darker side of human nature. Our exchange would continue, in the form of long letters, for years.

One afternoon I asked him what makes a person bad. He replied, 'Angela, in the twelve years I've been in prison, I have never met a man who committed a crime with evil intent.' I would have the opportunity to challenge this claim repeatedly over the subsequent decades and it would become key to my later work.

Looking back, I can honestly say that I never felt scared to be left alone with these men, nor did it occur to me to judge them. On the contrary, I experienced relief and a strange sense of homecoming. In their stories of incarceration and guilt, I found parts of myself reflected. I couldn't articulate it at the time. I couldn't make any link between their guilt for real crimes and my own apparently baseless sense of guilt. But there, in Sydney's clifftop prison, the cells in my body united in unanimous approval of my mission.

'This is it,' they told me. 'This is it,' I agreed. 'This is what I want to do with my life.'

I was twenty-three and I was where I needed to be: locked up with the culpable, transforming guilt into rehabilitation and redemption through art. Within that labyrinth of blank walls and complex psychological needs, I would not only develop as a mural painter but also do some good.

But to do it well, I needed more training.

I returned to England and enrolled on the only relevant course I could find: a three-year artistic therapy diploma. My parents were baffled by and sceptical of my life choices – so many of my friends and contemporaries were following the signposts towards marriage, babies, mortgages and domestic bliss. 'Why do you want to work with prisoners and not more deserving people, like cancer victims or children?' my mother asked, while my father quietly despaired at the idealism of reforming the prison system through art.

Nevertheless, determined to support each of their children through further education, they generously agreed to fund my diploma.

The course took place in the West Sussex countryside and was based on the teachings of Rudolf Steiner, whose holistic view of life focused on the human as an essentially spiritual being. . Steiner investigated the spiritual world with the rigour of science, but also drew on the intuitions of age-old wisdoms rather than modern Western perspectives that increasingly separated mind from body. The resulting philosophy – anthroposophy – was a fusion of Eastern and Western traditions that touched on everything from education to architecture to farming. Each subject was brought to life through a multi-dimensional approach. We looked at changing concepts of good and bad in the study of ancient civilizations and religions and followed the development of human consciousness in the artefacts of world cultures. My mind was in heaven.

In guided practical exercises, we plunged into the world of colour and into the subconscious, idiomatic realm from which our language draws its inspiration: we 'see red', 'get the blues', 'turn green with envy'. We were encouraged to search for the truths underlying the hundreds of similar expressions. Looking through a prism, we could see how the colours of the rainbow emerge where light and dark meet. Our constantly changing emotions were referred to as the weather of the soul, and illnesses of the mind or body were shown to be the result of imbalances or extremes in how a person relates to the world through thoughts, feelings or actions.

We practised 'reading' the paintings of real case studies, intuiting the ailments of their creators. I was good at that. The course made sense in ways that nothing at school ever had. But I would frequently rebel against the prescribed painting technique of gently building up thin layers of colour, alarming my tutors by paint-bombing my paper in destructive outbursts. Until I learned from a visiting teacher that it is not the final picture that is the artwork, but the transformation of the human soul while making it. 'The human being becomes the artwork,' I was told. That I could relate to. It was exactly the kind of work I wanted to do in prisons.

Once again, however, settling in one place led to my demons catching up with me. This time, my mental turmoil was augmented by physical symptoms – stomach cramps, amenorrhea, food allergies – for which, according to main-stream medicine, there was no apparent cause. I sought help in emerging new-age treatments and consulted ancient philosophies, from homeopathy and Chinese herbs to aroma-therapy and Bach flower remedies. I described to various therapists and practitioners the discomfiting feeling that plagued me: of being split in two, as if by invisible forces. I talked about the grey fog that hovered around me. I self-medicated with food, using dieting and bingeing as pressure valves to release or sustain the build-up of energy. My moods were erratic, yanking me from heights of elation to depths of depression. I meditated and walked, worked myself to exhaustion, tried to be nice, to please, to help. I couldn't let anybody know how tightly I was holding myself together. But I was on the brink of a messy unravelling.

Extreme behaviours and addictions can indicate a trauma seeking resolution or release. Some people spiral and crash spectacularly. Others seek oblivion, silently withdrawing or sinking to rock bottom. Like pain tolerance, the limits of what we can physically or psychologically withstand vary from person to person. And either response can lead to death or suicide.

For those who have never suffered with addiction, it must be hard to comprehend the enslavement to a particular substance or state. Eating disorders must seem particularly bizarre. Surely self-discipline and willpower are enough to curb the ravenous madness that makes you want to consume and consume or, alternatively, starve until you faint? It is easier to relate to drug, nicotine and alcohol addictions, because, superficially, they offer more reward, even fun. Abstinence, as expounded by the Anonymous groups, is the foundation of recovery. But you can't abstain from food and stay well.

I was living in Switzerland when I reached my own rock bottom. It was the summer of 1991. I had fallen for a German man I met during my final year at art therapy school. He promised neither commitment nor even particular kindness, but I followed him none the less to Switzerland on the pretext of deepening my colour studies. Amid the pleasant fluttering of early attraction, weight dropped off me effortlessly and the gradual protrusion of bones under my clothes left me feeling light, empty, strong and in control. Over the course of the summer, the affair and my studies blossomed.

By autumn, both were faltering. My eating habits responded accordingly. I began to eat excessively: chocolate, ice cream, biscuits and bread were the drugs of my madness. And I did feel mad as the cycle rolled out over the days, weeks and months. Food filled my thoughts from the moment I woke. I had to bombard my body with enough edible bulk to dull the pain or send me into intoxicated oblivion. A period of punishing starvation would follow to combat the guilt. The cycle seemed unstoppable. In rare lucid moments, I was plagued by a vision of myself as a vast and blubbery and beached on a kitchen chair in slippers with an open tin of biscuits. This was where I was heading. It felt real and terrifying. Depression wrapped me in its cold, grey cloak. Occasionally it shifted to give a glimpse of a bright future, swiftly followed by the agony of not being able to reach it. I felt a screaming aloneness, separated from everything save for the ghostly companion following me, haunting me, prodding and poking at me. And darkness like never before.

I am in my car.

It is raining heavily. The windscreen-wipers do their best, but it seems to be pouring both inside and out. I am crying so hard I can't see. I wind my way higher into the mountains, weighing up each bend for its potential efficacy – its proximity to a sheer slope. The descent has to be steep enough. I need this to work.

At each bend, I am ready to be deliberately inactive, to not turn the steering wheel, to simply go over the edge and plummet. A tragic car accident. Nobody will be hurt more than necessary. Nobody will have any cause to reproach themselves. And I will be free of pain, blissfully free of my loathsome body and weak-willed mind, of the shame and the failure.

A sharp corner comes towards me.

I freeze and time freezes with me. A split second stretched towards eternity. I hear the voice of a woman, kind but vehement, from the passenger seat: 'I so wanted to live, and I am dead. You so want to die, but you are alive.'

I instantly recognize it as the voice of a friend of my parents who had been tragically killed earlier that year in an avalanche. She had been a wonderful, free-spirited woman, full of life and curiosity. She had taken me seriously at a time when I was relentlessly questioned for my unconventional lifestyle. She didn't judge. She encouraged. Now she was saving me.

I turn the wheel.

4

Lives Trapped in History

The dead are invisible, they are not absent.

St Augustine of Hippo

I HAD ALWAYS KNOWN MY grandfather was a soldier. In the
only two photographs I had seen of him – the portrait on
my mother's writing desk and a picture of him showjumping
that she kept in her bedroom – he was in full uniform. What
I didn't know then was how related his absent presence was

Karl competing in a showjumping event.

to the symptoms I could catalogue so well but whose source eluded both me and, it seemed, all therapists.

Karl von Graffen had been born in 1893 and grew up on the shores of the Great Plön Lake in the north of Germany. The Graffens were a noble family. The men held titles: budget or imperial councillor in the 1600–1700s, and mayor of Hamburg and member of the military Cabinet in the early to mid-1800s.

Karl was naughty as a boy, often in trouble with his parents for skipping school. At the age of ten, he was enrolled as a cadet and sent to board at the military school in Plöner Schloss, the vast castle not far from his home. In this complex of white buildings overlooking the lake, the characteristic Prussian virtues of duty, honour, bravery, obedience,

Karl as a ten-year-old cadet.

discipline, humility and incorruptibility were instilled in him. And of them all, it was duty and honour that he valued most.

Karl was eleven when his mother died unexpectedly of cancer. His father soon remarried and his stepmother came to love him like her own child. Successfully completing his training at the main cadet institute in Berlin, he quickly climbed the ranks. By the time he was twenty-one, he had been promoted to first lieutenant and was serving in the 60th Artillery Regiment in the First World War. There is little information about his activities then, except that he fought in Crimea and was temporary battery leader of the 65th Reserve Field Artillery Regiment that saw action in the trenches of Ypres, Ginchy, Arras and Yser. In 1914, he was awarded the Iron Cross second and first class for exceptional courage. He came home four years later emaciated, with lingering symptoms of malaria and a large shrapnel wound in his neck.

When Germany signed the armistice on 11 November 1918, many of the returning soldiers felt undefeated in military terms. They believed it was the food shortages caused by years of Allied blockades that had forced them to surrender. And that, among other negative traits prejudicially attributed to Jews, the 'cowardice and treachery' of Jewish German soldiers had also played a decisive role. With the ratification of the Treaty of Versailles in January 1920, their bitterness hardened into a sense of deep betrayal – by the Kaiser, but most of all by American president Woodrow Wilson. They had put great faith in his fourteen-point peace proposal which championed 'peace without victory'. But the punitive and vindictive terms of the resulting treaty left Germans feeling humiliated. The nation lost its colonies, its most productive industrial and coal regions were placed under foreign control for at least fifteen years and huge sums were to be paid to Britain and France in reparations.

The financial consequences were devastating, but the most unpopular part of the treaty was the war guilt clause, which lay full blame for starting the war at the feet of the Germans. This didn't make sense to many of them, nor did it seem fair.

Conscription was also banned – soldiers had to be

Karl during the First World War, 1917.

volunteers – and the army was reduced dramatically to just 100,000 men. Karl was selected to be one of them.

From 1920, Karl was stationed in the majestic town of Schwerin, due east of Hamburg. Presiding over the town's tangle of cobbled streets, the fairytale Schloss Schwerin rises out of the flat surrounding landscape that breaks up to float like icebergs into a series of lakes. Across the water from the castle – a stretch my grandfather had once swum in full uniform for a bet – were the red- brick army barracks that housed the young officers. Karl was a fun-loving and popular thirty-year-old, a handsome man with high cheekbones and soulful eyes. He was also an excellent sportsman, winning countless prizes including the army high-jump and long-jump championships in 1922.

He met my grandmother, Ilse Bornhöft, in 1927 and, after three meetings, they were engaged. She was thirteen years his junior and had enjoyed a happy childhood with her brother and three sisters at the farming family's home, Wildenhorst. As a teenager, she had lived through the turbulence of war, the abdication of the Kaiser, the birth of the Weimar Republic and the extreme poverty brought on by the hyper-inflation of 1923.

My grandmother married Karl when she was twenty-one and they rented a six-room apartment overlooking the castle. By the end of 1928, she was a mother. Adolf was born that December and Marlen in November 1930. These early years as newlyweds were carefree, filled with laughter, tennis, riding, parties, dancing, music, literature and art.

But between the births of their first two children, the 1929 Wall Street Crash prompted America to call in its massive loans, including one made to Germany following

Ilse Bornhöft, my grandmother, 1927.

the hyperinflation. Much of the country descended into mass unemployment, malnutrition and resentment of the Jewish community, which appeared to some to be immune to the financial depression. The paralyzing headlock of the Versailles Treaty intensified, leading to political chaos and civil unrest as the Weimar Republic, under Paul von Hindenberg, began to collapse, preparing fertile ground for Hitler's rants and promises.

These were desperate times and people longed for someone to bridge the gulf between the warring left and right and heal the country. In the elections of 1932, the Nazi party gained a bigger share of the vote than any other single party. The contempt in which Hindenberg, the president, held the 'Bohemian corporal' was well known but, in January 1933,

convinced by his advisers that, with no party holding an overall majority, the Weimar government needed the support of
the Nazi party to function, he reluctantly appointed Hitler
chancellor. In return, Hitler, in the guise of offering friendly
co-operation, promised not to threaten the Reichstag, the president, the constituent states or the churches.

In March 1933, the ensuing Enabling Act – officially
entitled 'Law to Remedy the Distress of the People and Reich' –
granted the chancellor and his Cabinet arbitrary powers and
the freedom to act without parliamentary consent or constitu-
tional limitations. The Supreme Court did nothing to challenge the legitimacy of this measure, accepting the two-thirds
majority vote, even though it had been achieved through
the intimidation and repression of political opponents. Hitler
immediately took full advantage of these privileges, construct-
ing the apparatus of totalitarianism by abolishing the powers of
the states and formally outlawing all non-Nazi parties. When
Hindenberg died on 2 August 1934, Hitler fused the roles of
president and chancellor into one and declared himself the
supreme leader, or Führer.

My mother, Jutta, my grandparents' third child, was ten
weeks old.

The Nazis' ascent had an instant impact on her father's
career. Hitler immediately reorganized the downsized Weimar Republic's army and residual navy, the Reichswehr, into
the Wehrmacht, the regular unified armed forces of Nazi
Germany, adding a new air force, the Luftwaffe. In blatant defiance of the Versailles Treaty, he ordered massive
investment in defence spending and the reinstatement of
conscription. This would ensure a military force capable of
fulfilling his expansionist vision of repossessing lost German

territory as well as gaining new terrain in the east. He appointed himself commander-in-chief of the Wehrmacht and required all members to swear an oath of allegiance to him personally. These are the words my grandfather, in his position as chief of the 10th Battery of the 2nd Artillery-Regiment of the new Wehrmacht, would have spoken in 1934, unaware of the deadly consequences to which his sense of duty would lead.

> I swear to God by this sacred oath that to the Leader of the German Empire and people, Adolf Hitler, supreme commander of the armed forces, I shall render unconditional obedience and that as a brave soldier I shall at all times be prepared to give my life for this oath.

In the course of the following years, Karl became a highly respected artillerist and the author of an instructive book on ballistic missiles. In October 1935, at the age of forty-two, he was promoted to the position of adjutant (administrative assistant to a senior officer) and, later, to the head of the artillery school in Jüterbog, a medium-sized garrison town 75 kilometres (just over 45 miles) south of Berlin, where he was to teach war theory and tactics.

The family moved into a ground-floor apartment in one of the many red-brick, gable-fronted buildings that lined the wide, cobbled streets in the military part of town. The children attended the local school, where a picture of their father in full uniform hung proudly on the classroom wall. When there was no shooting practice, they were allowed to play on the firing ranges and gather mushrooms, nettles and chamomile to boil as soup or tea. Being close to Berlin gave my grandparents access to all the wonderful opera, theatre and exhibitions on offer, as well as the zoo for the children. A highlight was the 1936 Olympic Games. Karl had very nearly qualified for the decathlon but, at forty-three, was considered too old to compete. Nevertheless, they had a pass for all the events and attended every day, my normally highly disciplined grandfather often scrambling to stand on his seat for a better view. My grandmother recalled in her twilight years how, along with many others, they celebrated the performances of the black American athlete Jesse Owens, whose four gold medals blew Hitler's myth of Aryan supremacy out of the water.

The arrival of Dorothee, in February 1938, completed the family and the four children were brought up with what my grandmother termed 'loving strictness and consequence'. Karl demanded unconditional obedience, something she would occasionally have to compensate for, but the parents were united in their shared goal always to be there for their son and daughters.

The artillery school was the scene of one of my mother's more chilling childhood stories: the visit of Hitler and Hermann Göring (referred to by my grandmother in her old age as Fat Göring), who was his deputy, commander-in-chief of the Luftwaffe, and founder of the secret police – the dreaded Gestapo. My grandfather was in charge of showing them round and reporting on the durability and stability of the bunkers to withstand artillery shelling. He later revealed to his wife how surprised he had been, impressed even, by Hitler's extensive military knowledge and informed questions. On completion of the tour, he accompanied these highest-ranking Nazis through the town in the widely admired *Führerwagen*, the large, open-topped Mercedes from which

Hitler so often greeted jubilant crowds, their arms raised in passionate salutes.

Jüterbog was no different. As the car proceeded past his house, my grandfather pointed out his family, standing outside to watch the parade. Hitler looked directly at them and waved. The children waved back, though little Jutta's most vivid memory of the occasion was her preoccupation with having caught her foot in the railings. But I would shudder at the thought of the world's most murderous monster sitting beside my grandfather, locking eyes with my mother.

What my grandmother knew or didn't know, saw or didn't see, did or didn't do, I can only surmise. In her eighties and nineties, she would painstakingly record her life in a memoir of which I did not become aware until several years after her death. While this would shed fascinating light on her personal history it provided only tantalizing glimpses of her opinions and feelings about events of the 1930s and 1940s still too harrowing for so many of her generation to recall or discuss, even over half a century later.

It is certain that neither she nor my grandfather joined the Nazi party. And I would learn from relatives that her mother, my great-grandmother, used to listen to the BBC every day after lunch to 'learn the truth' about the German political and military situation and took great pride in never once having raised her hand in a Hitler salute. I imagine that – like so many – my grandmother may initially have welcomed Hitler. He was supportive of women who embodied the *'Kinder, Küche, Kirche'* (children, kitchen, church) ethos and focused on providing secure, healthy and happy environments in which to support their husbands and raise children for the fatherland.

My grandmother (L) with two of her sisters and (L–R) Jutta, Marlen, Adolf and their cousin Bernd.

Hitler was adept at drumming up a positive sense of national identity, welding the disparate tribes of the German principalities into a racially unified 'people's community', or *Volksgemeinschaft*. Citizens were given a spade to work the land or build thousands of kilometres of roads. 'Nobody,' my grandmother would later note, 'had any idea these would be used for war purposes.' The government-run *Kraft durch Freude* (KdF) – Strength Through Joy – programme organized leisure activities for workers: cheap holidays and cruise trips, hikes and theatre outings. He promised peace as well as rearmament and protection from Bolshevism and the 'Red hordes'; he promised to solve Germany's economic problems, develop and modernize industry, and to give the country and its people back their pride. The widespread criminality and incessant street fighting abated as freedom of speech was

curtailed and offenders and political opponents were 'reha-
bilitated' in the early work camps, or 'correctional facilities'.

Life improved for many and the media, controlled by
Joseph Goebbels, portrayed Hitler as a healer and saviour.
My mother thinks she remembers my grandmother saying
that he was sent by God and, if she did, she wasn't alone in
believing this. Finally, here was a strong leader vowing to
steer the nation out of its troubles to greatness again.

My grandmother would surely have hated the suppression of intellectuals and the swift and total clampdown on
opposition parties. And, like a lot of parents, she resented the
growing influence of the Hitler Youth and military service
for children. But the Nazis were widely seen as the only ones
capable of fighting Communism.

As the persecution of the Jews and those who thought
differently took increasingly dangerous forms, her fears evidently grew. She would describe in her memoir the infamous
Kristallnacht of 1938 – the 'Night of Broken Glass' when
the Nazi party's paramilitary forces expelled Jewish families
from their houses and destroyed their synagogues while the
authorities looked the other way – as 'horrendous, a total
nightmare'. She wrote of how 'deeply serious conversations
were had, full of worry and concern about the whole escalation'. On top of that were the worries about the consequences
of being branded a 'defeatist'. 'One friend who was not very
careful in what she said was taken away with her small children and vanished.'

When war was declared on 3 September 1939, my grandmother wept. She, along with so many others, had genuinely
believed that peace would prevail. Still, the war was largely
perceived as a necessary act of defence for Germany. Had

Hitler not made repeated offers of peace? Why had these been rejected and had Britain and France opted instead to respond to his refusal to withdraw from Poland by putting their relationship with Germany on a war footing? Some Germans felt that reclaiming the territories they had been forced to concede after the First World War was completely justified. Others believed that the threat posed by Bolshevism in the east had to be quashed once and for all.

While numerous visitors to Germany in the years leading up to the war were appalled by the climate of jingoism and warmongering they found, countless testimonies demonstrate how widespread the desire for friendship with Britain was, as Julia Boyd documents in her book *Travellers in the Third Reich*. As well as recording the kindness, warmth and consideration Britons were shown, they reveal incomprehension of the British position. Why couldn't Britain let Hitler achieve his Lebensraum, or 'living space', in the east without violence? 'Their earnestness is almost tragic,' wrote one young traveller, a member of the Charterhouse School hockey team. 'They find it impossible to believe that we should prefer as an ally the French, the friends of Russia and Czechoslovakia, to them – fellow Saxons.' For some there was just resignation. 'Hitler is now our destiny.'

Within a month of the outbreak of war, Karl von Graffen was transferred to the Oberkommando des Heeres (OKH), the Supreme High Command, near Berlin, where he was put in charge of artillery and munitions. His military theories and teachings were immediately put into practice.

In August Hitler had signed a non-aggression pact with the leader of the Soviet Union, Joseph Stalin, under which they agreed not to aid the other's enemies or to engage in hostile acts against each other. It gave Hitler a guarantee that he could invade Poland without any resistance from the east and Stalin breathing space in which to build up his armed forces. But Hitler reneged on the deal, invading the Soviet Union in June 1941. Although he acted against the advice of his senior staff, given the success of their Blitzkrieg, or 'lightning war', in the west, victory was none the less expected to be quick and decisive. With over 3 million German soldiers lined up along a 2,900-kilometre front, some 1,800 miles, it was the largest invasion force in the history of warfare. In addition to troops, the Germans deployed 600,000 motor vehicles and between 600,000 and 700,000 horses.

Due to his front-line battle experience and extensive artillery expertise, Karl had been given command of his first regiment, the 129th Artillery Regiment, a few months earlier, and was stationed in East Prussia. Three German army groups – North, Centre and South – were charged with capturing Leningrad, Moscow and Soviet Ukraine respectively. On 22 June, Karl advanced into Belarus towards Smolensk and then Moscow.

My grandfather would remain on the Eastern Front for just over two years, marching thousands of miles through the vast expanse of Russia. He would write to my grandmother every other day, using a code to disguise his whereabouts and other confidential information. She would meet his every request – for his field cap, a towel, cigarettes – as best she could.

In March 1942, he was appointed leader of the 58th Infantry Division and then promoted to commander until September 1943. He took part in the notorious Battle of Volkhov in the birch forests and swampy peat bogs south of Leningrad (now

St Petersburg) and was awarded the Knight's Cross for his courage and leadership.

Meanwhile, the family apprehensively followed events on the radio. My grandmother had to complete an assistant sisters' course to tend the wounded and dying arriving in Jüterbog from the Eastern Front: men laid out in rows, some on the train platforms, others in cattle trucks. Often she worked through the night, changing bandages by candlelight. Sometimes she took my mother.

As the tide turned against the Germans, Karl avoided the fate of the over 3 million soldiers and officers who were captured by the Soviets before the end of the war. Of those sent to Siberia, many froze or starved to death. Instead, in September 1943, he was transferred south to Italy, where he became higher artillery commander 316 (Army High Command 10), a role that took him into raging battles against the Western Allies at Monte Cassino, San Marino, Rimini and up to the Dolomites in the north. In the final days of the war, Karl was delegated the leadership of LXXVI Panzer-Corps near the small hamlet of La Stanga in the foothills of the Dolomites. It was here that he received the order for the unconditional surrender of troops in the first days of May 1945, just after Hitler killed himself.

This was where my grandfather's war ended and his time as a prisoner began.

5

The Power of the Unseen

*What haunts are not the dead but the gaps left within us
by the secrets of others.*

Nicholas Abraham, *Notes on the Phantom*

'So HOW MANY TIMES a day do you think about death?'
The Swiss doctor asked her question almost matter-of-factly, her hand poised to write a single digit in the little square box. The close encounter between my car and a mountain edge had spurred me to seek help at the local clinic.

'Once? Twice?' she prompted, not even looking up.

I knew it was normal to contemplate death and dying occasionally, so I answered immediately and with total candour. 'Every few minutes.'

Now she looked up, abruptly and with undisguised shock. Then referred me to her more senior husband. Her sense of urgency felt startling. He questioned me further and eventually proclaimed his diagnosis with surprising nonchalance: 'Anorexia and bulimia. And you've had them all your life.'

Although I was very aware of these disorders, I had no idea that you could have them both simultaneously. I imagined that people suffering from anorexia had downy skin and were always life-threateningly underweight. I might lose two stone in as many months and become painfully thin but I could gain them back just as quickly.

Still, I was relieved finally to be able to put a name to my dark secret. I was no longer mad or weak, or even unique, with my unnaturally obsessive thoughts and shameful behavioural patterns. It was a medical condition and, as with most of them, there was a mapped-out path of treatment leading towards a potential cure.

It later transpired that the doctor's diagnosis wasn't entirely accurate – I was never bulimic – but he was right when he said that, from a medical perspective, my system was cold, 'as if you aren't wanting to inhabit your body fully; as if you don't want to be here'. Even my stomach, my metabolic core, was cold to the touch. I was to be regularly massaged with oils and wrapped in warm towels, bathed in water and rubbed back to life. I was also to take a variety of drops and perform certain physical exercises daily. And to attend weekly meetings of OA.

'What's OA?' I asked.

'Overeaters Anonymous.'

Was he serious? Even at the peak of my weight gain, I wasn't obese. Did I really have to do this? Apparently, I did.

Embarrassed, I sneaked off to a meeting in Basel a few weeks later and was surprised, as I walked into the small, wood-panelled room, to find four women of around my own size, and age waiting there.

I was familiar with the principles of self-development groups. As a child, I was a bit of a daydreamer and growing up through the calendrical cycles of church services instilled in me a sense that spirit and soul were as real as the more tangible physical body. My English grandparents were excellent examples of Christian faith in action, not only in their innate belief in some greater force at work behind the scenes, but also in their day-to-day humility. My German grandmother had a different, less overtly religious way of looking at the world. After witnessing such devastation, her philosophy was expressed through an effusive appreciation of beauty, nature and culture.

By my early twenties, I had already begun exploring various religions and spiritual practices and had come to see them all as routes on a map, each starting from a different base and defined by different words, but all heading towards a similar, unifying destination beyond the limitations of everyday consciousness. But what I was most interested in were those serendipitous moments when we simply feel or know something: those invisible channels of communication.

I was sure that the ability to intuit in this way was something we all had, if only we attuned ourselves to it and trusted its subtle signals, and I was keen to develop mine. That had been my reason, while living in Sydney, for signing up for a two-day workshop designed to awaken the hidden powers of the mind. As we sat in a large hall, a polished-looking man in a suit took us through various visualization exercises, first alone and then in pairs. I partnered a middle-aged woman in flip-flops. The slick-suited leader encouraged one of us to imagine a friend or family member and the other to close their eyes and express what they saw, felt or thought without censorship or judgement.

I saw things that seemed ridiculous: clouds in front of a pair of eyes, a camera tripod shooting from somebody's head, three severed tubes sticking out of a heart. But these things made sense to the woman sitting opposite me: cataracts, a frustrated photographer, a triple bypass operation. In another exercise, our eyes closed, we were instructed to look for the person or thing that had hurt us in the past, forgive them and let them go.

I found nothing. I tried to fix in my mind images of my mother, then Ivano from Florence, but neither would stick. Then, as clear as if they were present in the room, two figures: me, as a small child, big-eyed, almost frightened, walking hand-in-hand with a soldier.

This bewildered me. Who could the soldier be? And when had any soldier done me harm?

Strange as it may seem, the fact that my grandfather had been a soldier never even crossed my mind, still less the notion that he could ever have hurt me.

The image remained a mystery. It would be many years before I would attach any significance to this scene.

The Overeaters Anonymous session commenced. Everybody was given an opportunity to speak. I sat there, dumbfounded, as I listened to the other four young women. Their words were like sublime music to me. I could relate to almost everything they expressed. They talked openly and gently, as if stuffing your face was as common an activity as filling the petrol tank of your car. They spoke of traumatic experiences they had endured, of an overbearing or emotionally absent parent. They described low self-esteem, guilt, feelings of despair and loss of identity.

I had spent years holding myself together, trying in vain to control the urges and blaming myself for being weak, pointless and lacking willpower. Here I could finally let go. In fact, the very concept of willpower was abandoned in favour of surrender. 'Giving up' was what you had to do to get better, just not in the way I so nearly had. The first step towards recovery involved giving up the belief that we can control an addiction and the fruitless struggle to do so. Acknowledging our powerlessness opens us to the possibility of accepting help from a higher power than ourselves, whatever form that may take.

I subsequently attended many OA sessions and, by following the twelve-step programme, I gradually step-by-stepped my way out of a dark labyrinth and back on to a main road with signposts, street lighting and other human beings. I began confiding in a few carefully selected friends. When my siblings came to visit, I talked to them, too, about my eating disorder. With their love, support and shared family humour, they helped me heave myself back into the world.

Talking was key to the recovery process, as was speaking the truth. On a trip to England, I tried to speak to my mother honestly – about my experiences, my feelings of worthlessness and what was required from her to prevent it happening again. 'It really got quite bad, Mum,' I said, as we stood together on the platform of a railway station, deliberately keeping my tone as light as possible to avoid triggering a predictable knee-jerk reaction in either of us.

She didn't seem to hear.

Any allusion to weakness or failure always seemed to evoke the opposite of sympathy or compassion. 'Everybody eats too much at times, and then diets,' she said, and with that, my attempt to name the shame I carried and to speak the truth was trivialized and dismissed.

I knew all too well the absence of self-reflection I was up against. Defences would spring into place; somebody else or something else was always to blame. Instead of attempting to breach them, I stepped back to try to understand what might have happened to my mother to engrain this default response. I knew that my grandfather had been away at war and that my grandmother had brought up four children singlehandedly. Might that fatherless decade explain my mother's dominant role in our family? I tried to imagine how she might have felt on being separated from her own mother, on losing everything she knew and valued overnight. I wondered how she felt about her nationality in the light of everything that came out after the war; if wanting to escape her stained and shamed homeland was one of the appeals of living in England. And whether she believed that she, or maybe we all, had to be perfect in order to be accepted.

I wanted to understand. I longed to talk openly about some of her feelings, to get through to her warmth, talk about her needs and heal her past wounds. I wanted her to acknowledge that perfectionism, control, criticism and judgement, even when offered with the best intentions, weren't always supportive or helpful. I wanted to forgive her for not meeting my needs. But her continuing criticism and dismissal of my lifestyle caused my anxieties to flare again. Where we had once breezed effortlessly in and out of each other, we were now a big, knotted ball, mangled and forged together like the metal components of a car crash.

'I hate my mother,' I said out loud to the OA group one day. It was a horrible emotion but, like lancing a boil, saying those words popped its potency. I never said this again and I never needed to. Once I had stepped off the self-destructive eating disorder rollercoaster and liberated the huge amount of energy I had expended in avoiding my pain, life began to bubble in technicolour. I had got to the bottom of my problems and was at last ready to start my prison vocation in earnest.

I decamped to Cologne in Germany. I had written to the progressive prison there offering to run a mural-painting project. They supported the arts as a tool for rehabilitation, as did an innovative trust I was interested in working with. Later, I would ask myself if, unconsciously, I might also have been driven to work with German perpetrators of crimes as a result of a visit to another of Germany's prisons. One that had become an emblem of evil and whose horrific back story posed huge questions about guilt.

Auschwitz.

The Poland of 1990 was perhaps not an obvious choice of destination for a summer holiday, but something – possibly the word 'budget' – had inspired me and a close friend to board a coach heading for Zakopane at the foot of the Tatra Mountains. As we travelled through the recently opened German Democratic Republic and former Eastern bloc countries, a grey gloom filled the frames of the coach windows. Shabby buildings pockmarked with bullet holes lined the empty streets. In the absence of street lighting, at night whole towns disappeared.

Our hotel was as basic as the stodgy meals included with our stay. The shelves of the surrounding shops were more or less empty. At the weekend flea market, rows of tatty blankets, camp beds and tiny plastic tables laid out in waterlogged fields offered rusty collections of redundant-looking machinery parts or tiny piles of cucumbers or potatoes. Women in headscarves and men in caps waded between them, heads down, as they hunted for what they required.

One of the outings offered in our package was a coach trip to Auschwitz. My friend didn't want to come but I signed up, wholly unprepared for what awaited me. The oppressive desolation of the site, like nothing I had ever encountered anywhere before, pervaded everything. It followed us as the guide led our small group through the rows of two-storey brick buildings. It blanketed the silence as we stood in front of the huge, glass-fronted vitrines packed with mountains of leather suitcases, spectacles, shoes and human hair. It hung in the corridors lined with row upon row of the framed black-and-white faces of former inmates. It clogged our imaginations as we were told how soap had been made from the body fat of corpses.

I tried to place little feet into the shoes, to see eyes blinking behind the spectacles, to pack favoured belongings into the suitcases. But I couldn't.

The gas chamber and crematorium were housed in an empty, bunker-like space with low ceilings and concrete beams. There were ovens, the kind into which you might slide loaves of bread or pizza. The guide told us about the poisonous gas. He gave us some figures too large to take in. The rest of the group snapped a few photos and left. I lingered behind. A silence more visceral and powerful than any sound filled the space. It was as if the present was being sucked out like air leaving nothing but the essence of the voiceless horror of hundreds of thousands of murdered people.

The experience of visiting Auschwitz shook me to the core. I was utterly unable to form a mental image, either at the time or afterwards, of the suffering that had taken place here. Instead, I was haunted by the human capacity for depravity; by the incomprehensible, calculated, methodical extermination of human life carried out by the perpetrators: the Germans. And these weren't historical Germans from some bygone age, but people who might have dined, danced and talked with my own grandparents.

Questions nagged for weeks. I didn't know enough about history, about Judaism and Nazism. That would all come later. At this point, my primary concern lay with the people who had committed these atrocities: how they became evil, how much ordinary Germans had known, whether they had agreed with it, what they – or anybody else – could do to redress the wrongdoing, if redemption were even conceivable. I didn't yet recognize that I, too, might be entwined in this horror story through my familial roots. This possibility had passed me by. But it wouldn't for much longer.

'Right,' I announced enthusiastically to the class of eight men standing in front of me. It was September 1992, day one of my first project in Cologne's large remand prison, JVA Ossendorf, and we were all locked in a dark, grey hobby room at the far end of the wing, empty but for a battered ping-pong table. I tried not to think about the fact that I had no key.

Most of the prisoners were looking at the floor with their hands stuffed down the fronts of their tracksuit bottoms. I wanted to break the ice and tried to sound upbeat. 'We'll brainstorm ideas for a mural, and then we'll all agree on one.'

Eight pairs of eyes looked up sharply, unexpectedly, with undivided attention. Encouraged, I expanded on the plan for the day, outlining the exercises we would do and introducing them to the blatantly insufficient selection of materials provided. I was vaguely aware of the exchange of glances and wry smiles, which I put down to the novelty of doing an art class and being in a room with a young woman.

It was several days before one of them explained just how upbeat my opening statement had been. By muddling the verbs *einigen* and *vereinigen*, I had suggested that we brainstorm ideas for a mural 'and then all go to bed together'.

Despite this particular exercise failing to materialize, they all seemed excited about the mural.

I, too, was excited by the road ahead. I believed in art's capacity to restore dignity, offer an emotional outlet and inspire change. I had found refuge and recognition in the art room at my sixth- form college and was determined to create a similarly safe space for the misunderstood within these walls. Colours would provide a non-verbal language for the unutterable. Guided exercises would gently open doors that had long been locked shut. Murals, if not quite of the calibre of an Italian fresco, would humanize the environment. And prisoners would feel seen, heard and cherished. I knew I could genuinely make a difference here.

I was employed by the Maßstab Trust, founded and run by two visionary lawyers who worked with prisoners in ways that chimed with my ideas, and soon my weekly classes and mural-painting projects were full and attracting long waiting lists. It felt like more than just a new start in a new city or a new job. Everything seemed to be coming together for me. In that prison, all the apparently contradictory parts that made me who I was could work in harmony. My English and German sides knitted themselves into a single entity and I was able to draw on every one of my disparate experiences – study, travels, inner searching and suffering, mental illness, addiction and creativity – to meet the artistic, emotional and practical demands of my students.

Furthermore, surrounded by people considered 'bad', I could relax in the knowledge that any innate badness of my own wouldn't stand out. Among those deemed guilty by society and by a formal justice system, I was unquestionably on the side of good.

6

Prison and Perpetrators

*If you treat an individual as he is, he will remain as he is. But if
you treat people as if they were what they ought to be, you help
them to become what they are capable of being.*

Johann Wolfgang von Goethe, *Wilhelm Meister's Apprenticeship*

EVERYTHING ABOUT LIFE IN prison is extreme.
Time sometimes contorts and sometimes stands still.
Seasons leave few distinctive marks on the bland, neon-lit, air-
less spaces. Flaccid bodies shuffle through the corridors. Pallid
complexions prematurely age young faces. Uncertainty buck-
les backs and roams freely through the pathways of prisoners'
minds.

The clang of large keys grinding in metal locks defines
the rigid rhythms of each day. In the evenings, the soundtrack
changes: a crossfire of desperate howls and long, wordless
yells that ricochet between cell windows as radios tuned to
different channels are turned to full volume. The inmates
prop photos of their loved ones on tables as mush is scooped
from tin trays and they prepare themselves to face the empty
hours of another night behind bars.

For most people, prison is a simple concept: criminals
have done something wrong and deserve to be excluded from
society, locked up and punished. Within weeks of arriving in
Cologne, I felt very differently.

In the art room, a small generic space with four tables pushed together and a lockable metal cupboard for basic materials, I introduced the inmates to the colourful world of my studies. Blank pieces of paper provided a safe space for tentative expressions of emotions long locked away, too dangerous or painful to feel. Playful exercises broke through fortified personal boundaries and connected each man with the group. With their paintbrushes, they planted seeds in a cold blue ground, let them grow roots and watched as shoots magically turned into green plants on contact with the painted yellow sunlight. Here, on their paper, there was no right or wrong, just an awakening to possibilities, uniqueness: their other selves.

My heart sang as I saw them lose themselves in deep concentration and wrestle with creative challenges. They moved colour around the paper as though it were a stretch class for their taut nerves and compressed emotions. And my initial concerns that this might result in the contents of their dark, criminal minds being spewed all over the walls in scenes of mediaeval or comic-book hell were not borne out. It soon became clear that what the prisoners really wanted to express was their longing for open skies, nature, beauty, home, the people they loved.

The German for 'to understand' is *verstehen*. The word implies a movement away from your own perspective into someone else's in order to comprehend the meaning and intention behind their actions. Between art classes, I visited the cells. Being an employee of an outside organization rather than of the prison itself, I wasn't obliged to report anything I heard, and I was therefore considered a safe pair of ears. I sat on the beds of heroin addicts, robbers and simple fraudsters, of

One of many mural-painting projects in Cologne Prison, 1994.

mafiosi, murderers and rapists, as they recounted their stories, often for the first time. I was finally learning how evil begins.

'I just lost it. They pushed me too far ... First my mother, then her. I was at breaking point. I was unloading the shopping from the car. We had bought a kitchen knife. I stabbed her again and again. She was pregnant with my child ... They both survived, but I can't forgive myself.'

'I was sexually abused by my father's friend. He owned a small shop and would give me sweets and cigarettes afterwards. My father knew about it. My mum was a drug addict and so was my sister. My older brother pimped them out. He raped four women and murdered his wife ... I really wanted to be different from them and yet here I am.'

'It just happened. I was bouncing my young daughter on my knee and I became aroused. I did it because I love them so much.'

'After I murdered her, I lay her on the bed and placed roses around her body. They accused me of being coldblooded in court, because I showed no remorse, no feeling. I feel it all, though. It's just that my feelings get stuck here.' The man pointed to his upper chest and throat. 'They just don't come out further. But I feel all of them.'

In many cases, unrequited longing for respect, purpose, justice or love was raw and barely disguised. Most were suffering widespread emotional illiteracy, resulting in each negative feeling morphing into a single faceless tormentor. For a number of prisoners, punching someone or 'getting out of yourself' with drugs were the only measures that offered relief, albeit temporary. Some could pinpoint identifiable events that cut across their life and changed its course, like the track points on a railway line. Often it was a single decision, a yes instead of a no, usually, made against their better judgement and in turn propelling them towards a series of more bad decisions and, ultimately, their cell. These are not justifications for their actions, simply some of the steps that led to them.

Just as hard to hear about as the crimes themselves were the catastrophic family circumstances that had left young boys emotionally scarred and severely disadvantaged. The stories of domestic abuse, deprivation and ignorance made me question whether violence, addiction, criminality and mental illness are inevitable reactions of once-sensitive, open-hearted kids to a cold, cruel world and a childhood that didn't make sense. It was not difficult to look past the tattoos and shaven heads, the pumped-up muscles and the inflated bragging, and see in the perpetrator in front of me the little boy cowering at the top of the stairs, watching helplessly, his hand shielding his younger brother's eyes, as his mother is brutally attacked by her boyfriend. How do you process that? The answer for some, it seemed, was by becoming 'tough', 'male', 'strong' and 'brave'. By becoming a criminal.

There were times when I would be amazed by the courage of these offenders, by their determination, their capacity – as children – to survive. Dysfunctional upbringings and inadequate parenting hadn't equipped them with the tools or the moral compass with which to navigate their way through life. Usually, they offered justifications for their actions. The man jailed for punching a stranger who made advances to his girlfriend? 'Protection,' he said. (Of her, or of his pride? I wondered.) The young Jamaican who smuggled drugs to help finance his mother's cancer treatment. The sexual assault on a woman who was 'asking for it'.

Setting aside psychosis and severe mental-health problems, I discovered that, just as the bank robber in Sydney had claimed, these offenders hadn't intended to be or to do 'evil'. Even the man who dropped breezeblocks on to the heads of prostitutes believed he was 'ridding the world of scum' and thereby making it a better place. The reasoning was invariably deeply flawed, of course, but I didn't judge. I just listened and tried to understand: a fly on the wall of their minds.

There are always back stories, and yet this significant factor is largely ignored by most justice systems around the world, which are too often founded on the principle that yet more degradation, punishment and shame will make offenders repent. It isn't always easy, or possible, to see beyond the crime. But finding the capacity to do so is one of the ways to prevent repeat offending.

I would only much later realize why I instinctively felt

such love for these ostracized men. And why I so urgently wanted to help them.

Gradually, the years in the system began to take their toll. I loved my work and it grew in all directions, but every day, people took from me and a part of me remained with them. I could feel the absence of this part as I moved freely through the streets outside.

A prisoner who had been in several consecutive art groups summed it up over a mug of instant coffee. He spoke of how I took the prisoners' problems away, worked on them and returned them solved. He said I had pulled him out of a real hole, helped him to stand on his own two feet and brought out the artist in him.

'You can be very proud of yourself,' he declared.

Suddenly, I saw clearly that for nearly five years, pulling others out of holes was exactly what I had been doing: going down into that deep pit again and again, hauling people out, carrying them on my back and setting them on their feet on solid ground. I was heartened to know that my work was helping people. But now I felt absolutely incapable of carrying another soul for even one step. I had zero creative energy left. I felt exhausted and overdrawn.

'You're too open,' said my colleague and friend as she stirred crushed lime and sugar at the bottom of her glass.

We were in our favourite bar sipping our weekly caipirinhas through straws after our shared drawing class in the segregated unit for those who had committed particularly serious crimes. Without any real supervision of our work, we were regularly left alone to digest other people's problems.

Here, every Wednesday, we decompressed by exchanging tales with the black humour characteristic of surgeons or soldiers. 'What a job!' we would sigh fondly to each other.

I knew that she was right, that I gave too much to the prisoners, let them pick and choose what they wanted of me until they had emptied me out. We often talked about their positive responses to authenticity and displays of trust but also of the importance of boundaries to their rehabilitation. After all, every crime is the overstepping of a boundary – the crossing of a physical, personal or legal line. Yet here, too, jail – with its walls, bars, locks and guards – was wholly ineffectual and counter-productive. This quadruple reinforcement of boundaries both prevented inmates from learning how to respect the normal lines in society and compounded the emotional and psychological damage of dysfunctional childhoods by inducing even greater levels of passivity and irresponsibility.

As we finished our drinks, my friend turned to me and asked, 'But what about *you*? What about *your* life?'

It was a fair question. I had to face the fact that I was becoming isolated and estranged from the outside world, losing myself in the relentless regimented rhythms of the system. I had relationships and friends, but they had to compete with work for my time and my heart. I was heading for another edge.

The link between trauma and addiction has been well documented. According to Gabor Maté, a renowned physician and author and an expert in both spheres, any behaviour to which we become a slave can be defined as an addiction. The cycle is the same as that of any other addiction: craving, short-term pleasure or relief, longer-term harm and, ultimately, an inability to give up the behaviour. And, by its very nature, no addiction can satisfy the need at its source.

To really understand and heal addiction, you have to get to the wound that is driving it. Initially, the activity or substance involved is seen as a helpful solution to a problem. It gives the person relief from their suffering. It offers a short-term escape, makes them feel whole, fills an emptiness, soothes pain. I saw plenty of evidence of this among the many drug addicts in the prison. I often heard how heroin emulates a mother's unconditional love, how cocaine increases self-confidence and energy levels, how extreme bodybuilding encourages respect or guarantees protection.

Maté and other trauma specialists confirm what I have both experienced in myself and witnessed in fellow sufferers: that an addiction is neither a choice nor an inherited disease. It is not even the primary problem. It is, in many cases, a response to trauma, to some event that has led to a disconnection from painful emotions and, ultimately, the self. Sometimes it might not have been solely the event itself that has proved overwhelming, but the lack of any help.

I had previously succumbed to the allure of various substances and was lucky to have recognized that they were a dead end. And I had used food – or starvation – as a drug to control my inner monster. Now I was somehow back in the clasp of another addiction: work. I was responding to the constant flow of adrenaline. The validation of being good at my job and making a difference were far preferable to the deep-seated feelings of guilt and shame that still lived inside me. And the sense of being needed had displaced the feeling of being unlovable. But my previously sharp antennae for danger were becoming blunt.

It came to light one day that a member of my art class, an unassuming man who was always polite and diligent, had told his brother, another inmate, in a written note that he intended to commit a violent act in the run-up to his trial for multiple rape and murder. I had been teaching him for over six months, unaware, by choice, of his crime. His plan was to take me hostage.

Fortunately for me, the brother – who was also one of my art students, and with whom I had a good rapport – reported him and he was immediately transferred to a top-security wing. But the experience shocked me. I sat in on his trial as often as possible, trying to comprehend not only the identity of this man as a monstrous sexual predator, but why the jeopardy lurking in every corner of that prison had never previously worried me. I had been locked in countless rooms with potentially dangerous and desperate men without any kind of alarm, key or guard. Yet I had never felt frightened. Though some chose to inform me, I never asked what crime they had committed. That way I was able to see each individual as a multi-dimensional human being and to work with their strengths as well as their weaknesses. And I had always been able to make a distinction between the doer and the deed, which enabled me to unreservedly condemn the deed – if I knew it – without condemning the person. I also genuinely believed that some protective sheath rendered me untouchable. Most of them are as likely to harm me as I am them, I had thought. But that evidently wasn't true, and now doubt contaminated almost every area of my work.

Even more disturbing to me was my slight sense of disappointment. I realized that, perversely, I almost wished I had been taken hostage. Why was that? Was my self-hatred really that great? Was there a part of me that saw myself as a victim? Or perhaps I even aspired to be a victim?

There were no rational answers to these questions at this point in my life. This episode would, however, prove to be the final straw for me. With only porous boundaries in place to separate my feelings from those of others, I had absorbed the messed-up lives and thoughts of the prisoners and I was losing control.

Over the course of a few weeks, my life bolted like a runaway horse, galloping me into a string of high-stress and high-risk situations, car accidents, relationships and illnesses, before bucking me off completely. The light in my eyes flickered and dimmed to a glazed vacancy. I could barely move.

I was admitted to a hospital in southern Germany that took a holistic approach to diagnosis and treatment. The whole period is a blur. All I knew was that it was 1997. That I was exactly thirty-three-and-a-third years old. And that the identity I had worn for the past six years was unravelling like an old woollen jumper. I was in freefall, toppling from the hard-won heights of my successes. Without the validation of my various roles – artist, teacher, campaigner, organizer, team member – I was nothing.

7

The Unspeakable

In a way we are all haunted. I am haunted by the shadow of
something and it's on the periphery of my life all the time . . .
but I have no right to be haunted.

Rita Goldberg, *Unspeakable*

I HAVE OFTEN FANTASIZED ABOUT what I would take with me
if a sudden catastrophe forced me to abandon my home.
My item of choice has changed over the decades: from my
beloved childhood doll, Gigi, to my dachshund, Scampy; from
my silver watch to photograph albums and diaries. Nowadays
it might be a mobile phone and hard drives. I have also had
nights broken by dreams of flight. Usually I am hurriedly
packing before running desperately for a train. Or trying to
rescue as many things as possible from a burning building.
Sometimes I have to decide which family member to save.
Every time I am burdened with too much baggage. A stubborn course of obstacles litters my path and I rarely make it to
where I am going.

As a child, I would pile my most precious possessions on
my bed – always Gigi, maybe a chocolate or a postcard, once
a life-size dog on wheels. Even for daytime outings, I would
pack a little bag with essentials: a clean pair of pants, a comb,
a little bit of pocket money in a purse. I always needed to
be ready. I never made the link to my mother's escape, her

distress at having selected the wrong toy, the terror of losing her mother on the platform.

Back in the forties and fifties, young children were seen as immune to psychological wounds. It was assumed that they were sufficiently robust for devastating events to wash over them without lasting impact. Gradually, psychologists identified a link between a parent's child-rearing habits and the development of a child's personality. We understand now that our deepest sense of self is created in minute-to-minute exchanges with our carers, that nurturing emotional interactions are an indispensable requirement of human development and that the brain's stress-response mechanisms are programmed from the very start of our infancy.

In his now famous theory, the psychoanalyst John Bowlby attributed mental-health and behavioural problems to a lack of attachment in early childhood. Babies experience hunger, thirst, cold and even new noises as stressful and rely on the comforting responses of the primary carer, usually the mother, to learn the vital skills for regulating their moods. Bowlby suggested that children, as part of their survival instinct, are biologically pre-programmed to form attachments with others. Initially, their natural communication system develops through one primary bond with an adult, and it is the quality of this first relationship that will serve as the prototype for all future relationships.

This theory has been expanded over the years and we now understand that the formation of deep, healthy and secure attachment relies on parents who are sensitive to their children's signals, emotionally available and responsive to their infants' needs. The quantity and quality of both physical and emotional contact – from facial expressions and touch to tone of voice – help the child to feel at ease in their environment and reassure them that they are loved and worthy. The ensuing attachment becomes the secure base from which a child moves out into the world. It promotes the development of a healthy sense of self and empathy for others.

More recently, it had been shown that what a foetus experiences in the womb – even at the embryo stage, indeed, from the moment of conception – is instrumental in the formation of neural circuitry and lays the groundwork for our future emotional and mental skills. As the foetus grows, it is exposed to the wider world via its mother, from sounds such as her voice to the food that she consumes. Her thoughts and feelings, positive and negative, are conveyed by neuro-hormones.

If a mother, or other primary carer, has experienced trauma, they may find it harder to respond sensitively and effectively to their infant's needs, or to offer security, consistency and protection. Trauma can result in emotional volatility, numbness or dissociation, leaving a person feeling unsafe or ill at ease in their own body. Without the responses of a parent figure to regulate their emotions, without anybody there to hold them, babies can become over-stressed and overwhelmed by their feelings. Over the years, repeated expressions of anger, depression and coldness from a carer might lead to a child learning to shut down, give up easily or overreact. When a child fails to develop empathy, they may be excluded from games, parties or even school. Negative or inadequate responses to their behaviour can consolidate into lowered self-esteem, distrust of others, feelings of being lost, abandoned and unlovable – all incentives to succumb to the allure of compensatory substances or activities that can in turn form the basis of addictive, violent or criminal behaviour.

This might sound reductive to some, but I had witnessed this cycle repeatedly in prisons. And although my mother was in many ways consistently attentive and loving, and enabled me to develop a healthy sense of self, on closer analysis, it seemed that some of my symptoms were almost textbook indicators of the child of a traumatized mother. Yet nothing in my mother's experiences or behaviour appeared to constitute a severe enough trauma to warrant the intensity of these effects.

In the sixties, classical psychoanalysis was still based on Freud's theories, which saw the internal psychic reality of the patient as the major cause of their issues. The influence of external world events – war, barbarity, diaspora, politics, both current and historical – was not a consideration. In fact, it was thought to 'muddy the waters'. At that time, there were also conversations about whether or not the analyst, consciously or unconsciously, might avoid paying attention to certain world events due to having experienced similar ones in their own lives. Nazi atrocities, for example, might have been off limits for a Jewish analyst and Jewish client due to an unspoken mutual preference for keeping their shared trauma shrouded in silence.

However, evidence of 'battle exhaustion' in soldiers had been noted for centuries. By this time, the First World War hypothesis that 'shell shock' – the term coined by the British to describe the symptoms that appeared in large numbers of combatants exposed to the stress and terror of constant bombardment in the trenches – was down to an overall lack of moral fibre, and afflicted only those with some pre-existing weakness, had largely been abandoned. Abram Kardiner, who treated US war veterans in 1923 and published *The Traumatic Neuroses of War* in 1941 in anticipation of a new wave of shell-shocked soldiers, recognized that any individual could be affected by war and that traumatic symptoms were a normal response to an unbearable situation. However, while hypnosis remained the primary treatment used by psychiatrists, the psychological scars were unacknowledged. And from 1947, traumatic neuroses had all but disappeared from official psychiatric language.

The seventies saw more research into trauma in general. After the Vietnam War, which stretched over twenty years from 1955 to 1975, US epidemiologists, psychiatrists and neuroscientists, among others, began to revisit soldiers' experiences, as many veterans were displaying incapacitating symptoms to such a degree that they led to violence, homelessness, depression, unemployability, substance misuse and mood disorders. There was also growing recognition and openness about the influence of the Third Reich on those who had experienced it first-hand.

It was only when the survivors of German concentration camps showed a similar range of emotional, cognitive and behavioural tendencies that the previously individually labelled and treated trauma symptoms were combined into one psychological trauma diagnosis: post-traumatic stress disorder (PTSD). But it was not until 1980 that this term would finally be included in the bible of psychology, the *Diagnostic and Statistical Manual of Mental Health Disorders*.

As the struggles of the children of Holocaust survivors – the second generation – came to light and were systematically studied for the first time, psychoanalysts began to expand their understanding of PTSD to encompass the notion that personal internal worlds and wider historical, societal and political external worlds are intertwined. By the end of the eighties and early nineties, and in the wake of other dramatic global events – the collapse of the Eastern communist bloc; the Yugoslav wars; the end of the Apartheid era – these expanded theories became widely accepted.

The family dynamics of second-generation survivors of the Holocaust revealed children who had grown up in atmospheres steeped in trauma, not only that of their parents but also of their entire communities. Many of the first generation had coped by suppressing what they had experienced, often unaware of the impact on their psychological and physiological health. This in turn affected their marriages and parenting.

Overwhelming past experiences of grief, fear, distrust and depression, and haunting memories of the ever-present hunger in the camps and ghettos, would manifest in many forms within the present. Some children complained of the emotional coldness and unavailability of their parents. Others of the exact opposite: so precious were they to their parents that the anxiety for their safety this engendered reached a point where they felt they were being controlled.

Many suffered from confusion, guilt and shame. On the one hand, they took on the burdens of the damaged parent, wanting to heal them and feeling guilty for being unable to do so. And on the other, they longed to extricate themselves from the damage, which would mean pushing their parents away. Some unconsciously replicated the extended periods of uncertainty endured by their relatives at the edge of life and death in their choice of career, opting for front-line jobs such as medicine where their skills could be employed to pull someone back to the solid ground of life. Rita Goldberg, author of *Motherland: Growing up with the Holocaust,* describes a permanent sense of fear or anxiety. What, after all, had ever happened in her life that could compare with what her parents had gone through?

The nineties offered a vocabulary to describe the mechanism via which second, and third, generations of survivors were affected by the suppressed memories and experiences of their parents and grandparents. Coined by the Romanian professor Marianne Hirsch, 'postmemory' defined an inherited form of post-traumatic stress disorder. The term was first used in an article about the American cartoonist Art Spiegelman, whose graphic novel *Maus* had been serialized between 1980 and 1991. *Maus* is made up of two stories. The first presents the Holocaust as endured by Spiegelman's Polish father, Valdek, from the years leading up to the Second World War to the liberation of his parents from a concentration camp. The second, parallel narrative depicts Spiegelman's troubled relationship with his father and his reaction to the suicide of his mother in 1968. According to Hirsch, the fact that his childhood – and subsequent adult life – were affected by events that he had not, and could not, experience personally was indicative of 'postmemory'.

This term has since come to be applied more widely and is now used in many contexts beyond the sphere of Holocaust survivors. It is generally accepted that subsequent generations can absorb the trauma of forebears through images, stories, attitudes and the behaviour of family members.

When the effects of past traumatic events continue into

the present they may, in some children, be transmitted so deeply and thoroughly that they manifest themselves as memories. The connection to the past is not actually 'remembered' but constructed through imagination and projection, putting the lives of those with overwhelming inherited memories at risk of being dominated and shaped by the experiences of parents or grandparents.

I hadn't heard the word 'postmemory' back in the nineties but, if I had, it would have come closer than any other to naming my own growing collection of symptoms. My mother's childhood stories had been deposited in my memory like a cuckoo's egg in a host bird's nest. And my life had, to a degree, been dominated and shaped by her experiences. But nobody was looking at the children and grandchildren of perpetrator nations then. And how could one possibly relate what was going on in me, or in anybody else, quite frankly, to the devastating impact on the descendants of Jewish Holocaust survivors?

In any case, my mother's traumatic experiences were of fear and dislocation, not of guilt and shame – the two feelings that afflicted me most acutely. It was not until 2004, with the publication of German journalist and author Sabine Bode's seminal book *Die Vergessene Generation: Die Kriegskinder brechen ihr Schweigen* (*The Forgotten Generation: The War Children Break Their Silence*), that the traumatic effects of the Second World War on non-Jewish German children would be first acknowledged. And it would be another five years before Bode's third book on the subject would reveal the extent of traumatic transmission to the third generation. My generation.

*

My weeks in hospital extended into several more weeks at a small recuperation centre somewhere in southern Germany, nestled in woods filled with the sounds of spring. The gentle rhythms of the day allowed me to reflect on my life and the process that had burned me out.

I had blossomed in Cologne with its vibrant lifestyle of beer gardens and street festivals, concerts and vernissages. I liked the culture of order and structure that assured efficiency on a practical level and left the mind free to indulge in creative, philosophical or intellectual thinking. And I loved the open-mindedness and liberalism of young Germans, with their earnest authenticity and progressive views. I had made friends quickly, appreciating the refreshing clarity of their communication. People said what they meant and did what they wanted, rather than bowing to pointless etiquette. I even began to see my mother's direct manner in a new and more positive light.

There were times, however, when the plain-speaking candour of my friends came across as, at best, ungracious, and at worst outright rude.

'Would you like to come to the cinema?' I remember once asking my flatmate.

'No,' came her answer, with an abruptness that almost winded me. Unadorned by a thank you or a reason, from my perspective, she might as well have said 'Fuck off.'

No less insulting, it transpired, was my response to her genuine inquiry about my wellbeing. I was surprised when my typically English 'Fine, thanks. And how are you?' met with the exasperated retort: 'I wouldn't have asked if I hadn't wanted to know.'

Throughout the time I lived in Germany, very few of

those who had been children during the war talked of it openly. In my circles, the war never arose in ordinary conversations. It wasn't out of bounds exactly; it just wasn't within them, either. My absorption in my work, and the fact that I possessed neither a television nor a broad enough vocabulary to appreciate German newspapers, left me ignorant of the huge national reckoning with recent history that was taking place on political and cultural levels in the wake of the 1989 fall of the Berlin Wall and the early years of German reunification. I was even unaware that the grassy park in which I regularly picnicked with friends rested on top of the pulped remains of the Allied bombing raids.

Cycling through the old centre of Cologne, I might catch sight of a display outside a shop of black-and-white postcards showing a city of ghostly façades, hollowed-out windows like shocked eyes surveying the bombed devastation. In every picture, the blackened spires of Cologne's cathedral rose defiantly from the rubble like the spire in Hamburg that had puzzled me as a child. Sometimes I would stop and remove the cards from the stand, examining the photographs to try to bridge the fifty years between then and now. But I felt strangely detached from these scenes. I could neither condemn nor celebrate the city's destruction. Nor could I fully empathize with the wartime civilians who'd lived on these streets.

Part of me simply relished life without the tensions of historical conflict. In general, Germans seemed to look upon the British with fondness. And during my time working in prisons, I heard only one reference to the Second World War, and that was when the building was evacuated and we were sent home because an unexploded British bomb had been uncovered on the premises. Nobody made a single jibe.

Behind the scenes, however, on the personal level, and within families, the still unspoken horrors of the past leaked their unprocessed secrets into the lives of the third generation, burdening and debilitating them in ways very few people understood or recognized. I must have picked up on them. Because, in my efforts to comprehend my innate sense of badness and my compulsion to help prisoners, I had flirted with the idea of reincarnation. While a totally far-fetched concept to most Western secular or Christian thinking, reincarnation is a well-established strand of Jewish mysticism and other spiritual teachings and some kind of rebirth or continuation of the soul offered a potential explanation for my struggles. I contemplated in my diary: 'Within my belly lies evil, past karma undigested and indigestible . . . I have this niggling thought that I was alive in the Second World War and was responsible for the death of many innocent Jews. I was a Nazi, dedicated to an idealism based on a huge misunderstanding.'

The memory-like familiarity I felt with anything I experienced relating to Nazi Germany was always from the point of view of the culprit. The image in my mind's eye of me hauling one person after another out of a pit as a form of repentant restitution seemed to chime with reincarnation. Yet even if such a karma were possible, I reasoned, how would I ever know for certain? And what could I do to 'digest' or work through it?

In spite of the years of physical distance, the relationship between my mother and me remained fragile. I often felt confused during visits home and family reunions. It was always lovely to see my family: our mother continued to put flowers in our bedrooms and prepare beautiful meals; our father would open a bottle of champagne and we'd all raise a glass. They were generous and would ask with genuine interest about our lives. And I loved telling them about my work, making them laugh or gasp at the often absurd situations I encountered on a daily basis. They had become deeply proud of what I was doing and my father quietly revelled in responding to inquiries from friends as to where or how I was with 'She's in prison!' As we shared news, stories and traditions, all seemed well. But I still had a strong sense of being tangled up in my mother's psyche by what felt like an invisible umbilical cord.

My parents once visited me in Germany and we tried to talk. But nothing landed and we all became upset. The conclusion we reached was a familiar one: that all my difficulties were of my own making. But, as I would discover many years later, they actually weren't. Some of those 'problems' could be attributed to a psychological state defined as 'symbiotic entanglement'.

In their work with trauma, psychologist Professor Franz Ruppert and psychotherapist Vivian Broughton looked closely at the way in which experiences of trauma are split off and consigned to the unconscious in a process of dissociation. This disconnection of the mind from the emotional and psychological impact causes the psyche to fragment into three different selves. The 'traumatized self' is frozen in time and can be suddenly triggered. The 'survival self' guards the trauma and protects us from it through suppression, control and avoidance. The 'healthy self' feels safe but knows something is amiss and yearns to be whole.

The 'survival self' quickly develops strategies and structures that keep the trauma at bay. Over time, these mechanisms become increasingly subtle, sophisticated and organized, forming everyday actions and reactions that the person comes to believe are part of their nature. Consequently, they mistake this 'survival self' for their real self.

When a mother undergoes such a process of dissociation, it is possible that the psyche of her child will, to a degree, take on this split structure. Particularly if the trauma occurred, or is re-stimulated, during pregnancy, when the mother and infant are almost entirely fused. The foetus developing in the womb might feel all that she feels – her confusion, terror, ambivalence and anxiety. It cannot be separate from any of this and does not have the cognitive means to make sense of its experience.

The mother's emotional structure, assumed by the child as its own first psychological imprint, becomes the gateway for the transmission of trauma or any other unresolved experiences. The resulting dynamics – known as symbiotic entanglement – can be very confusing for both child and mother. Both are affected by similar symptoms of trauma and yet, for the child, these symptoms are not their own. This compromised relationship may preoccupy the child throughout their life, informing all later relationships and leaving them unsure which feelings are their own and which really belong to others. They may struggle to feel loved by their mother, may idealize or hate her, may copy her survival strategies or may try to save her from her suffering.

I have come to the conclusion that this is what happened between my mother and me. But neither of us could see it.

'I don't know what you're talking about!' she had pleaded when, yet again, I clumsily knocked against her wounds while trying to navigate a way through the minefield of our sensitivities. Her face was steeped in such authentic exasperation that I finally believed her.

I could hear that we had reached the end of the road. It dawned on me that only three options remained for us. I could walk away from her for ever. I could try again at a later date to make her understand how I believed her life had somehow impacted on mine. Or I could let it all go.

I recovered, gradually, but it felt impossible to return to my job in the prison, or even to resume my work with young offenders. Acknowledging this was one of the hardest truths I had ever faced. But I had to accept that I had served my time and a new stage of my life awaited me.

For several years, when I needed to recharge my batteries, I had retreated to the west coast of Ireland. Its shifting fogs, rainbows and the magical serendipity that effortlessly shaped each day offered the perfect antidote to the prison's rigid order and razor-wired boundaries. There was one place that beckoned in particular: Sligo, the seaport nestled between cairns and clouds in a land steeped in Celtic mythology. In the late summer of 1997, I packed up my flat in Germany, bought an old car and moved to Sligo to watch and paint the dramas of the sky as they unfolded from minute to minute. Sitting in bed in the draughty house that became my home for a while, wrapped in eiderdowns and blankets with hot-water bottles and mugs of tea, I began to read Sergei O. Prokofieff's book *The Occult Significance of Forgiveness*, given to me as a leaving present by a sympathetic colleague in Cologne. I pored over every word, not turning a page until I had fully absorbed the lessons of the previous one.

I had no single act to forgive. My mother had never deliberately harmed me. But, as became apparent, forgiveness is rarely about just one thing.

First I learned how to overcome what Prokofieff called the 'lower ego,' with its resistance to forgetting and forgiving. My grudge against my mother had remained a black clot in the flow of our relationship; a tangled knot of painful accusations and memories that was distinct from the positives of our bond. It had blighted my adolescence and it was still clogging the present, too. Acknowledging it in my OA group had been a first step towards dissolving it but, whenever we met, that knot was there, precluding any possibility of a fresh start.

I learned to free myself of expectations of how people should behave. This was like a grieving process. I mourned the lack of emotional closeness that prevented me from being able to include my mother in the highs and lows of my life. I mourned the fact that she had so rarely seen me anywhere other than on her turf, where the old rules prevailed. I mourned the opportunities she had missed to know the professional, successful and happy version of a daughter in her element on more liberal ground. And then I let it all go. The third lesson was to stop blaming her, to overcome my lower ego with its self-righteous sense of justice, anger, revenge and begrudging hatred. I had to give up these responses and accept her as she was, just as I wanted her to accept me. The final challenge was to learn to love her from the 'higher ego', the level of consciousness that forms the spiritual or divine essence of a human being and lies beyond body and mind.

It would take many months, but I would learn to forgive my mother.

8

Matters of the Heart

Have patience with everything that remains unsolved in your heart . . . live in the question.

Rainer Maria Rilke, *Letters to a Young Poet*

RELATIONSHIPS, WITH THEIR ACCOMPANYING smorgasbord of emotions and challenges, were often the main arena in which my conflicts and inner shit-show played out. They'd be beautiful and passionate, often dramatic and impractical and usually doomed to fail by conventional standards. But then, reliability and long-term commitment had never been attributes that attracted me. And the establishment of a nuclear family within a till-death-do-us-part marriage was not a cultural norm I aspired to. I remained hungry to venture off-road and eager to experience life's remote corners.

Behind the scenes, however, two patterns were discernible.

The first stemmed from the powerful chemistry of damaged people. I was still drawn to tricky men and found a role for myself in their suffering or dysfunction. I'd mistake intensity for intimacy, see creativity behind addictions. I'd hang on too long, ending up battered by my partner's emotional unavailability and finally by disappointment and pain.

The second scenario saw me pushing away good people who tried to get too close. I carried my guilt so tightly that there was little space left for any other form of intimacy. It was like a dead or jealous lover. I would feel it stirring whenever I made plans to settle. Eventually, in a battle between head and heart, I would be dragged down by another failed attempt to join my contemporaries in the sunlight of 'normality'.

My German grandmother had once accurately captured exactly how I felt. 'It's as though you have two souls in your chest,' she had said compassionately.

Torn between a longing for nun-like spiritual devotion and fulfilment and a daring life on the edge, breaking norms, I was coming to see the source of my split soul as a residue of the conflict between the two warring nations I embodied. But I seemed incapable of negotiating a peace treaty. Was it even possible to have two souls?

Ireland, with its mercurial skies and rugged coast, promised endless inspiration and a sense of future. I filled sketchbooks, painted, wrote, walked and ran workshops. I was building a more balanced life, developing as an artist. But after eighteen months and the birth and death of a wonderful but doomed relationship, I returned to England and moved to the banks of the Severn estuary in Gloucestershire. I was really happy in my new life. Inspired by the beauty of my surroundings, I would scoop up mud from the riverbed at low tide and mix it with my paints, squelching them between my fingers before dancing paintings of big skies and weather into existence with my hands.

My artwork started selling well and, for a while, I felt at peace and whole. Not least because everything had now changed between my mother and me. I had noticed it the first time I hugged her on arriving back in England. Like a miracle, forgiveness had dissolved the long, exhausting fight

One of my 'mud paintings': Silent Night.

between us and, in its place, a gentle, mutual support had grown that promised to endure.

But my tendency to curtail intimate relationships continued with the collapse of another chance of marriage and children, security and a settled future. Much as I had wanted this relationship to work, part of me couldn't breathe and my inspiration and creativity had dried up.

I sought out a therapist and, with her help, revisited the potentially traumatic Florence incident with Ivano. We established that I had probably been given an early form of the date-rape drug Rohypnol, whose effects matched mine exactly: loss of muscle control, trouble standing or walking, feeling drunk, sleepiness, all lasting for four to six hours, followed by strong amnesia resulting in limited or no recollection of assault. Yet, regardless of what actually happened between my flashbacks, it remained an experience devoid of fear. Dramatic, fascinating, horrifying, strange as it may have been, it was not the source of my problems.

We re-examined family dynamics and boarding school. I even challenged the therapist to try to identify the persistent fox of my dreams and find out once and for all what it wanted. I was an old hand at this now, with answers of my own: maybe the fox was a form of bouncer to my heart, poised to defend me from rejection when others discovered the rottenness at my core. Or was it a part of me that felt lonely? It seemed hopeless.

However, with the therapist's help, I came to see my fox as a guardian rather than an enemy. There was something important I had to find or do in the tangled undergrowth of that dream and the fox was benignly holding me in that trench until I could adjust my eyes enough to see in the dark. It just wasn't my time to frolic gaily in the sunlight – not yet.

This made sense to me.

I can now recognize certain traits of inherited trauma and guilt in this inner dynamic: the model of the fragmented 'survival self' protecting the stuck 'traumatized self' while the 'real self' looks on and seeks resolution. The physical coldness – picked up on by so many doctors – was a form of dissociation. I needed the intensity of dramatic or painful relationships and incessant action, high risks and new challenges to make me feel anything. I pushed away nice, kind boyfriends for their own protection and delighted in unsuitable men because their tough independence and emotional unreliability freed me from the pressure to be good.

'I don't want to be a mother until I feel more confident

that I can keep my shit to myself and not be a victim of the shit my parents gave to me, which they picked up from their parents,' I had written to a friend in 1989. If I was bad or half-evil, I had reasoned, I didn't want to bring another version of myself into the world. And if I wasn't, I didn't want to pass on my struggle to my own child.

The idea that a 'generational curse' of transgression, sickness or hardship can be passed down by parents to their offspring has been around for a long time. The Old Testament declares that the 'iniquity of the fathers' will be visited 'upon the children, and upon the children's children, unto the third and to the fourth generation' and that 'the fathers have eaten sour grapes, and the children's teeth are set on edge'.

When the field of psychoanalysis emerged in the late 1800s, such ideas were expanded on through the study of the impact of parents' neuroses on their children. All subsequent schools of psychology examining trauma looked at the implications of this handing-on of neurotic traits. In 1913, Freud talked about events experienced in one generation being replicated in each succeeding generation in *Totem and Taboo*. But he didn't know how this happened. He suggested that unconscious conflicts might be primed to be triggered into action by subsequent conflicts and explored the occult notion of telepathy as a form of cross-generational communication.

Later, in the 1960s, Swiss psychologist Carl Jung described feeling 'under the influence of things or questions which were left incomplete and unanswered' by his parents, grandparents and more distant ancestors. It often seemed to him, too, that he had to 'complete or perhaps continue things which previous ages had left unfinished'. I had felt much the same for my entire life. But, with no academic or scientific knowledge of psychology, I had never found the words to articulate it so clearly.

The idea gained further currency when similar problems were recognized in the children of American veterans of the controversial Vietnam War, regarded by many, like the Germans in the Second World War, as perpetrators of brutality rather than its victims. The term 'transgenerational transmission' was coined to define the psychological wounds and baggage of one generation being passed on to the next, leaving them to grapple with the trauma and find ways of venting it without re-triggering it in their parents. As Dr M. Gerard Fromm describes it: 'What human beings cannot contain of their experience – what has been traumatically overwhelming, unbearable, unthinkable – falls out of social discourse, but very often on to and into the next generation as an affective sensitivity or a chaotic urgency.'

But none of this information was commonly known and, as I was striving to understand my mother and my relationships and to interpret my recurring dreams, I had no access to such cutting-edge research in science and psychology. Instead I relied on my instinct and periodic exploration of the energetic wisdom of age-old practices.

Quite by chance, while living in Ireland several years earlier, I'd met a man at a friend's house who came from New Zealand. He told me that he had been sent by Maori elders to tell his story and to heal. He had a beautiful face but he didn't look like a magic man. Open as I was – and still am – to alternative and ancient lore, even I doubted that the odd process he outlined would have any impact.

And yet it did.

Sitting in the warm kitchen, I obeyed his quiet instructions. We both kneaded a ball of clay the size of a small lime in the palms of our hands. As the clay warmed, he talked to my pain, his gentle words penetrating the wall behind which it was hiding. We pressed a relief of an ancient labyrinthine spiral on to each surface of the little orbs and then I followed him outside into the cool afternoon and we buried them in a kiln he had carved in the earth. As they baked, he called upon ancient beings from the bogs and seas to return from exile.

Bizarre as it may sound, it was a profound experience: as if he were reaching deep inside me, talking directly to the depths of my body and gently touching my core. When it was over, in a soft voice, he gave his diagnosis: 'There is a memory cell set deep in the waters of your etheric. It has been passed from generation to generation, like a gene, waiting to be talked about and let go.'

Later, he pressed the still-warm talisman with its snake-like relief into my hands and thanked me for letting him get so close.

I would remember his words years afterwards, when they surfaced clothed in the academic language of scientific books on the field of epigenetics.

As if returning to a default setting, after the break-up of my latest relationship, I fell back into prison work, this time in the bowels of London, in jails as grim as any from a Solzhenitsyn or Dickens novel. I moved back to the city and was soon at full throttle again, in the role of arts co-ordinator for the leading prison arts charity, Koestler Arts: facilitating projects, fund-raising and passionately presenting the case for the arts in public talks. With the full support and encouragement of two former chief inspectors of prisons, Sir Stephen Tumim and Lord Ramsbotham, and other big names in prison reform, I established a Learning to Learn Through the Arts scheme. Its aim was to break down barriers to learning and serve as a springboard into education, vocational training, and – ultimately – into work.

We employed visual artists in a full range of media to run intensive projects, each designed to deliver differing learning styles, to raise self-esteem and levels of emotional literacy and to inspire in prisoners the desire to change. Once again, I watched the arts unlock creative talent and provide outlets of expression for the prisoners' trauma, anger and yearnings. I saw defences drop and trust grow; postures change and faces relax as they came to feel both accepted and respected. I witnessed men crying as they received their home-made certificates – worthless as qualifications, but priceless to them. However, in England I was – like so many others keen to reform the English penal system – up against the prevailing, punitive attitude that 'prison works'. The political desire for the prison service to be seen as being tough on crime had created a culture of resistance and risk-averse policies. My experience had taught me that my scheme would only bring about positive change if the huge, dysfunctional systems changed, too. After four years, I was in danger of dropping from exhaustion once again. This time, in a conscious admission of defeat and the need for self-preservation, I surrendered to the stubborn illogic of an overcrowded, underfunded institution and handed in my notice.

That was when my German grandfather stepped out of the wings and on to the stage of my life.

9

The Ashtray

We shall never surrender.
Winston Churchill

I HAVE ALWAYS BEEN AWARE of the presence of the dead. They exist in the empty spaces between the living, in the objects they have touched or worn, in the clouds of memories we carry around with us: silent and invisible, but present.

It is 1981 and I am seventeen years old, sitting with friends around the kitchen table, which is littered with the customary assortment of coffee mugs and cigarettes. A rainbow of plastic lighters claims personal ownership of each packet as smoke curls upwards to hover under the ceiling like fine cobwebs. In the centre is a round, black object covered by a shiny brass lid, with pincers on one side.

As we chat about diets, boys and parties, or complain about our parents, we draw long and hard on our cigarettes and tap the ash on to the lid. Somebody leaves theirs resting in one of the grooves to burn itself out, a long, grey sausage of wasted poison.

When the lid is full, one of us pinches the pincers between thumb and forefinger. It opens like a trapdoor, releasing ash and stubbed-out butts into the black cavern below before snapping shut. Once the base is also full, I unscrew the lid and shake the debris into the bin.

My grandfather's ashtray.

We think nothing of this ashtray until, one day, my sister and I are smoking at the kitchen table while our mother rolls out pastry for one of her famous apple cakes with the almond topping, and she tells us that it had belonged to her father. It was the ashtray he used after the war, as he sat in his chair in the back room of their house, or on the balcony, staring out on to the garden beyond. He would sit there, lighting one cigarette from the glowing butt of the last, sometimes up to seventy a day, until he died of lung cancer. The scraping of its levered lid as he dropped one stub after another into the black bowl had been the soundtrack to my mother's teenage years, just as it was now the soundtrack to ours.

In 2005, I went with a friend to see the newly released German film *Downfall*, a portrayal based on eyewitness accounts of the notorious events that unfolded in the *Führerbunker*, the underground complex that functioned as Hitler's headquarters in Berlin during the last ten days of the Second World War. Everybody, of course, knew the ending. Hitler commits suicide. His 'Thousand-Year Reich' collapses. Germany loses the war. There were no reasons whatsoever to cry. Yet I sobbed inconsolably for four hours after the credits rolled.

'What on earth are you crying for?' my bemused companion asked.

It was a valid question. My reaction was incomprehensible, even to myself.

I had just turned forty, the age when, according to an older friend, you see the horizon of your life. My birthday had indeed felt like reaching a summit. Looking back over the landscape of my past and forward to the years stretching ahead, they appeared, for the first time, equidistant.

In most cultures, the past is visualized as being behind us and the future in front. But there are those, such as the Aymara people of the Andes, for whom it is the past that lies before you, because it is something you can already see, and the future that stalks you from the rear, dark and unknown.

Sitting in that London cinema, I experienced a huge collision of fragments of time. An event from the past had popped up in my present like a roadblock. But what was it about this film that had unleashed such a reservoir of tears? It was definitely not Hitler's downfall. I had been distressed by the killing of the six Goebbels children by their own mother, but it wasn't that, either. It was witnessing the generals confronting Hitler, trying to turn him back from the catastrophic course to which he was committed and which would cost the lives of countless German civilians. Hitler retaliated by denouncing the entire army as 'a bunch of contemptible, disloyal cowards, traitors and failures, the scum of the German people . . . without a shred of honour'.

Honour.

That word jumped out at me, striking within the context of this otherwise wholly dishonourable historical episode.

Hitler had continued to rant, accusing the generals of having hindered his plans for years, of putting obstacles in his way, of betraying and deceiving him from the very beginning. 'I should have liquidated all the high-ranking officers, as Stalin did!' he shouted, ignoring their shocked – hurt, even – protests and ordering that some of them be shot.

For the first time, in my memory at least, we were seeing these soldiers in a halfway human light. Here they were trying to save lives rather than take them. The two camps had always been so clear-cut: the British were good; the Germans were bad. Here, for a brief moment, the distinction had been blurred.

I had always been told that my grandfather valued honour above all else. He had been a Wehrmacht general. Might he, too, have stood up to Hitler and tried to stem the tide of destruction?

Back at my flat, I turned on my computer and Googled my grandfather's name: Karl von Graffen. A photograph appeared on the screen. He was instantly recognizable, his peaked cap casting a shadow over his eyes as he stood against a backdrop of mountains, a cigarette in his hand, talking to two other soldiers. They were dressed differently, and wearing helmets. It looked as if my grandfather was the senior officer.

Other than the few stories my mother had told us, I still knew very little about him. Over the years, both the familiar monochrome face and the green-and-gold leather frame that enclosed it had faded in prominence as a garden of younger generations bloomed around him on my mother's writing desk. But he was always there, unblinking eyes peering from beneath the peak of his cap, lips slightly pursed and sealed in silence.

The surrender of 76th German Corps to 337th Infantry, 85th Division at La Stanga, Italy, on 2 May 1945. L-R: Colonel Oliver W. Hughes, commanding officer of 337th Infantry, General von Graffen, German Corps GG 76th, Lieutenant Lamm, interpreter.

Now, studying this photograph I had never seen before, and reading the accompanying text, I learned that what it showed was my grandfather surrendering. The other two soldiers were not his men, they were Americans. This was the moment his war was lost and he was taken prisoner. It was 2 May 1945. Two days after Hitler had killed himself.

I couldn't take my eyes off this man who might, in another world, have become a much-loved grandfather to me. He was standing upright, sandwiched between an officer and an interpreter, looking dignified, polite, honourable, even.

The photograph had been taken in somewhere called Stanga in the Italian Dolomites. Why on earth would he have been in Italy? It dawned on me that I knew very little about what my grandfather actually did in the war. There are other soldiers in the background, clustered along what looks like a railway line. It was hard to believe that this was him in action – or, rather, non-action – as the loser, the captured enemy.

I'd found the photograph in an online album dedicated to the memory of someone's father. I left a message in the comment box and, to my surprise, received a reply almost immediately.

To my even greater surprise, the reply was from my Tante Marlen in Germany. The tone was both amused and pleased, as if my mother's older sister had been patiently waiting for me, indeed for anyone, to take an interest in her father. She told me that she was in the process of typing out the hundreds of letters he had sent my grandmother – who had died two years earlier – from the front and, later, as a prisoner of war. Written in the old-style handwriting, often in pencil on very thin paper, they were now almost illegible. She offered to send me some typed examples.

A week later, Tante Marlen's transcripts arrived by email. Clicking on the attachments, I was abruptly transported to the Russian Front.

> *1.41*
> *My darling sweetheart,*
> *Today I received your lovely parcel with 150 cigarettes. Thank you so much. I now have managed to put aside a good reserve for when things get bad.*

> *3.6.41*
> *My darling,*
> *I don't know if I will be able to write in the next couple of days, so I just want to send you my love now. And it might be a while before I hear from you because I am constantly on the move.*

These were the first words I heard from the sealed lips of the stern man in the photograph. And they were words of love. Stunned by the tenderness of his voice, I felt almost awkward slipping into the intimacy of his marriage without even knocking.

> *22.10.41*
> *Today I slept, for the first time since 22.6, in a bed with a mattress. Otherwise I have always slept in my sleeping bag. It keeps me warm and is where I feel most at home.*

7.11.41
Yesterday I sunk as low as to become a cigarette-butt
smoker. I collected the stubs from ashtrays and rolled a
cigarette from them. I've managed to have half a cigarette
a day that way. It's sickening to be so dependent on the
incompetence of a so-called intendant . . .

15.6.42
Yesterday was an intensive day as the Russians attacked
several times with tanks and broke through our lines in
the north, albeit only with a few single tanks. We
destroyed 15 of them and I was congratulated by the
supreme commander: 'Under your well-established
leadership . . . ' etc.

Like a fist slammed on a tabletop strewn with iron filings, this small photograph and these short excerpts rearranged the constellation of my entire life. Suddenly my grandfather was a momentous presence. I could hear the rumble of the tanks, smell his cigarette smoke, feel the comfort of his sleeping bag and share the frustrations of his position.

Looking back, I can identify *Downfall* and the discovery of that photograph in Italy as the marker of a significant crossroads in my life. My grandfather's surrender was a turning point for him too, but while my road was leading me out of darkness, his was taking him towards it.

After leaving my job with Koestler Arts, and with my paintings flying off the walls of galleries, I decided to return to Gloucestershire and focus on my own art. On a visit there, I had instantly fallen in love with the derelict gate lodge to Stroud's Victorian cemetery, which was up for sale. I was thrilled when the offer I made for the property was accepted, and set about transforming it into my first permanent abode. I stripped its interiors of intruding ivy, damp woodchip wallpaper, gloss paint and potentially deadly wiring and slowly breathed life into its walls. They seemed to smile as I brushed them with colour and filled the spaces between them with love, laughter and the paraphernalia of my life. In this neglected little stone building that had housed the former guardians of the dead, I knew I had found home.

While unpacking boxes that had long been stored at my parents' house, I came across the black ashtray that had been my grandfather's constant companion in his final years. I hadn't seen it in the decades since it sat on our kitchen table when we were teenagers.

I turned the ashtray in my hands. I had enrolled on a fine art degree course in Stroud and, experimenting with new techniques, I was beginning to investigate how memory can reside in places; how history can remain resonant in the earth; how the essence of a person can be held in objects. I knew that the ashtray was an important relic of my grandfather.

In May 2007, Tante Marlen finally completed the Herculean task of typing up the hundreds of letters my grandfather had written to his wife during his years away. She bound this chronicle of his war years in a blue cover and sent a copy to me. Dictionary in hand, I set to work reading it. Although she had emailed me a few snippets previously, I had little sense of what the rest might reveal.

A letter from my grandfather to my grandmother, March 1942.

The letters begin in Poland in the early months of 1941. The war has been going well for the Germans. My grandfather sounds relaxed and confident, a man in his element as a soldier:

> *I think in the coming months we will first of all be throwing the English out of the Mediterranean so that we have an uninterrupted connection to Africa . . . I've already made myself a bit unpopular as I really insist on discipline, so anybody found on the streets misbehaving will be put into a cold room with no furniture for a night . . . I'm refreshing my Russian but I don't think I'll have an opportunity to use it . . .*

I didn't like him. He came across as a macho bully, the kind of war-justifying army officer I would have vociferously challenged had he been alive. I didn't like the tone he used towards my grandmother, either. Sometimes he sarcastically chastises her for not writing enough, other times he barks orders at her to send things that he has forgotten: gloves, a thicker coat, tobacco – above all, tobacco. He was clearly a nicotine addict and his war was going well or badly according to how many cigarettes he had or, more crucially, didn't have.

I also found the letters confusing; too full of references to places, military terms or German words I didn't know.

> *We get wonderful fresh bread rolls with butter,*
> *marmalade and sausage and then I am on the road in the*
> *car from morning to evening . . . In four weeks the*
> *Balkan story will probably already be history, our losses*
> *are laughably low and in Italy nothing much more can*
> *happen. In Berlin and Kiel the English have been making*
> *themselves uncomfortably noticeable, though – have you*
> *felt any of it? The time of our separation is now becoming*
> *too long, but I think in 6 months we won't be separated*
> *any more . . . A thousand thanks for the 200 R6.*

R6 was a German brand of cigarettes. This rang a bell. Weren't these what my brother Christopher smoked?

What is my grandfather doing in Poland? He is clearly very busy meeting people, but who? He mentions 'delicate matters' and training his regiment to march long distances – but what for?

On 21 June he writes only four lines:

> *My dearest,*
> *Just to quickly send you my love. I unfortunately don't*
> *have time for more. When you receive this letter you will*
> *know why! A loving kiss for the children and for you,*
> *Yours,*
> *Karl*

My grandmother would indeed soon know why, and so would
the whole world. The secret invasion of Russia, Operation
Barbarossa, had begun. His division is about to march hundreds of miles towards Moscow.

I paused and looked out of my window. Heavy spring
rains were falling on the trees and graves in the cemetery,
threatening to pulp the last of the pink blossoms. I lit a fire,
settled into an armchair and read on, marking in the margins
wherever my grandfather mentioned the names of places or
used words that were unfamiliar to me.

What was the OKW? Why were the Russian villagers
greeting the Germans with flowers and milk, as if they
were liberators? Who were the 'terrorists' and 'partisans'
who committed horrendous acts and massacres against the
soldiers?

> *1.7.41*
> *The roads are so bad, and the dust doesn't let you see more*
> *than 2 metres in front of you . . . There are abandoned*
> *Russian tanks everywhere . . . But in 2–3 weeks at the*
> *latest we'll be in Moscow and then that's Russia sorted.*

Sorted? Really? Even with my scant knowledge of Second
World War history, I knew this was wildly over-optimistic.

The conflict there would rage on until Germany's defeat four years later. I read on, following his advance into the hell of the Eastern Front and the interminable Siege of Leningrad, through freezing winters and spring mud.

The Soviets, recovering from their surprise, fought back with increasing confidence and intensity. As the bombs dropped, so did the temperature. And then my grandfather's supply of cigarettes ran out and his letters stopped, too. It was June 1942. His division was under heavy artillery fire in the Volkhov region. The Germans had encircled 40,000 Russians, trapping them in a mudbath, and the Russians were trying to 'box' their way out with tanks. And then, silence. It was as if several crucial chapters had been ripped out of a novel. I was left teetering at the edge of a chasm.

My mother filled in some of the background details to her childhood memories and my father, fascinated by modern European history, consulted the books lining the shelves of his small study. His collection wasn't restricted to works written by the victors – he was married to a German, after all – and his understanding of events not confined to a narrow British perspective. As I began Googling some of my questions, more floated up straight away, like spores released into the wind. Hungry for visual information and tangible experiences, I scanned online images to flesh out and bring these scenes to life.

A trickle of letters restarted in February 1945, when I found my grandfather in Italy. He was still optimistic, still in charge, still smoking. The war ended in May 1945 but his letters didn't. The third section of the chronicle was dedicated to his life as a prisoner of war, first in camps in Italy and then in Germany. These last letters connected me to a human condition that made sense to me. I viewed my grandfather in a more sympathetic light as a prisoner than I could as a soldier. And, when his mood descended into blackness as incarceration took its toll, I felt his devastation as though it were my own.

His later letters, in which the British become his jailers, brought me face to face with my own inner enemies. I felt the tug of a familiar conflict of loyalties. He was a German prisoner of the retributive British. And yet the British had conquered an evil regime. I read on, trying to get inside his head, desperately searching for signs of self-reflection, regret, remorse, horror – anything that would help me cast him as a 'good soldier' who obeyed orders out of a sense of duty rather than conviction.

10

Like Grandfather, Like Grandson

When we look at our parents, then we see that behind them
are their parents, and behind their parents are other parents,
and so on through many generations. The same life flows
through all of them until it reaches us.

Bert Hellinger, 'Introduction to Family Constellations'

'YOUR BROTHER HAS ALWAYS reminded me of my father,' my mother remarked one day.

I'd never heard her say that before.

Christopher bore no obvious physical resemblance either to my parents or to me and my sister.

'He looks like the moon,' we would joke, a reference to his round face.

Christopher had been working for General Motors in Wiesbaden and Frankfurt since the mid-1990s. His arrival in Germany had coincided with my departure. Though quieter and more private than the rest of us, he was clearly accomplished and respected in his job and always fun and generous when we saw him. But contact with him was increasingly sporadic. His visits became shorter and less frequent. Emails remained unanswered for months. My parents worried but wanted to believe his excuses: he hadn't received the last message; he'd been exceptionally busy with work or away on a business trip abroad.

We knew he was a heavy drinker and smoker, and it was obvious that he was troubled by something. However, it was a subject none of us could broach with him without risking further withdrawal. Caroline and I tried to gently coax him to communicate, offering unconditional support and the promise of confidentiality, but our efforts were met with silence.

The timing of my mother's comment was astonishing. A few weeks earlier, I had participated in a 'family constellation', a powerful exercise developed by German psychotherapist Bert Hellinger designed to uncover the underlying – usually unconscious and often destructive – dynamics within families, particularly those that extend over generations. It builds on ancient ancestor-honouring practices as well as the idea that our individual wellbeing is intimately linked to the wellbeing of our wider family system, or 'family soul', past and present.

The format is simple. It involves a large circle of people (generally strangers), one of whom has requested to be the subject of the constellation. The facilitator asks the subject to pick people from the circle to represent members of their family and place them in a spatial arrangement that seems to make sense. The mother might be in the centre, for example, the 'estranged' father on the periphery, the 'dead' grandmother facing inwards and the siblings at the back. Then each 'family member' is asked how they feel about their position.

It isn't role play. The participants are given no details of their 'characters'. Instead, the exercise draws on a form of intuition, encouraging everyone to express whatever words and emotions come to them. Afterwards, the facilitator shrewdly assists in a reshuffle, carefully moving people around within the circle to create a different constellation with different dynamics.

It was an extraordinary experience. I saw the dynamics of my family brought to life with uncanny accuracy through the individuals and arrangement I had chosen. Among many smaller revelations, one stood out. It was the dynamic between my brother and my grandfather, who I had placed on the far edge of the circle, a long way away from the rest of the family, like a star in another orbit. The man who was representing Christopher was drawn to our grandfather like a magnet, detaching himself from the core family to join him on the perimeter.

I couldn't explain this, but I left the workshop certain that if my grandfather was reintegrated back into the family circle, where he belonged, then my brother would follow. I didn't know exactly how I could accomplish that, but I decided then and there that I would make it happen.

I started by opting for an approach of light communication with Christopher without agenda or expectations. Maybe acceptance would work better than pressure. When I emailed him excerpts from our grandfather's letters, I had reckoned he would find them interesting but was fully prepared not to hear back from him. Unusually, I received an immediate reply.

'The letters are amazing,' he wrote, breaking months of radio silence. 'I have only skimmed them as I don't like crying at work! WHERE did you get them???'

This spontaneous expression of emotion moved me. I missed my brother. In our little email exchange, I discovered that he did indeed smoke the R6 cigarettes that my grandfather favoured. 'How come that brand?' I asked him. It was a pretty obscure one for an English person to choose. He could not come up with any concrete reason.

Was this all a coincidence? It didn't feel that way to me.

As the eldest daughter, Tante Marlen was the self-appointed guardian and archivist of the family history, and she held all the photo albums. The letters had resurrected my grandfather as a soldier. Now I wanted to create a fuller portrait of him as a father, husband, son, sportsman, poet and, ultimately, a broken man.

I planned a visit to Germany and my aunt and uncle offered to drive me to some of the places of significance to our family. I extended the invitation to Christopher. He accepted without hesitation.

As the trip approached, I felt excited and nervous. But I hadn't heard from Christopher in several weeks. He wasn't responding to texts and I feared that he was going to drop out. I hoped for the best, but braced myself for disappointment.

Twenty-four hours before I left, he finally replied to say that he'd muddled his dates and was in Detroit. I tried to be philosophical but I felt sure that he was not telling the truth. Sure enough, when my parents called his office in Frankfurt the next day, he was there.

The first thing he said to them was that he'd lied to me and felt awful about it. Apparently, a very open conversation ensued, in which he told them that he just couldn't face the questions about his life that our relatives were bound to ask. He acknowledged that he had problems to sort out. Precisely what this meant, we didn't know. Beyond the fact that, professionally, he was thriving in a position of considerable responsibility, we knew little of how he lived. Still, his admission that there was something to be sorted out was a chink in his wall of secrecy. And so, in spite of my sadness at his absence, I couldn't help feeling hopeful that Christopher was turning a corner.

I rang my mother, and she sounded much better for having talked to her son. 'At least we now know he's alive,' she said. She cried for a few moments before adding: 'You are a special person, darling.'

I was deeply touched by the rare expression of such an unfamiliar sentiment. I marvelled at how easy and close our relationship had become over the previous few years. Was it because my forgiveness had softened our edges? Or perhaps my interest in her family was enabling her to relax long-established defences.

I had been many times to Itzehoe in Schleswig-Holstein, where Tante Marlen and Onkel Wulf lived and our family roots were embedded. Sitting in the living room of their second-floor flat, with the traditional glasses of Sekt bubbling gently in front of us, we launched effortlessly into conversation. I was soon asking question upon question: what roles had my grandparents played in the rise of National Socialism? Had they welcomed it? Had my grandmother known anything about the Jews being sent to camps? Had they ever hidden anyone, or resisted in some more subversive way? Had they known people who had been part of the mobs that taunted Jews, making old men scrub the streets on their hands and knees? And, if they hadn't, what was it that had prevented them from feeling and acting that way when so many others were?

I had long seen Nazi Germany as a huge, grey rabbit hole into which many ordinary people had fallen, landing,

Alice-like, in a hall of locked doors with very few keys that fitted. I wanted to know how some people had become complying participants and others active resistors. How did some stand by as their neighbours were dragged away while others risked their lives to hide them? I wanted to understand the passivity that turned people into reluctant bystanders. I wanted to know what my family had chosen.

My aunt was unfazed by my barrage of questions and answered them openly and honestly. They had known that Jewish people were disappearing, but no, they didn't know about the concentration camps. Goebbels' propaganda had painted a very different picture. They were never part of the mobs, but they had never hidden anybody, either. Before I went to bed, she handed me a copy of the memoir Mummy-groß had written in her final years. After my grandmother's death, Tante Marlen had typed and bound her words into a companion volume to her husband's letters.

This was the first time I'd seen this memoir and, as my grandmother had never talked about the war, I zoomed in on that period. I read late into the night, hearing her dear voice as she described their lives, gently brushing up against the darkness of the times with the light touch of someone not wanting to stir it up.

I also devoured the few older family photo albums that had survived the flight and the war, staring at the black-and-ochre-white images, willing them to expand in any direction to reveal more context. I was seeing my grandfather from all angles, not just the face that looked out from beneath his cap. He was a handsome man: high cheekbones, soulful eyes. And there was one image that could have been an older incarnation of my brother. The similarities between them were so glaringly obvious to me, I wondered why they had never been remarked upon until my mother's recent comment.

The next day, Tante Marlen and Onkel Wulf took me to my grandfather's home town, Plön, where he was buried. Set back from the lake, in a well-tended cemetery, his grave was covered in a blanket of apricot-coloured flowers. I knelt down beside it, feeling simultaneously numb and overwhelmed.

'Hello, Großvati,' I said to him awkwardly. It was the first time I had addressed him by this diminutive.

There wasn't much to see at the red-brick house in which he was born, or at the imposing white castle that had housed the military school where, as a cadet, he had been inculcated with the values that would become the bedrock of his character. We weren't able to enter either and the fresh paint on their walls seemed to have wiped away all traces of the past.

After a coffee by the lake, we drove east for several hours to Schwerin, where my grandparents had enjoyed their first happy years of marriage. I peered through the rusty, bramble-strangled wrought-iron gates at the impressively large former army barracks and the huge, silent courtyard where once young men had jostled and assembled in their uniforms to be photographed, their lives still bursting with possibility.

Outside the red-and-white brick building overlooking the castle and the lake where my grandparents had set up home, I clambered through the flowerbed to peep through the window of their ground-floor apartment. I was hoping to catch a glimpse of the setting for the happy breakfast table scene I had studied in one of Tante Marlen's family albums. Net curtains cast the room into darkness, but I could just make out the carvings of the painted wainscoting.

In the centre of the town, crumbling and bullet-pocked render bore witness to postwar occupation by the Soviets, followed by decades as part of the Deutsche Demokratische Republik (DDR). I followed my aunt and uncle into one of Schwerin's oldest wine bars, its vaulted stone walls and small tables bathed in the orange glow of stained-glass windows. This had been my grandparents' favourite bar. It was here, in 1928, after just three meetings, that they became engaged. I looked at the white starched napkins standing to attention on the tables, ready for the evening's customers, and imagined my grandparents gazing into each other's eyes and smiling as they raised sparkling champagne flutes in a toast to their future.

We retraced their footsteps, wandering through the agapanthus- and box-hedged gardens along the shoreline of the serene lake. Inside the castle, my uncle pointed out a white spiral staircase which, I had been told, my grandfather had run up every day to report for duty. He filmed me running up the same stairs, euphoric at the affinity it made me feel with this energetic and talented young man, a new husband and father, living out a rich and happy life he had no reason to fear would not prove lasting.

I wanted to make some kind of symbolic offering at each of these places, to give him something, as you would bring a gift when visiting friends. I considered a rose or some other symbol of peace or love as a gesture of reconciliation, but when I thought about the real man who was my grandfather, it was obvious: tobacco. It had made his life tolerable, perhaps hellish, too, in his final years. Either way, it loomed large for him. And as I had been working with earth, mud and sand in my paintings, using them as carriers of memories of the sites they had come from, it seemed appropriate to perform a little exchange of soil from both countries. I couldn't help feeling that my grandfather might have thrown such esoteric claptrap back in my face. Nevertheless, at every significant spot, I dug a small hole, collected some soil in a labelled plastic bag and filled the cavity with earth brought from my garden in Gloucestershire, mixed with a pinch of British-manufactured Golden Virginia.

Our longest road trip was to Jüterbog, where the family had lived for the duration of the war. Tante Marlen, who had visited the town and the house a few years before for a school reunion, pointed out the landmarks of their childhood. There was the Schiller Schule the three girls had attended, where Nazi teachers had frowned upon their aristocratic surname, a clear pointer to the elitist lineage the National Socialists wanted to obliterate. There was the lake in which they swam in the summer, where incendiary bombs had on one occasion turned the water into a bubbling bath of fire and the young children had had to paddle quickly away from the dancing flames to the shelter of the surrounding bushes.

The home they had been forced to flee, in what had been the military part of town, was partly obscured by chestnut trees and unkempt shrubs. It was a large house, its tall, narrow windows in keeping with those of the other red-brick buildings around it. In those days it had consisted of two apartments, with my mother's family occupying the ground floor. Now it was divided into four.

My aunt knocked on the door. A short-haired woman in baggy jeans and red trainers opened it, strategically blocking the entrance as we crowded on the doorstep, explaining who we were and hoping to be invited inside. She didn't allow us into the flat, but she took us up a back staircase to the huge, empty attic where the children had once played. Tante Marlen tried hard to disguise her emotion as she stood, for the first time since their departure in the 1940s, in what had once been their playroom.

Outside, we wandered around the garden, an unimaginative grassy patch, instantly recognizable from a photograph taken there of the children a year before their flight. It had not, it seemed, changed at all in the intervening sixty years.

Across the road was a building that had been a shop, the scene of one of my mother's stories. It was a story that, as a child, I had found hard to comprehend. Little Jutta had walked in one day and bid the shopkeeper 'Good morning'. A teacher who was in the shop asked her why she hadn't said 'Heil Hitler'. Jutta explained that her mother had told her they didn't

L–R: Marlen, Adolf, Dorothee and Jutta outside their home in Jüterbog, 1944.

need to say 'Heil Hitler' to people they knew, an admission that had almost fatal consequences for my grandmother. She was reported, taken in for questioning and released only when she managed to prove that her husband was a high-ranking officer in the Wehrmacht.

My aunt spoke positively, even enthusiastically, about her childhood: her loving parents, the tricks her older brother played on his sisters; their family jokes and sayings. Unlike my mother, she insisted they never went hungry. And she recounted tales of night-time air raids, and being dragged out of bed and into the cellar, without any hint of trauma. I was conscious that the differing stories spoke not necessarily to different experiences but to different memories. I knew that it would be tricky to glean the full truth from those who were only children at the time and being shaped by propaganda from a very young age.

At the now abandoned artillery school, where my grandfather had taught war theory and tactics, I crunched through corridors still littered with shards of glass and rusting food tins left behind when the Soviet occupiers departed in 1993. I imagined him in his professional role, walking briskly between rooms and buildings, clicking across the floor in his knee-high boots and slate-grey breeches. Only a few architectural details of the school's former status survived: a stucco ceiling rose, a marble frieze, the stone body and wings of a huge, decapitated Nazi eagle.

I wished Christopher could have been here, standing in the bootprints of his grandfather as he progressed through a highly respected and successful career.

Back in Schleswig-Holstein, effortlessly skipping over the entire war to land in the family's life in 1945, we were

Karl at an artillery demonstration.

joined by my mother's younger sister, Tante Dörli, who had been eight at the time. Following the contours of the Baltic inlet, we pulled up in front of a large courtyard lined by low buildings that reached towards entry gates like welcoming arms. At the far end stood an impressive white house with a tall, red-tiled roof. This was Grödersby, my great-grandparents' farm, where the family had lived with other relatives and refugees after the war. My grandfather was to join them here in 1948, when he was finally released.

With no sign of the current owners being in residence, we crept around the back of the house to the large garden leading down to the shore. Once filled with flowers and veg-etables, it was now largely laid to lawn. There was nothing left of the neat rows of tomatoes my grandfather had grown to sell to the restaurants in the local town, and just one weeping

The vegetable garden at Grödersby after the war.

willow remained near the water's edge. There had been a jetty too, from which the family had often launched their sailing boat during the happier late 1950s.

This was my grandfather's view from his chair on the balcony. I could almost hear the click of his brass-topped ashtray as he lit one cigarette from the next, here, in his home, until the cancer finally claimed him.

There was sadness in my aunts' voices as they recounted their stories from those challenging postwar years. Before the war, my grandfather had, I already knew, been stern to the point of being over-strict. After nearly ten years' absence, he resurfaced into the bustling life of a family that had been obliged to steam ahead without him. With his former position at the head of the family filled by my grandmother, who had, in effect, been both mother and father to four children, three of whom were now in their teens, his authority had diminished.

My grandfather had become a relative stranger to his own family. With his son preparing for a career in agriculture and his wife running the household, nobody took him seriously when he talked about the little garden he'd begun cultivating. He was seen as irrelevant to their daily lives, and somehow unworldly. What could he know about anything after all those years away?

My aunts had nothing but praise for their mother, who, they said, had been remarkable throughout. She was only in her mid to late thirties when the war ended, and had held the family together, keeping her daughters fed, disciplined and, most importantly, imbued with a sense of safety. She never complained as she worked relentlessly, all the while supporting her husband on the front and, later, in prison, with letters and parcels.

Like their counterparts in England and elsewhere, German women had become far more independent and self-sufficient during the long years without their men, and all across Europe war-ravaged husbands were finding themselves largely superfluous to the functioning of their family units. It can't have been easy for women to adapt to having these unheroic, fallen men back in their lives. My grandmother would later reproach herself for not being patient or considerate enough, but she, too, had been changed by war.

An organic feminism had grown out of the wholesale defeat of the nation. In Britain, after a period of adjustment, the returning heroes managed to put women back in their prewar boxes, in spite of the huge contribution they had made to the war effort. But in Germany, the shift was deeper and more permanent.

In 1945, the anonymous author of *A Woman in Berlin* wrote:

> These days I keep noticing how my feelings towards men – and the feelings of all the other women – are changing. We feel sorry for them; they seem so miserable and powerless. The weaker sex. Deep down we women are experiencing a kind of collective disappointment. The Nazi world – ruled by men, glorifying the strong man – is beginning to crumble and with it the myth of 'Man'. In earlier wars, men could claim that the privilege of killing and being killed for the fatherland was theirs and theirs alone. Today we women too have a share. That has transformed us, emboldened us. Among the many defeats at the end of this war is the defeat of the male sex.

My heart ached for my grandfather: not as a soldier, but as a man. My grandparents' relationship had blossomed as a marriage between a strong, successful husband and a cultured and feminine wife. But those roles had been ripped into pieces which it was proving impossible to stick back together. I could feel the impact of his fall from grace within the family. In the light of the horrors that emerged after the war, it would not have been surprising if his wife and children, like so many others, had harboured conflicting feelings about him and his professional commitment to the cause he had fought for. But if they did, none of those thoughts was expressed out loud.

My aunts described their father as a romantic: a poet and a

thinker, and apparently hopeless with money. He would spend what little they had on impractical if heartfelt gestures. He had once splashed out on a flowery negligée for my grandmother, a touching gift from a husband who had been deprived of intimacy but an unappreciated extravagance when broad beans were having to be grown to the size of small eggs in order to provide food for hungry mouths. He also bought an open-topped Opel, his favourite car, as a surprise for my grandmother's birthday, propelling her, and their tight budget, into spasms of panic.

I couldn't help but pick up on another connection between my brother and his grandfather: Christopher was working for Opel in his job with General Motors.

The saddest story of all was Tante Marlen's memory of my grandfather, at one family lunch, reaching across to place his hand on his wife's. My grandmother quietly pulled hers away. I shivered, even though the day was warm and sunny, and excused myself to return to the weeping willow. Beneath the tree, I performed my small ritual of remembrance and reconciliation, digging so furiously into the rootbound soil that the head of the trowel broke away from the handle.

Over the following months, and out of sight in Germany, my brother was unravelling. His last-minute absence had alerted us all to the fact he was struggling, not least with alcohol. I knew from experience that there would come a nadir of suffering, the proverbial rock bottom, at which a person is confronted with the extent of their dysfunctions, denial and pain. It is a place where you must make a choice, sometimes as stark as the choice between living and dying. In order to live, you need to choose to change. At that moment, rock bottom can transform from an inescapable quagmire of despair into a firm base from which you can push up towards the surface, towards recovery. In spite of its darkness and isolation, rock bottom is a good place to reach. It is a chance to break the spiralling freefall of self-destruction.

Christopher reached his rock bottom over the Christmas of 2007, six months after my visit to Germany. We had been unable to make contact with him for months and, with no way to reach him, we all feared the worst. We sang carols with faltering voices and my father remained on his knees for longer than usual after communion.

On 2 January, my parents received a call from one of his colleagues. Christopher hadn't shown up for work in the New Year and had been found in his flat, alive, but only just. He was in a hospital in Frankfurt, where machines were preventing his body's systems from shutting down. Without hesitation, the whole family rallied round. My parents suddenly began to look old as they faced another challenge from their little brood of misfits.

Christopher spent weeks lying on the floor of his dark pit, too weak to push himself to the surface. But he pulled through. A period of rehabilitation followed, during which – to our mutual amusement – he was exposed to some of the practices and vocabulary familiar to him from my therapies which he had tended not to take too seriously. He eventually got back on his feet, slayed his demons, or at least managed to lock them up, returned to work and, most importantly, rejoined the family.

I watched in wonder as this episode unfolded. Behind the drama, I could see how my grandfather's growing presence in our conversations was shaking the bedrock on which we all stood. My trips and research were like stages in an operation to remove a bullet. This one had been festering deep in the entrails of our shared past and it had taken a collective fever to draw our attention to its existence.

But now, as I had hoped, we were reinstating my grandfather and my brother was returning to the fold along with him.

11

Shadowlands

Vision is the art of seeing what is invisible to others.

Jonathan Swift, 'Thoughts on Various Subjects,
Moral and Diverting'

I WAS SEVENTEEN WHEN I had my first experience of the power of place. While studying art history in Florence, I was absorbed in sketching Michelangelo's four figurative sculptures in the heavily marbled Medici Chapel when the guard on duty ambled over to see what I was doing. Picking up on my passion for the sculptor, he beckoned me to follow him through a small door in a corner of the chapel, leading me down a steep, narrow flight of stairs and into a tiny vaulted space.

As my eyes adjusted to the dim light, amputated limbs materialized on the white plastered walls; hands gesturing, flexed shoulder muscles, a foot resting. I felt the prickle of goosebumps. The guard waited, not uttering a word, until he saw recognition dawning on my face. These were the same postures as those I had just been sketching. Barely able to contain his excitement, he explained. Until a short while ago, this had been a coal cellar. It was only when the coal was cleared out that they had discovered these drawings. I was standing in the room Michelangelo had used as his studio while he worked on the chapel. It was as if the passage of over four centuries ceased to exist. The usually taut threads of time spanning past and future lost all tension, slackening into a quiet heap that was the current moment. Here, in the presence of these priceless sketches, I felt a thrill like none I had ever known. I didn't question or judge my experience. I just knew I was as close to the spirit of the long-dead man as could be possible.

That was when I realized how, on some level, the essence of a person can linger in a place, connecting them to the present even when their physical form has long been absent.

Artists quickly learn that 'negative space', the space between or around physical forms, is as important as the objects themselves. Empty space is the silence between musical notes, the pauses in poetry, the stillness of a dancer. Therein often lies the meaning or drama of the piece. To experience the fullness of empty space requires a suspension of left-brain – logical, linear or analytical – thinking in favour of the right brain's more dreamy, creative, feeling style. Only then can you begin to properly see, and include or reproduce in your art, its energy.

We used to practise the technique of 'seeing' in my art therapy training. We'd compare a dead leaf and a fresh green one; a baby's hand with that of an old person. The differences are not purely visual or sensory. If you allow yourself, you can *feel* the quantity and quality of the life forces within the physical forms.

This led me to many questions about what it is that we humans feel in the presence of religious relics, antique collections and museums. Or former battlefields and ancient cultural sites. Or even family graves.

Animism, the belief that every object, living or non-living, has a soul or spirit, is a feature of many ancient cultures. What is it that compels us to preserve and value certain tangible objects, buildings and landscapes? Imagination, fantasy, wishful thinking? Do we imbue the material world with meaning, or does the material world itself hold resonant memories in a similar way as our bodies do, deep in our muscles and cells? And, if memory hovers like an aura around a physical object or place, could we develop a cognitive method of gaining access to it, just as artists train themselves to use the right side of the brain to access the energy of negative space?

Psychologists describe a memory of a past event that has not been recalled for a considerable period of time as a 'recovered memory'. Like a smell or tune or piece of material heritage, a particular location can instantly evoke a past that appears to have been buried. The multi-sensory dimension brings it to life, just as the stories of contemporary witnesses add colour, detail and emotion to the black-and-white facts of history.

It was after visiting the landmarks of my family's life in Germany that I began to wonder whether it was possible that a person's unresolved traumas or crimes do not die with their physical bodies but persist, trapped within whatever essence or memory of that person remains, waiting for subsequent generations to dig them up and lay them to rest. If time is not linear but relative, or even an illusion, as is claimed by some philosophers and even certain physicists, could the past, present and future co-exist in each and every moment?

*

Knowing some of the facts about my family's past was not enough to process them. I had many lightbulb moments in terms of understanding, but my intense responses came from a deeper place. For over forty years, these stories, their traumas – as perpetrators or victims of war – had lived disquietingly inside me. I had tried suppressing them and escaping them. I knew nothing about the mechanics of trauma then, but I intuited that *feeling* its impact was an important element of recovery. And, to feel the whole story in all its potency, I needed to travel to the sites where memory, conscience and emotion collided.

There were two places I knew had witnessed key moments in my grandfather's and mother's lives. The first was Stanga, north of Belluno, where my grandfather had surrendered in May 1945.

It was from the military service record among his letters that I had learned how, in September 1943, he had been transferred from Russia to central Italy to fight the Allies around Bologna, San Marino and Rimini and then in the notorious 1944 Battle of Monte Cassino. In the final weeks of the war, he had been made leader of the LXXVI tank reserve in the Dolomites, which explained why it was at Stanga that he received the orders for unconditional surrender to the Americans.

I invited my sister to come with me to Italy to try to find this place and, always supportive, she agreed. With only a printout of the photo I'd found on the internet and the sparsest of information to go on, Caroline and I drove through chocolate-box Tyrolean valleys to the little town of Vipiteno, 5 kilometres from the village of Stanghe I had identified on a detailed map of the Dolomites and which I had assumed was an Italian spelling of Stanga. But it soon became obvious that Stanghe wasn't the place in the photograph. The landscape was all wrong. Confused, we inquired at the tourist office in Vipiteno. It was late in the day but the young assistant happily rose to this novel challenge. The three of us pored over local maps of the hilly area north of Belluno and leafed through guidebooks until the assistant unearthed a minuscule hamlet several hours' drive away, just a cluster of little squares with a road running through it.

The following morning, we made our way along the winding road that knits the Alps to the Dolomites until a sign announced our arrival in La Stanga. The map at the tourist office had not lied: there really was nothing here other than a tiny collection of buildings and a roadside guesthouse. We scanned the scenery in vain for landmarks resembling those in the picture. We were already through the hamlet when I looked in the rear-view mirror and saw them. We both did: huge rocks rising like parted thighs on either side of the valley. And there, nestled between them, was the chalet from the photograph. A handful of other houses had been built around it since. The railway line was gone and the modern tarmac road had distorted the 1945 scene almost beyond recognition. But the landscape of mountains and rocks was identical. Our hearts thumping, we turned the car round and approached a woman hanging out her washing.

At first I was afraid to bring out our photograph, for fear of a strong anti-German reaction. But she was interested and happy to help. The original chalet, she told us, had been built in 1942. Caroline and I walked around, looking for the spot where our grandfather and the two Americans had stood, but the angles and relationship between the buildings and

La Stanga.

rocks were always wrong. The woman advised us to ask at the guesthouse, as that had also been around in the forties. Ordering two beers in their bar, we cautiously showed the landlord the picture. He reacted with excitement, calling over his wife, who told us that her great-aunt had run the guesthouse during the German occupation, and that this was where the generals had stayed. Her mother, thirteen at the time, remembered it well. The soldiers had been billeted 50 metres further down the road but often congregated here to eat and drink.

My grandfather had probably been standing right in front of this building when he was taken prisoner. Maybe the Americans had arrived early in the morning and caught them by surprise before they could get to their positions. If there even were still positions by that stage. Or perhaps he had wandered out to greet the victors. Greet? Is that what you do to people who are about to capture you? It was hard to imagine his state of mind. After years of orders to advance, destroy, kill or hold positions, he was now being told to put down his weapons, wave the white flag and surrender himself and his men to indefinite detention. I willed this place to reveal the events to which it had borne witness, longing to yank back the curtains of time and step into my grandfather's boots.

The landlords invited us to dine in their restaurant that evening. Exhausted, we found accommodation at another, smaller guesthouse nearby, run by a welcoming couple who quickly joined the growing troupe of intrigued locals. My knowledge of wartime history was so pitiful, and so focused on England and Germany, that I had overlooked Italy's own Faşcist past under Mussolini – a past that meant many Italian family histories featured wartime allegiances to the Germans. I was just relieved to be received with warmth rather than the customary loathing.

Dinner was served by the great-niece of the woman who had served our grandfather. It was quite possible that we were sitting at the same table, on the same terracotta tiled floor, beside the same tiled stove. Tiramisu and grappa appeared on the house. In a small adjoining room, complete with more original tiles, a fire crackled in a 360-degree open hearth flanked on three sides by wooden benches. I sat down and stared into the flames. The interlude between 1945 and 2008 closed. It was beyond doubt that my grandfather had sat here, talking and smoking, flicking his cigarette butts into the embers, either aware or oblivious of the imminent denouement of his war making its way towards him through the mountains.

The following morning, Caroline admitted to feeling emotionally hungover. She was not used to exposure to the huge shadowlands, not just of our family but of Germany. She, too, had broken ranks with parental hopes and societal expectations by returning from her own travels in South America with a young man called Dante in tow, a 'penniless Peruvian panpipe-player', as his best man would fondly describe him at their wedding. For years, her priority had been stabilizing a marriage perceived by the outside world as a mismatch and raising their two gorgeous boys while holding down a job in the tailor-made travel industry. Yet I was glad for her sake as well as mine that she had made this journey. This was her heritage, too, and I was convinced we were all carrying some of it, even if our responses were different.

There was one more task to accomplish before we left La Stanga: my soil ritual. With its fusion of site-specific rite, remembrance and reconciliation, I had come to see this on one level as a form of acupuncture, using a trowel instead of needles to stimulate the healing of wounded places and wounded people, and on another as a means of helping me to process and release the vestiges of any burden of trauma or guilt held within me.

With tarmac having replaced the stony road where my grandfather had stood, I exchanged my blend of earth and tobacco for the soft sand and pebbles of an almost dry riverbed. As I did so, an apology spontaneously welled up in my heart.

I apologized – to whom exactly I couldn't be sure – on behalf not only of my grandfather, but also my grandmother, the wider family and myself. I asked for forgiveness for any real or perceived culpability we continued to bear in relation to the war. And I sent healing and love to all those – on either side – affected by the horrific actions of fellow human beings.

Performing my ritual in La Stanga.

We concluded our ceremony by folding our paper copy of the photograph of my grandfather's surrender into a small origami boat, like those we used to make out of chocolate-biscuit wrappers as children, and launching it into a vestigial trickle of the river. As we drove into the Dolomites, I felt the afterglow of this powerful meeting of third-generation war descendants whose family destinies had crossed once again.

The second place of special significance was Berlin, the city that had provided my grandparents with many happy memories but had also been the backdrop to my mother's trauma.

I had always regretted never having seen East Berlin while the wall was still up. In my imagination, it was an urban landscape of spies lurking on gloomy street corners and brave souls being shot attempting to escape, tangled like crows in a barbed-wire curtain. The whole notion of an Iron

Curtain snaking from north to south, slicing Europe in two like a sandwich and severing families, intrigued me.

As it was, I made my first visit there soon after the jubilant scenes of the fall of the wall had burst on to our television screens in 1989. In the former Eastern Sector, more bullet-pocked walls and crumbling façades betrayed the failures of Soviet life. Low cloud made the air feel clammy and stale, as if you were entering a damp cellar in which time has been trapped. A cold wind whistled along the wide strip of rubble-littered wasteland that meandered through the city, following the course of the partially dismantled wall. Occasionally a pop-up café lit by candles would offer some respite from the echoes of the heavy boots that had once patrolled the streets. Beneath the bleak surface of desolation, however, was an unmistakable sense of release and the promise of spring.

Through the 1990s, Berlin hummed with the activity of cranes and diggers. As capitalism trampled its opportunistic feet over the decaying remains of Communism, the raw uniqueness of the early post-reunification years was gradually transformed into the new, shiny conformity of contemporary cities everywhere. Norman Foster's sparkling glass dome crowned the restoration of the Reichstag, reflecting the new German parliament's forward gaze and insistence on transparency. Watchtowers and checkpoints, stripped of their deadly power, became part of the tourist playground.

In the back streets and suburbs, however, a darker energy persisted, pulsating through the cracks in the pavements and skulking in the unrenovated doorways in which people had once taken cover from the gunfire ricocheting through their neighbourhoods. No amount of cosmetic surgery could disguise the impact of the city's near-destruction etched on the faces of the people who had lived through it. No amount of fresh tarmac and render could banish the ghosts that brushed against you as you walked through a history that refused to be relegated to the past.

It took me a while to work out that Berlin's contemporary main railway station, the Hauptbahnhof, which opened in 2006, stands on the site of the old Lehrter Bahnhof, the station from which my mother escaped the city. It was 2008 before I sat on its main concourse, trying to feel the atmosphere. But the passage of time and comprehensive rebuilding had robbed the location of access to any sense of my mother's most terrifying moment. Her station had been a chaotic, crushing mass of desperate humanity, pushing and shoving in panic. Mine exuded the calm of German punctuality and the orderly sale of pretzels and coffee to people going about their everyday lives.

It was later that day, while exploring Berlin's expanding contemporary art quarter with an old friend, that the past punched into the present with a force that alarmed us both.

We had been happily wandering streets lined with cool, glass-fronted galleries, dipping in and out of minimalist white rooms so bright it seemed the decorators must have vacated them only hours before. But as the day wore on, I became increasingly aware of an uncomfortable sensation rising inside me. Something seemed to be seeping up from the pavement through my feet and weighing down my legs. It rose further, turning my stomach hard. By the time we stopped at a café, it had reached the level of my heart, at which point it spilled out in a huge wave of sobs that seemed to have come from nowhere. My friend was baffled. So was I. Until I saw where we were. To our left was Christian Boltanski's powerful 1990 installation *The Missing House*. Plaques commemorating the Jewish people who had lived in the now empty space climbed walls that had once sheltered whole families. Almost directly opposite was the site of Berlin's oldest Jewish cemetery. In front of it, a huddle of small, bronze figures represented the 55,000 Jews who had been held here and gathered in this square to be deported to concentration camps. We hadn't known it, but we had been meandering our way through the formerly bustling Jewish quarter of Scheunenviertel. I remembered a line in *Fugitive Pieces* by Anne Michaels: 'Truth speaks from the ground.'

I wondered how anyone could walk past this place and not feel the assault on their psyches as I did. Like a photograph in a developing tray, I had been overtaken slowly by this heavy, creeping sadness. But by the end it had my whole body clamped in a vice, demanding acknowledgement.

12

Layers of Silence

The world is full of guilt that has never been forgiven
and which can now no longer be forgiven.
Bernhard Schlink, *Guilt About the Past*

I AM AT A FRIEND's wedding. I am in high spirits, sipping sparkling wine, chatting to strangers and feeling the love directed at the happy couple. After a sit-down lunch, the band starts up. Klezmer music. I learn that the bride is half-Jewish. As the wedding guests joyfully take to the floor, dancing and clapping in a circle, I remain on the periphery. Usually I love dancing to the escalating rhythms of this deep, soulful music. But this time I find my eyes filling with unwanted and embarrassing tears. Something peculiar is happening to me. My ears are ringing. My mouth is dry. My vision blurs as the dancers in front of me metamorphose into what appear to be images of the 1930s and 1940s. Jewish men, women and children maintaining what they can of their traditions.

I want to howl as the figures transmogrify further, dissolving into emaciated, naked bodies being shovelled into mass graves by huge mechanical diggers. I want to disappear, to say I am sorry, beg forgiveness. But I can't speak. Suddenly, I am an enemy infiltrator. I feel conspicuous. I freeze as people beckon me with smiling faces to join in. They are only doing this because they don't know who I am, what I am. I am deceiving them even by being here. What would they do if they knew?

Unpacking and discovering half of yourself in your mid-forties is a strange process, like being reborn into a familiar world as an unfamiliar character. My burden of guilt was beginning to assume a clearer shape, and a potential crime. My diaries and art were both witness to and instrumental in this unfolding, documenting it like time-lapse cameras focused on a butterfly emerging from a chrysalis. That, at least, was how I tried to see it.

'Some part of me feels responsible. Not me, Angela Findlay, but something that flows through my blood, genes, culture,' I wrote.

I could understand my sense of guilt only by comparing it with what many Germans of my age might also have felt, but had possibly long ago processed. It seemed so dark, like an indelible stain on my own clean(ish) slate; irreversible and almost unforgivable. And yet it was not really my guilt. I was impatient to further prise open the lid of my subconscious, to take out its contents one by one and turn them around in my hands, as I was doing with the lives of my mother and grandfather.

On my return to college for the second year of my fine art degree in Stroud, I started collaging together copies of my growing collection of photographs, maps and writing to create abstract representations of the stories I knew about my German family. I stuck them on to large bits of paper that I ripped, stitched and splattered. And then, almost by accident, I 'came out'. It happened at the end-of-term presentations of our work. I was usually unafraid of presenting my work to my peers, most of whom were mature students like me, but this time I was terrified. My voice and body shook as I confessed what I was doing: 'My grandfather was a German . . . a German general. And I am researching his life.'

If I had been confessing to murdering a child, I don't think I would have felt more afraid and vulnerable than I did revealing my German roots to these people, who had known me for little more than a year.

My fears were not entirely unfounded. Nobody said anything, but I felt the mood in the room tighten as people silenced anti-German sentiments, prejudices even. Mocking the Germans was still a form of national hobby, a last bastion of legitimate discrimination. Blatant racism still went largely unremarked, only occasionally triggering indignant or angry reactions, even among liberal-minded Europhiles. You merely had to scratch the surface and it was there. And I wasn't admitting simply to being German; I was admitting to being the granddaughter of a German general, a functionary of the Nazi regime.

Gradually my course-mates began to disclose how their lives had been affected by the Nazis. One woman had recently converted to Judaism because her husband was Jewish. She found what I was doing challenging, her husband even more so, to the extent that he reproached a mutual friend for continuing to associate with me. I felt the familiar sting and angst of exclusion that comes from being 'othered'. And I could not defend my otherness. When it came to the Holocaust, I had no defence.

Another fellow student who found the whole subject

deeply uncomfortable turned out to be the son of one of the first British soldiers to have arrived at Bergen-Belsen concentration camp in 1945. One man summarized his views during a social visit to my house without mincing his words.

'They are all to blame,' he said, pronouncing a guilty verdict on the entire German nation.

'What, even my ten-year-old mother?' I asked in genuine bewilderment, showing him a picture of her at that age.

'Yes!' he replied, so emphatically that the guest who had accompanied him walked out in disgust.

His words hurt, possibly more now that the generic Germans for whom people's hatred was ingrained had begun to assume the faces of my relatives. But I also felt anger at his certainty of his own place on the moral high ground.

There was another reaction that also surprised me: a crumbling of some of the walls of this fortress of inbuilt antipathy. With tears streaming down his face, one of the art teachers thanked me for telling the stories of actual people living through the times. His uncle had been killed by the Germans and he had been brought up to hate them. Being able to feel compassion for them freed him from a loathing resentment into which he had been bound his entire life. Even the man whose father had helped to liberate Bergen-Belsen softened as he helped me Photoshop an image for my project, clearly moved by what I was doing.

But what *was* I doing? As I tentatively picked my way through the territory of my family's past, I felt naked and exposed. On one level, I was simply researching and making art about my grandfather's role in the war. On another, I was an archaeologist carefully scraping away at compacted layers of silence to untangle my family's unprocessed experiences and emotions, thread by thread, inching deeper and deeper into a darkness whose edges I could not see. I felt very alone.

In 2002, a study by social psychologist Harald Welzer uncovered some of the ways young Germans were dealing with their family stories. In *Opa war kein Nazi* (Grandpa was No Nazi), Welzer examined conversations about National Socialism and the Holocaust between three generations from forty volunteer families. It revealed how, during their collective reconstruction of the past, each generation tended to conform to a specific pattern. Those with first-hand experience of the war often recounted events in abstract, fragmented or even contradictory ways, possibly anticipating accusations or judgement. Their children and grandchildren then filled in the gaps, adding details to create their own versions, largely to cast their relatives in a more favourable light and dissociate them from the 'bad Nazis' they had heard so much about. Frequently they would see their grandparents more positively than the grandparents saw themselves.

Focusing on small incidents of bravery, two thirds of the young Germans interviewed perceived their family members as resisters, heroes or victims of National Socialism. Half the interviewees claimed their relatives had disapproved of the Nazi regime, while only 2 per cent thought they had a 'very positive' opinion of it and 4 per cent 'quite positive'. Just 1 per cent acknowledged their parents or grandparents to have been directly involved in crimes, whereas 63 per cent mentioned their suffering during the war. According to this data, 25 per cent of the wartime adult population had helped the persecuted, 15 per cent had been active resisters and a mere 3 per cent had been anti-Semitic.

These findings were clearly at odds with reality. But I

could empathize with the younger generations. Loyalty plays a significant role in blocking inquiry into the misdeeds of relatives. It is deeply painful to throw suspicion on people you love. I myself felt utterly daunted in my efforts to embed the enormity of the Holocaust into my family's story. One of my aunts said that nobody in the family saw anything of the expulsions of the Jews, but my mother remembers seeing a cattle truck full of people. Maybe she did, maybe she didn't. Maybe it was one of the cattle trucks bringing back wounded soldiers. She recalls the mother of one of her best friends disappearing after her husband defected to the Russians. She never heard what became of her friend.

Titbits of information, but not enough to exonerate anyone of the guilt that is now attached to the more passive choice of 'non-action', or *wegguken* – looking away – that had drawn so many Germans into unassertive complicity with Hitler's dictatorship. It was inaction, after all, that enabled the heinous actions of others. Today people are encouraged to be 'upstanders' rather than 'bystanders'. And I have since made it part of my life to speak out about uncomfortable truths. But I didn't – and still don't – feel qualified to pass judgement on my family's role in those times. I just wanted to understand and learn the lessons.

While I was unable to see my grandmother as anybody other than the kind, loving, 'good' person I had known her to be, I couldn't be 100 per cent sure of her 'goodness'. And I wasn't going to allow myself to dismiss the possibility of an uglier truth, as many contemporary Germans choose to do, by focusing on isolated acts of resistance as proof of innocence. In her memoir, a tiny crack appeared in her silence on the question of the responses of ordinary people.

We had heard of concentration camps but not in any detail. People who were released from them never talked about the horrors they witnessed. That was later never believed – but those who say that have never lived under a dictatorship. With the benefit of hindsight, it is so easy to judge and condemn . . . But even the foreign diplomats couldn't see through things, and we civilians only got our knowledge through Dr Goebbels' propaganda on the radio or in the press. Hitler's pathological hatred of the Jews frightened us, but how intensively we were spied on. Every critical word was a big danger. Of course there was an underground resistance but not everybody felt themselves to be a martyr. I'd like to know how today's critics would have behaved.

She's right, how would I – or any of us – have behaved? The question had become fundamental to me. Am I, or would I have been, brave enough to risk my life to harbour persecuted people in my attic? Could any of my own beliefs and idealism ever tip over into aggressive fanaticism? Have I stood up to bullies?

Sometimes, maybe; no doubt not enough. I once instinctively intercepted a fight in which a young man's head was being kicked in. And in my prison work, I frequently challenged discrimination, sexism and unfairness. But do I – do we – always actively defend people against prejudice and racism? Or are we at times too frightened or complacent to call out uncomfortable truths, even round a dinner table or in the office?

We might spend hours on Twitter or Facebook sharing news and signing petitions for or against things. We might write a blog or join a march. But what would we be doing if some of the wars, injustices, oppression or atrocities happening in other parts of the world were taking place on our doorsteps? Would we always be honest or courageous enough to protest? I imagine the answer, for most of us, is no.

We have probably all, at different times, been weak and strong, brave and cowardly in different measures. Maybe that was how it was for my grandmother. I believe she certainly makes a valid point on two counts: many of us have never known life under a dictatorship, in which acts of heroism, resistance or defiance may not only place us in mortal danger, but our families, too. And secondly, we now have the benefit of hindsight.

My almost unhealthy determination to look the evils of that time in the eye went on for several years. I read harrowing testimonies of witnesses and survivors of atrocities. I learned about the staggering scale and methods of the systematic murder of 11 million people. I visited the sites of some of the worst wickedness and inhumanity.

At Dachau, among the first Nazi concentration camps and the one that was in operation for the longest, a permanent exhibition conveys just a tiny fraction of the suffering endured here. At Oradour-sur-Glane in France, crumbling ruins, abandoned bicycles and rusting sewing machines left untouched since 1944 tell the story of the massacre of the village's 643 inhabitants by the Nazi occupiers. In Budapest, on the Pest side of the Danube Promenade, a memorial of assorted footwear made of iron and in the styles of the period line the riverbank: worn-out men's boots, women's heels with straps,

Shoes on the Danube Bank *(2005), Budapest.*

the tiny, buckled shoes of children. I placed my feet between them. This was the last piece of solid ground on which some 3,500 Hungarian Jews had stood before being shot, losing their shoes as they fell into the icy water.

It was another experience in Budapest that eventually gave me permission to stop repeatedly immersing myself in accounts and images of the Holocaust. In the sinister House of Terror, headquarters for a decade of the Hungarian Nazi party, I wandered through artistic installations depicting the cruelty of consecutive Fascist and Communist regimes. In one dark room, forcing myself to watch yet more footage of piles of skin-and-bone corpses being bulldozed into mass graves, swallowing hard to prevent the rising emotions from clattering into the hushed space, I received, from somewhere, an order: 'Enough.' It was a gentle instruction, like a hand on my shoulder turning me away. And, wherever it came from, it was right: I had seen enough.

I acquiesced on one condition: I vowed that if I stumbled upon any story in my family with even a whiff of anti-Semitism or atrocity about it, I would pursue and face it.

But when it came to my grandfather, I knew it was going to be complicated.

13

'A Good Soldier'?

No one who either knows or believes that there is another course of action better than the one he is following will ever continue on his present course when he might choose the better.

Socrates, in *Protagoras* by Plato

The von Graffen family, 1942.

I AM IN TANTE MARLEN's attic and she is holding out a dog-eared black-and-white photograph. It was taken around 1942. My grandmother is seated, surrounded by her four children. They are all dressed up, their hair neatly brushed, and they are looking up at something in the corner of the room, or pretending to; putting on photograph faces, half-smiling, possibly because this is what they have been told to do.

My aunt offers me one of the new copies she has had made, pleased by their crisp edges.

'The original is the picture your grandfather carried in the breast pocket of his jacket all through the war, that's why it is a bit tatty,' she says. 'These are nice and clean.'

As if a switch had been flipped, my eyes fill up. Suddenly, he is so close. My aunt notices and casually hands me the old photograph instead. She finds it strange that I would prefer this to a pristine copy, while I am bewildered by her lack of sentimentality or attachment. She appears to have no sense of it as a precious object, treasured enough for her father to have tucked it away next to his heart throughout the war on the Eastern Front.

For him, this picture must have represented home. For me, it verged on a holy relic, a tiny doorway into the world he had inhabited. I could see him taking it out and propping it up against a lamp as he sat in his self-made dugout or wooden hut to write one of those hundreds of letters to his wife. This delicate artefact had survived a war that had destroyed whole towns, tanks and millions of lives. I looked at the photograph, just as he must have looked at it over the years, missing his wife and each child in turn as they grew up without him. Yet even his huge love for these five people could not free him from his oath to Hitler and sworn duty to his fatherland.

A part of me genuinely believed what we had been told as children: that not all Germans were Nazis and that my grandfather had been one of the good soldiers in a 'clean' Wehrmacht. I desperately wanted to distance him from the horrors of the Holocaust and place him in history as nothing more than an apolitical artillerist and division leader. Studying his letters and the notorious invasion of Russia offered me the chance to look for clues to the man beneath the uniform. Had he believed in Hitler's vision for Germany? Or had he simply felt bound by patriotic duty? What kind of soldier had my grandfather been?

I joined an online forum for Wehrmacht militaria enthusiasts. I had no idea who I was communicating with – whether they were geeks, collectors or something more sinister. Tapping my grandfather's name into the search box, I was excited to find a thread in which three members were examining black-and-white photographs of various German generals and trying to determine who they were from the medals and other insignia hanging on their uniforms.

I wouldn't have recognized my grandfather from the picture alone. He was standing in profile, wearing the familiar German army helmet, flanked by two senior-looking uniformed officers. One, established as a Philip Keffel, was looking on while the other, Alexander von Pfuhlstein, fastened a medal around the neck of the soldier between them. A poster going by the name of Elwyn identified the central soldier as von Graffen – 'skinny, but just a tad bigger and shorter than von Pfuhlstein, with a longer upper torso'.

How did these people know my grandfather in such extraordinary minute physical detail? I messaged one of them, Pete, a little fearful of who he might be and how he might react. He responded immediately with a friendly willingness to engage, followed by a tentative inquiry as to whether Angela

Karl (centre) receives his Knight's Cross on the Eastern Front from Alexander von Pfuhlstein, 13 August 1942.

was my real name. It was apparently rare for females to appear on these websites. As our correspondence progressed, I began to relax. He emailed me photographs of my grandfather I had never seen before and filled me in on aspects of the war I didn't know about. Which was basically everything as far as the Eastern Front was concerned. I hadn't even been aware that Leningrad and St Petersburg were the same place.

Pete also alerted me when photographs of my grandfather came up for sale on eBay in the USA. There was one of him being awarded a medal; another of him leading a memorial ceremony in Russia. I hadn't seen either of them before. I got up at five in the morning for the final hours of open bidding. I watched as the bids rose: $25, $30, $35 . . . I was able to snap up one of them for $40, but the others continued to climb to ridiculous prices. Who were these people

My grandfather, on the right, in Russia.

who were interested in such pictures? And what did they know about my grandfather?

I messaged Elwyn via the website asking him for any information he might have about General von Graffen. He, too, asked about the reason for my interest. Once again, I found myself hesitating. This man could be a Nazi-hunter who might name and shame me or a Neo-Nazi who might see me as a trophy. I decided to trust him, took a deep breath and told the truth. He reciprocated by explaining that he was an 'information collector', a passionate categorizer of military detail and facts. He had a wide knowledge of

Knight's Cross-bearers, generals, orders of battle, medals and so on, a decent library on anything Wehrmacht and a pretty vast collection of digital images. Then, as if to assuage any residual suspicions I might have, he deposited some photographs and bits of information into my inbox.

What grew out of this exploratory exchange must count as the jackpot of penpals. Over the subsequent months and years, Elwyn helped me to fill the extensive gaps in my knowledge. He drip-fed me names and photographs of people to whom Karl von Graffen had been subordinate or superior, sent me maps of battles and, best of all, added insights that brought my grandfather to life.

In exchange, I told him stories gleaned from my family and his letters: how my grandfather had struggled to control the Spanish volunteers of the Blue Division – Franco's contribution to the German forces as part-repayment for Hitler's help during the Spanish Civil War – who sang and danced around the night fires on the Eastern Front; how the division leader, Muñoz Grandes, had welcomed my grandfather, on a visit to Spain after the war, greeting him just as he had predicted: in his pyjamas and eating sardines from a tin.

When I mentioned to Elwyn in passing that my mother had worked for General Speidel at the NATO headquarters, I was staggered by his response. 'You mean General Hans Speidel, former chief-of-staff to Rommel? He was one of the only surviving plotters of the 1944 July assassination attempt on Hitler, probably the most significant act of resistance and defiance in the entire war!'

I'd had no idea. I had actually met General Speidel myself, although I knew him only as a benevolent elderly man who'd had us to lunch at his home on a family visit to Germany in

1976 – a lunch that would stand out in all our memories as one of our most regrettable displays of childhood bad behaviour.

Within minutes of our arrival, I had spilt my glass of Sekt over the pale upholstery of his silk sofa. Caroline and Christopher leaped into action like a well-trained rescue team to rearrange cushions. At lunch, as I politely blew on a spoonful of soup to cool it down, I caught sight of Caroline taking a gulp of sparkling mineral water and pulling a transparently disgusted face at what was in those days a filthy, soapy-salty brew. A burst of laughter blasted through my pursed lips, splattering soup all over the table. Caroline tried to stifle a guffaw with another gulp of her water, succeeding only in expelling it from her nostrils in a spectacular demonstration of the nose trick. My mother looked on, mortified, then sent us out of the room.

We left a few hours later, shamefaced and apologetic, for the general had shown us nothing but understanding and kindness. He gave us each a signed photograph of himself as a present. I had tucked mine into the pages of my first diary, sandwiched between red-and-gold marzipan wrappers and a postcard of a wild boar.

It turned out that our good-natured host had not only played a key role in sabotaging Hitler's orders to demolish Paris when the Germans withdrew but had also been assigned the task of persuading Rommel to join the plot against him. That's Erwin Rommel, widely known as the Desert Fox for his brilliant military tactics while fighting the British in North Africa, and the most respected field marshal in the Wehrmacht, both in Germany and abroad, not least for his efforts to make peace with the Western Allies and end the war. My grandfather was apparently often mistaken for Rommel in photos and people frequently remarked on their similarities as soldiers. That would have been taken as a huge compliment by my grandfather and his family.

Rommel, however, would not survive the war. After he was linked to the failed bid, orchestrated by Claus von Stauffenberg and fellow senior German army officers, to assassinate Hitler and topple the Nazi party, he was given the choice of facing trial or committing suicide. He opted for the latter to save his family from further punishment. Hundreds

'For Angela, with good thoughts of your visit in 1976, Hans Speidel.'

of people were arrested ostensibly in connection with the plot. Von Stauffenberg himself was shot by a makeshift firing squad the following day and many others, ranging from high-ranking officers to more peripherally linked conspirators, were hunted down over the next few months, tortured and executed by the Gestapo or forced to take their own lives, often after show trials based on the most tenuous of evidence.

Hans Speidel was among those interrogated by the Gestapo but, after refusing for seven months to betray anybody's identity, he was released. Apparently, Rommel had personally asked Hitler to spare him.

My mother didn't appear to know about this aspect of her boss's history, even though they had exchanged letters until his death in 1984. I winced with embarrassment and regret at the memory of how I'd let her down so badly at our only meeting.

It transpired that in Elwyn I had stumbled upon a contact who was widely respected as one of the leading online Second World War specialists. I didn't know his age, what he looked like or what he did for a living, and yet I had climbed into a virtual boat with him and set sail. It proved to be one of the most exciting voyages of my life.

The Second World War had for me been an ocean of question-marks but, with each email, archipelagos of understanding appeared. I began to grasp the structures and hierarchies of rank and authority within Hitler's Germany: the difference between the Wehrmacht – Germany's regular unified armed forces from 1921 to 1945, made up of the Heer (army), Kriegsmarine (navy) and Luftwaffe (air force) – and the SS, the Schutzstaffel, or protection squadron, the special police force founded in 1925 by Hitler to provide security for the Nazi party. The Waffen SS was its combat branch, politically indoctrinated and fanatically driven. Elwyn outlined the objectives of the invasion of Russia and highlighted the moral dilemmas faced by soldiers as they wrestled with conscience and duty.

The notions of military strategy and the ambitions of war were so alien to me that I struggled to imagine how anybody could have believed they could 'take over' a vast land mass like Russia. Hadn't Napoleon's defeat taught them anything? The blatant lack of foresight made me angry. It seemed to be about little more than the macho, power-hungry short-termism that lies behind so many conflicts, scantily disguised as a justified response to a perceived threat.

I liked Elwyn. His non-judgemental empathy with the spirit of the age allowed me to set aside my incomprehension and put me at my ease. I had never had anyone walk my path with me before. Nobody in my world needed to find out if their grandfather was a Nazi or not.

It was soon clear to me that I needed to go to Russia. This would be where I would get closest to my grandfather as a man at the top of his game: an outstanding artillerist and division leader, victorious in one of the most challenging battles of the war. Where I might be able to get a sense of what that involved in practical and human terms and perhaps to confirm to my own satisfaction that he had been a 'good soldier', ethical and courageous. This was where the veil separating past and present would be thinnest. Maybe a glimpse of the shadows behind it would show me what to do with the baton he had passed to me and put something to rest.

But where in Russia? I had already underlined all

references in my grandfather's letters to place names. As he wasn't supposed to reveal his whereabouts, some were coded: 'I am stationed in a village that starts with "B" and sounds like the place where we had that picnic on your birthday.'

I tapped names into Google and, on a large paper map of the country, traced the seemingly illogical, zigzagging course he had marched, each centimetre on my map representing hundreds of kilometres. The picture of the evolving Eastern Front that emerged, however, made no sense.

Elwyn told me not to worry: he intended to track my grandfather's path across Russia himself. I sent him my list of locations and he communicated with his contacts to resolve inconsistencies and the contradictions that arose from the ever-shifting borders and some place names being in German and others in Polish or Russian. I began to acquire some sense of the scale of the invasion and the responsibilities my grandfather carried as the conflict escalated and smashed through the rules of warfare as he knew them. I found it both fascinating and terrifying. A total of 148 divisions – 80 per cent of the German army – were involved. Seventeen panzer divisions with 3,400 tanks, supported by 2,700 Luftwaffe aircraft. It beat me how anybody could have failed to notice over 3.5 million German soldiers amassing on the borders of Russia. As I would discover, even Stalin hadn't believed it, and consequently ignored the many warnings of imminent attack.

I turned to memoir to gain a more visceral, personal understanding of the Eastern Front. I ordered a copy of *At Leningrad's Gates*, written by William Lubbeck, who had been a young soldier in the 58th Division – the one my grandfather headed at the time of the gruesome Battle of the

Volkhov – and, over a grey, damp weekend, I allowed myself to be transported south of Leningrad and into the depths of the freezing winter of early 1942.

The temperature is -20 degrees centigrade. The Soviets have begun a major assault on the German positions at the Volkhov River, trying to swing behind them to break the notorious 900-day siege of Leningrad. The 58th Infantry Division has been sent to the Volkhov front to cut off the enemy from the rear. Trudging through waist-high snow, German forces move both north and southward, trapping 180,000 Red Army troops in a *Kessel,* or pocket. The Soviets fight back with everything they have. The Volkhov air is filled with the incessant roar of artillery and machine-gun fire. 'The psychological strain generated by constant danger of attack from any direction ... is even worse than that created by the threat of snipers,' writes Lubbeck.

With the arrival of the spring thaw, the whole battleground swiftly turns into a muddy bog. The Germans have to construct five-foot high walls, 'corduroy' roads and walkways from fallen trees. 'We bunked in waterproof tents set up on a log foundation in order to keep us above the mud.'

Swarms of mosquitoes and lice plague them, allowing them little sleep. With hot soup a rarity, they live on crackers, canned tuna and sausage. 'Though our morale remained high, inadequate sleep, a poor diet and the stress of combat left us physically weakened and mentally exhausted ... My own weight dropped to an emaciated 160 pounds, but many other German soldiers endured far worse health problems.'

The battle rages on until the end of June, finally finishing in a German victory. Around 33,000 Red Army prisoners are taken. All that is left is a giant forest of tree stumps stretching to the horizon, body parts and the indescribably ghastly stench of death.

This man had fought alongside my grandfather in one of the toughest and bloodiest battles on the Eastern Front, wrestled with the same freezing temperatures and fathomless mud and been eaten by the same lice and the same mosquitoes. It occurred to me that William Lubbeck might be one of the few people still living who had seen my grandfather in action; the only man who might be able to tell me from first-hand experience what kind of soldier he had been.

His book had been published relatively recently, so he had survived into old age. But was he still alive? I wrote to him at the address of his publisher, Pen & Sword Books. A few weeks later, I received a reply from Mr Lubbeck inviting me to call him on an American number.

I picked up the phone.

His opening words set my heart pounding.

'I am familiar with your grandfather, Ms Findlay.'

I thanked him for his willingness to talk to me.

'I was very interested to read your letter,' he said in German. 'All my memories came back.'

Suddenly, I felt guilty. I realized I was unprepared for the impact this odd conversation between two strangers on opposite sides of the Atlantic would have on him, as well as on me.

Mr Lubbeck began to recall, in his hybrid German–American accent, the scene after the Battle of the Volkhov. 'All that was left of the landscape five miles to the west of the river were tree trunks, mud and dead Russians,' he said. 'It stank.'

After a while, I plucked up the courage to voice the

question that was the most urgent and terrifying to me. 'So, can you, er, tell me what sort of man my grandfather was? What sort of soldier?'

As if reaching into the recesses of his mind to sift through piles of memories, he replied slowly. 'He was a very strict, forward individual; a good soldier, very active.' He paused. 'A very forward, active soldier,' he said again.

I understood him to mean that my grandfather had led from the front. He had not been the type of soldier to hang back barking out orders from the safety of his bunker.

I longed to ask Mr Lubbeck more but I felt that posing difficult moral questions would be an abuse of his generosity and willingness to place his dim-lit past in the harsh beam of my contemporary gaze. My vocal cords were already starting to quiver with emotion, so instead I just thanked him and told him how incredibly special it was for me to talk to him. He was silent for a moment, as if lost in the memories I had stirred up.

'Yes . . . Yes, I understand,' he said eventually, with such thoughtful gentleness that I really felt he did.

14

'They Were All Murderers'

*'We' – this 'we' is everyone who has never experienced anything
like what they went through – don't understand. We don't get it.
We truly can't imagine how dreadful, how terrifying war is – and
how normal it becomes. Can't understand, can't imagine.*

Susan Sontag, *Looking at War*

'I'M COMING WITH YOU,' my mother declared over the phone,
her voice conveying reluctance and determination in equal
measure. I was in the process of booking a complicated train
journey across Russia that followed in the seventy-year-old
footsteps of my grandfather.

'Really?' I replied, surprised and relieved. I hadn't wanted
to make this trip alone but who else would accompany me on
such a personal journey? 'Are you sure you want to?'

Far from wanting to, it transpired, she felt a responsibility to travel with me. She couldn't bear the thought of me
going on my own and knew she wouldn't be able to forgive
herself if something happened to me on my 'pilgrimage'. I
was as deeply grateful to her as my father was horrified. She
was seventy-five by this time, severely diabetic and her life
depended on a fine balance of regular meals and insulin injec-
tions. But her mind was made up. And I was excited by the
prospect of sharing this adventure with her.

On 14 September 2009, we set off from Cologne, where I

had been spending a few days visiting old friends. There was a sense of role reversal as I handed my mother a tinfoil package of black pumpernickel and salami sandwiches in anticipation of her first diabetic low. Standing on Platform 7 at Cologne Hauptbahnhof, my mind was unsettled by the parting utterance of one of those friends, who I'd met for a quick cup of coffee a few hours earlier.

'They were all murderers.'

She had hissed the words, recoiling as I brought out a photograph of my grandfather.

I was totally shocked. We had known each other for fifteen years but this was the first time the Second World War had come up in any of our conversations. Her father had deserted, she told me with manifest pride. The implication was that this was what my grandfather should have done.

I struggled to follow her reasoning. Was she saying he should have abandoned his men? Put his family in danger of repercussions? Would that have been the right thing for a senior army officer to do? I was amazed she saw it in such black-and-white terms. We'd had endless discussions about the nature of crime and criminals and I had always completely respected her views. But I had evidently underestimated the revulsion and anger some Germans still felt towards their armed forces. 'Can you really lump professional soldiers who kill in the line of duty together with the people in prisons who have murdered innocent people?' I asked.

Of course, many Nazis had indeed been murderers, but surely Wehrmacht soldiers had been different. Or did she see all soldiers as murderers?

'Apparently, my grandfather was really *korrekt*,' I

continued, coming to his defence with a term that conveys not only punctiliousness but decency.

'Urgh!' She flinched again. 'I can't even hear that word.' I hadn't known that for some Germans, *'Korrektheit'* encapsulated blind obedience to the Nazis' utterly 'incorrect' policies.

She said it again, as if to shake me out of my naïveté. 'They were all murderers.'

I was stunned by the passion with which my friend had dismissed the entire regular army and hurt by her repugnance for a member of my family. But the seeds of doubt over what I was attempting to accomplish were already sprouting roots. Maybe I shouldn't be trying to find the good in him. Maybe contemporary Germans knew something I didn't and I, too, should be delivering an unequivocally guilty verdict on my grandfather and exiling him from my family tree. That's what many Germans of my age were doing, after all. But to me it felt unnatural not to even try to understand a person before condemning and disowning them, especially when that person was my own grandfather.

I kept my thoughts to myself as a piece of Russia chugged into Cologne station, arriving at Platform 7 as if from a distant world. Approximately 5 feet wide and 7 feet long, with light grey Formica walls and green seats, the first-class compartment in which my mother and I had thought it wise to invest was a far cry from the luxurious Orient Express-style cabin I had imagined. A rude Russian guard released the top bunk using a special key and, shoving a pile of sheets into our arms, told us we had to make our own beds. Soon afterwards, lying between sheets starched to the point of stiff dysfunction and rocked by a lullaby of clanking metal and the jolting rhythm of a carriage with no suspension, my mother fell asleep. But my mind remained wide awake the entire night. I imagined my grandfather marching every step of the way, through Przasnysz, Chelmo, Soldany, Elk, Grajewo and Osowiec, deeper and deeper into this unknown territory.

There is no record of how my grandfather felt about the outbreak of war. I remembered what Elwyn, my online adviser, had suggested his mindset was likely to have been. 'He would have been so excited, lining up with his men on the border between Poland and Russia on the eve of the massive 1941 invasion of Russia. Finally, he would be able to put into practice all that he had trained his men for.'

When my grandfather's letters start, on 13 March 1941, he is somewhere in East Prussia, now northern Poland. They give the impression of an extremely busy man with significant military responsibilities, almost champing at the bit to get going. He describes his men as a motley lot but is confident he can get them into shape. He asks my grandmother to send him a Russian dictionary 'just in case'.

On 24 June it all kicks off as Operation Barbarossa commences. His tone is optimistic. It becomes clear that he wholeheartedly believes in the necessity of combating the Bolshevik threat from the east. For him this is a pre-emptive strike to prevent a Russian invasion of Europe and the huge arsenal of weaponry they discover only confirms that conviction.

> *We are now sitting in the swamp firing at enemy artillery. I've been in the same clothes for the past 3 days. If anyone is able to rest, they do it sitting up . . . You can't imagine in what kind of huts the people here are living and how filthy everything is . . .*

I have brought with me a copy of the letters for each of us and, as my mother and I follow his course through Belarus, we follow his narrative and allow his words to bring the passing landscape to life: infinite, flat expanses, birch forests, little domed churches and brightly painted wooden houses with corrugated tin roofs and sandy tracks running between them. In other places, swampland disguised as solid ground leaks on to the tracks, small houses built on islands floating on its surface like wooden arks.

> *The people are very friendly and welcoming and give us bread, honey, eggs and potatoes with butter. All of them are cursing Bolshevism and the commissioners . . . Altogether, the war suits me perfectly and I think that we can already plan our winter sports holiday because this won't take long.*

I couldn't comprehend how war could suit anybody, let alone perfectly. But his optimism wasn't altogether misplaced. The German blitzkrieg, advantaged by the element of surprise, was infamously swift and met with little resistance. In fact, the German troops were initially welcomed by some subjects of the Soviet regime as liberators from Stalin's cruel dictatorship.

> *In general, the population is peaceful . . . but today we had to shoot a lot of the inhabitants because they are leading the partisan war.*

I was shocked by how casually my grandfather talked about shooting people. I tried to tell myself that was just a normal day's work for an active soldier. Or murderer.

> *There are also partisans floating around in the woods and*
> *villages. In one place the Russians had established a forced*
> *labour camp with a torture chamber and shortly before*
> *we arrived they murdered all the inmates, among them*
> *many women. They cut off their breasts, slit open their*
> *bellies. Until now I had thought that kind of thing was all*
> *just propaganda.*

He was conscious, then, that there was anti-Russian propaganda. This felt important. It suggested to me that, even if he believed it now, he had not always accepted the Nazi argument that expansion into the east was essential to create Lebensraum for the German people. He goes on:

> *Behind our backs the SS are clearing up.*

'Clearing up'?

At this point – as at so many stages of my search for the truth – I wasn't cognizant of the full implications of these words. I was too focused on my grandfather's potential personal culpability to see the fuller picture. I would later learn that, since the mid-nineties, the actions of the SS in the wake of the Wehrmacht's advances had officially been recognized as atrocities. That this had been an intentional war of annihilation in which many soldiers had all too willingly complied. That the brutality had at first genuinely appalled the Wehrmacht soldiers who reported the deeds of the SS as unacceptable aberrations of warfare. But that they had then turned a blind eye. Or joined in.

My grandfather's oblique allusion to 'clearing up' can only have been a reference to the mass murder of millions of

Communists and Jews in villages and towns across German-occupied territories. Whole communities were eradicated overnight with the collusion and co-operation of local people and militias. Even in my relative ignorance, I found it disturbing that he could talk of the actions of the SS as if they were polite catering staff clearing the tables and washing up after the army had eaten.

My mother and I rattled on towards Minsk. With our black bread and salami sustaining us in the absence of anything resembling a dining car, we spent our second night travelling parallel to the main road to Moscow along which her father had marched. I tried to visualize soldiers hiding among the spindly silver trunks of the starlit trees, dragging their guns and provisions; young men, thousands of miles from home, thinking about those left behind, wondering what lay ahead.

> *Yesterday I drove through an area where two Russian*
> *companies that had been cut off were marching,*
> *5 minutes behind me. I only just made it to a protected*
> *place and personally had to shoot them all.*

I glanced over at my mother in the seat opposite, also reading these pages. She had always believed that my grandfather hadn't shot anybody. My brave and vulnerable mother. I hoped she would skim that bit or maybe have a little diabetic low that would prevent it from sinking in. I felt bad exposing the family myths for what they were: myths. I felt guilty about unsettling my aunts' positive view of their father. I felt disloyal reading letters written privately and intimately between my grandparents, prodding them with

185

the sharpened probes of modern inquiry and unfair benefit of hindsight. But this quest for truth was mine, not theirs.

I think my mother must have passed over that entry, whether deliberately or not. But she could see I was bothered by something. I told her what my friend had said.

'They had to obey orders, darling,' she said kindly. 'Your grandfather, just like many other officers, felt bound by duty. They had had to swear allegiance and obedience to Hitler. Some younger Germans with very modern or left-wing views now think about the soldiers as murderers, but not all.'

Her protectiveness of him and, by extension, me was the hug I desperately needed. Yet I knew none of this was as straightforward as she believed. We continued to read. It was now July 1941.

> *I don't think we have slept for more than 10-12 hours in the past 8 days . . . The whole area is a dust cloud through which the darkened sun tries to shine. The main streets look like a crater landscape, cars can go no faster than walking pace.*

The Red Army had split into leaderless groups which were easily captured by the Germans. Around 6 million Russian prisoners were taken, many of whom were summarily executed. But the German troops were wrong-footed. Their weaponry was wholly unsuitable for the terrain. A good number of their tanks had no dust filters and were rendered useless, and the dust clouds they created attracted air attacks by the Red Army, whose KV1s were far superior. The Russians would also start forest fires as a delaying tactic and leave timed bombs in buildings as they retreated.

It was the partisans, however, who gave the German soldiers some of their biggest problems. My grandfather described how they would hide in the forests, barefoot, and pretend to surrender by raising their hands. Then they would attack with machine guns and hand grenades. The wounded Germans were murdered in the most gruesome ways, 'eyes gouged out, skewered with rifle butts and bayonets, their bones crushed and robbed . . . Our people are now so livid about this style of war that there is no pardon'.

Poring over the letters in the weak sunlight as the train carved its way through the miles of birch forests, it was clear to me that, in the eyes of the German soldiers, the Russian partisans were not only ambushing them but also their deeply embedded military values. And with such wild violence that the soldiers felt compelled to abandon their training and ingrained sense of 'fair warfare' to fight for their lives like street gangs. I wondered how my grandmother had felt reading all this. Had her husband's honesty contributed to the coolness between them once he returned home?

> *I am sitting in a meadow under a cloudless sky. In the past month we have marched over 1000km and still have 800km to go before we reach Moscow. You only get 2 hours rest on these marches, other times 24 hours and longer are marched at a time. I'm sick of this torture. Our marching orders are changed daily so who knows where we are going to end up.*

Increasingly, there are complaints about 'ridiculous orders' from the 'idiots above'. I underline each one, as if gathering evidence for his defence.

I was glad when, with 2,000 miles and two days and nights behind us, my mother and I finally arrived in Moscow and could turn our thoughts to getting a good meal. No one spoke English and we considered it inadvisable to try German, so we followed the signs bearing the letter 'M', which we assumed stood for Metro, only to find ourselves heading into the men's toilets. Eventually we reached the huge open space of Red Square and the Kremlin and settled in at a restaurant with a view of the blue and golden domes perched like freshly made meringues on top of elegant white buildings. From here we could also people-watch. Hunched old ladies in headscarves sat silently on park benches, looking for all the world as if they had been cut and pasted from photographs of the 1940s, while some of the stereotypes of contemporary Russian society – deadly serious guards, all don't-mess-with-me expressions and guns, and long-legged women in tight jeans and killer heels – paraded by.

We rejoined my grandfather as all three of us headed north to Tver. His mood was changing as the weeks passed and the conditions deteriorated.

> *We have become used to digging holes to sleep in and putting our tents over them, except they are full of flies and ants during the day and mosquitoes at night. The weather is cold and rainy, there's nothing to smoke, to drink or to read. We can't listen to the radio either because we are too far away and because of the storms. Our straw stinks of cow shit and is full of fleas*

and I now haven't smoked or drunk for 4 days and 19 hours. It's disastrous. If only I could release my anger on some Russians as I can't stand this withdrawal much longer.

Now that would be murder, wouldn't it? I had met men in prison who had murdered for less, but my grandfather had already taken countless more lives than any of them.

I read his accounts with disturbed fascination. I could not, and cannot, relate in any way whatsoever to his actions or to the attitude of the aggressor. The violence of war shocks me and I imagine I wouldn't like him as a man if he was beamed into my life now in the way I was beaming myself into his. Yet on one level I am awestruck by the sheer stamina of these soldiers, of any soldier. I can almost taste the adrenaline. Take away the horror, and what they are achieving on the level of pure physical strength and endurance is remarkable, their bravery almost fathomless.

In places the letters touch me, too. He is upbeat and positive, reassuring his wife that he is safe, thanking her with all his heart for the parcels and letters she sends. He tries to give her hope and advises her on how to stay safe and healthy. I picture him taking out the tattered photograph my aunt had passed on to me and staring at the faces of his wife and children as the bombs drop around his wooden shelter, killing fathers, sons and husbands on both sides.

In spite of all that I found abhorrent about this man and his time-warped world, I still wanted to find a way at least to try to love a close relative forced to sleep in a hole in the ground.

It was pitch dark when my mother and I arrived at Tver, the strategically important city, known then as Kalinin, occupied by the Wehrmacht for two months at the end of 1941. It would also become the first major city in Europe to be retaken from them. My grandfather had arrived here a week after the initial troops had entered, having been delayed by the appalling 'road' conditions. There was little for his troops to do other than wait for their replacements. His main concern seems to have been whether he would make it home for Christmas.

We picked our way through the urine-smelling station underpass and emerged at a taxi rank that could easily have been mistaken for a scrap-metal yard. Rusty cars with chequered taxi lights Sellotaped to their roofs awaited us. There wasn't one that didn't look as if it would collapse into a flat pack of component parts the moment you closed the doors. Standing behind them was a selection of unsmiling men exuding an air of menace. It was a matter of choosing whichever driver seemed least likely to chuck us in his car boot and dispose of our bodies in a dark alley.

I selected a well-built, shaven-headed young guy who chauffeured us in silence through endless potholed streets where the only lights glowing were the give-away red ones in doorways and windows. I longed to be back home. But the town that had provided my grandfather with the luxury of a mattress for the first time in four months came up trumps for us, too. To our surprise, the taxi pulled up outside an incongruously brightly lit, modern business hotel.

The next day, it poured. 'The town looks miserable because even though there has not been much fighting, the Russians set fire to all the buildings – houses, shops and warehouses,' my grandfather had written. It didn't seem all that different seventy years later. Tver was full of the burned-out shells of what had once been beautiful, wooden chalet-style houses, apparently destroyed to make the price of the land they occupied more attractive to developers. Others stood crooked, rotten, held together with plasters of sheet metal. Everywhere were ancient tangles of electric cables and flaking rust, broken steps leading to patchwork doors, and dusty windowsills displaying vases of dead flowers behind filthy or broken windowpanes draped with ragged lace curtains.

What we didn't encounter in Tver was the bitter November cold and the snow that descended on the German soldiers, still in their summer uniforms as the vicious winter of 1941–2 set in. 'It has been -16 degrees [centigrade] for the past few days,' confirmed my grandfather. 'The poor foot soldiers have to sit in their rifle pits without winter uniforms and without heating or anything to smoke because the supplies can't get through.' And it got worse, above all for the Russians. The winter was one of the coldest of the twentieth century, with temperatures as low as -50 degrees being recorded in Tver. 'Outside it is -30 or 40 degrees. Close to my quarters they hung 3 Russians and put one in the snow as a signpost. There was another one lying frozen on the path. None of the inhabitants come to move them.' By the time the Wehrmacht departed from Tver in December 1941, leaving the city in ashes behind them, my grandfather had been given his first corps level artillery command – ARKO 18 – which put him in charge of six regiments of the 18th Army near Leningrad. On Christmas Eve he was presented with the Deutsches Kreuz in gold, awarded for repeated acts of bravery and leadership, and given home leave. When he returned to the front in mid-January, General Georg Lindemann had taken charge of the 18th. It was clear that the Siege of Leningrad was taking its toll. The scenes my grandfather paints in his letters from March 1942 are horrific.

> *The Russians . . . stream to and fro along the roads with their loaded sledges. Often you see very fragile people, who take more than an hour to hobble even 100m forwards. When one of them dies, the others sit around comfortably having their breakfast as if nothing has happened. In front of our position, there are thousands of dead Russians under the snow. There will be a horrendous stink when the snow thaws in spring.*
>
> *Yesterday I had to have a Russian woman shot because she had stolen. In general there's just a short trial, and those found guilty will be shot. The Russians have asked for it through their partisan warfare. We have to protect ourselves. They are used to worse from their own commissioners and are completely detached. You could blow their house up and they would just stay quietly in it. You feel sorry for the ordinary soldiers, especially the children. But even they are used as spies or partisans. So you can't trust anybody.*

All this makes stomach-churning reading. As our train clanked out of Tver, I felt that the picture of my grandfather was becoming more nebulous, not less. Sometimes he demonstrates sympathy, incomprehension – concern, even, for the people he is encountering – and I would soften a little towards him. Most of the time I was having to brace myself against his voice and my own rising nausea. One small consolation was the family's memory of this last incident, of him having the Russian woman shot for stealing. Apparently, it had haunted him, possibly more than anything else, long after the war had ended. I wondered what it was about her in particular that had scratched so persistently at his conscience.

Should I even be trying to understand him as a man caught up in a horrific history, a mere cog in a terrifying killing machine? Or should I be condemning him as a willing murderer of fellow human beings? Could I take pride in his achievements as a soldier, as British people take pride in their soldiers, even though they, too, kill? Or should I just accept that I didn't comprehend anything about this war and was not entitled even to comment, let alone condemn? Hindsight, after all, is an unjust judge.

From his point of view, one of the pinnacles of my grandfather's career was his promotion to commander of the 58th Division in April 1942. He was now in charge of a division originally led by the famous Erich von Manstein, regarded, thanks to his strategic genius and victories in battle, as Germany's most talented Second World War field commander. The appointment took my grandfather into the 'arse of the world,' as German soldiers dubbed the Volkhov swamplands between Veliky Novgorod and Petersburg.

My mother and I arrived in Novgorod with a sense of having landed in the city of 1942. Thick clouds of smoke hung in the air, penetrated by searchlights scanning the skies for enemy planes, while the sound of falling bombs whistled and banged all around. Thousands of people shuffled along in the same direction under black umbrellas, their heads bowed against the rain. It took a stirring rendition of the theme tune

Karl von Graffen (R) with Generalfeldmarschall Erich von Manstein (L) in Ropsha.

to the *Titanic* film, amplified to rock-concert volumes, to catapult us back into the present, resolving the bombs into fireworks and the searchlights into dancing laser beams celebrating Novgorod's 1,150[th] anniversary.

Depositing our luggage in what was clearly the last hotel room available – a hideous relic of Communism, complete with ripped and peeling wallpaper and cheap furniture on the verge of collapse – we made our way to the tourist office to organize a taxi. It was a public holiday and there were no taxis available, so the young assistant volunteered her boyfriend to be our guide for the day. Vladimir, she told us proudly, spoke English. A few hours later, we found ourselves climbing into his car. Thus far the language barrier had prevented us from conversing with anyone other than in two tiny exchanges on train platforms. But even those had been enough to demonstrate the ongoing hostility towards Germans. My mother and I agreed on a cover story that we were doing research for an English book about Second World War battles. Following copies of old hand-drawn combat maps from 1942, we headed north along the main route between Moscow and St Petersburg.

Abandoned tanks, overgrown bunkers and metal anti-tank hedgehogs still littered the open countryside, consciously preserved reminders of the 'Great Patriotic War'. One well-tended memorial after another lined the road, some display-ing the remains of fired munitions or rusty helmets complete with jagged bullet holes as crude testimonies to the fate of the wearer.

Many graves bore enamel photographs of the faces of the fallen, so many of them young boys. In other places, marble slabs listed the names of thousands upon thousands upon thousands of Russian dead.

It was overwhelming.

Nowhere I'd ever been, not even Berlin, made the war feel so close. So real.

So deadly.

In a deep voice and a heavy Russian accent, Vladimir, a strong, fit-looking young man in jeans and trainers, enlight-ened us on present attitudes towards the war, how it was celebrated as a triumph of Communism, not only over Fascism but also over the West in general, which was, to Russians, synonymous with concentration camps, torture and evil. It seemed that people made little mention of the gulag prisons and camps, where more people died than in the Nazi concentration camps. Or of how staunch pro-Stalin sentiments hid the truth that many among those nationali-ties who'd been subsumed into the Soviet empire, such as

The gravestone of one of the Russian fallen.

Latvians, Lithuanians, Ukrainians, actually saw the Germans as liberators. It was as if perpetuating this attitude of patriotic triumphalism was designed to make the immense sacrifices of the Russian civilians bearable.

We drove on down a bumpy track to the banks of the Volkhov, now a beautiful river dotted with fishermen. The peaceful scene belied the fierce gunfire and human carnage that had once churned its shores. An unsettling hum of midges filled the air.

I knew we were close to the 58th Division positions at the mouth of the pocket in which they had trapped 60,000 Russians. I discreetly consulted the letters. 'I am living in the middle of the bog again, 2km off the road that goes from

Novgorod to the North. Sometimes we have to wade through 70cm of water to reach our positions.' It is early April 1942 and the Germans are busy building log roads but the snows are thawing so fast that whole areas are turned into a 'muddy soup'.

> *If you haven't seen it, you can't even begin to imagine the mud and sludge . . . whole cars disappear in it . . . many horses have already drowned. They wade up to their stomachs in grey-black gravy and if there's a hole or a stone or a branch in the way, the horse trips or falls over.*

My grandfather's bitter commentary – the stinking, corpse-filled swamplands; the surrendering Russian soldiers; the air

One of the log or 'corduroy' roads. My grandfather is the officer in the long coat.

filled with incessant explosions and machine-gun fire – is punctuated by accounts of enjoyable social evenings in his quarters, lubricated by cognac and an apparent glut of cigarettes, which he distributes to his men.

It bears out William Lubbeck's view of him as an unusually 'forward' division leader. He frequently proceeds right to the front of the line, where the Russians are just 400 metres away. And a popular one, it seems: on his birthday in June he is treated by fellow division leaders to bunches of lilac and lily of the valley, phone calls, cigarettes and Hennessy.

The letters stop abruptly on 20 June 1942. Like a switch, the voice that has become so familiar is turned off and replaced

The Battle of Volkhov. My grandfather is on the right.

with the silence of letters long lost. A week later, he would lead his division to victory in the Battle of Volkhov.

The division's successes were frequently referred to in the reports of the High Command and, that summer, my grandfather was not only promoted to Generalleutnant (major general) but also awarded the Knight's Cross of the Iron Cross for extreme battlefield bravery and successful military leadership. It was the highest military honour a German soldier could receive.

I wanted to give myself permission to share in the satisfaction my grandfather must have taken from this recognition of the achievements of his men and himself; a moment of lightness amid the weight of all the other emotions dragging down my soul. In the photographs I'd acquired, his posture expresses the honour he felt in serving his country, in slaying its enemy, in winning the fight. It was the kind of recognition soldiers the world over strive for, the same honour you see in the eyes of British soldiers awarded the Victoria Cross. I wanted to feel the same pride as their relatives. But I couldn't. Not in the face of so much death and suffering. And not in the knowledge of who and what my grandfather had been fighting for.

[

Our expedition was talking its toll. I was growing numb with exhaustion. But my prime goal was to find the exact location of the 58th Infantry Division which, according to the map, lay a little further from the river, on the other side of the tracks at the railway station of Myasnoy Bor. This was the only site in Russia where I could know for sure I was inhabiting the same patch of earth trodden by my grandfather. I wanted to feel the aura of the place, to see him in action for myself, hear the world as he must have heard it. If I could just attune myself to the memories it held, I was sure this would be the key to understanding what kind of man he had been.

My mother's light chatter provided good cover as I scrambled along the track, eyes peeled and ears pricked, drawing on every fibre of intuition and imagination I could summon and focusing my mind on trying to penetrate the waterlogged birch forests that had grown up over the broken stumps. Like the searcher in a game of hide-and-seek, I sensed I was warm. But I could not reach the place I wanted to reach, neither in the landscape nor inside myself.

A sense of incompleteness nagged at my weary mind as we boarded our final train from Novgorod to St Petersburg at dawn the following morning. My mother immediately fell asleep, as did most of the other passengers. I looked across at her, in some ways so fragile and yet extraordinarily resilient and supportive. It felt such a privilege to have made this journey with her. It was a far cry from the comfortable and culturally rich kind of travel she was used to, and I loved her for coming with me. She had been a wonderful companion, surrendering herself to our peculiar itinerary without complaint and responding to everything we came across with her habitual curiosity and interest.

Quietly, I picked up my camera and went to stand in the noisy space between the two carriages where I could open the window. The rising sun infused the gentle mist hovering over the landscape with a pink and golden glow. I hadn't realized that the train would be passing through Myasnoy Bor.

As miles of birch forests passed in front of my tired eyes,

their stripy trunks merged hypnotically into one blurred image, like an abstract painting of a zebra. As I stared out at it, swaying with the rhythmic rocking of the train, I felt myself being drawn into a different world, staring into the eyes of the place, of the forest, and seeing into its soul. Gently touching something in the 'negative spaces' of the landscape.

Between the birch trunks I saw the men of the 58th Division, sensed the buzz of their hidden activity in the undergrowth, smelled the mud and the decay, heard the artillery fire. I felt the presence of my grandfather more keenly than ever before. Here he was, a professional soldier doing what he had been trained and ordered to do; doing it as well as he could, alongside thousands of others in the same situation. Could I condone it? No. But for a brief moment, I could understand.

It was only when I sat opposite my mother over our last dinner that the tears started to flow. There had been many moments when I had wanted to cry, but the practical demands of

Silver birch trees, Myasnoy Bor.

navigating Russia, as well as the need to take care of her health and vulnerabilities, had required me to keep it together. Now, with the end in sight and in the knowledge that I could soon deliver her safely back to my father, I was starting to relax and the accumulated strain spilled over. I found myself weeping for everybody and everything caught up in the hideousness of war; for my brave mother, who had come on this challenging trip without really understanding what I was looking for, or why; for the part of me that, for so many years, had been crippled by an invisible but enormous burden of guilt for one of the most horrendous episodes in history and for the hard, punishing part of me that somehow held myself responsible for it all.

My mother was kind. It was obvious that she couldn't fully comprehend the complexity of my emotions or my near-obsessive interest in her father. She could, however, see my exhaustion and how the word 'murderer' had shaken me and continued to haunt me. 'It was so different in those times,' she said quietly, and I felt the full strength of her, a mother comforting her child. 'It's all right, darling,' she soothed when the tears didn't stop.

But it wasn't all right at all. Nothing about it was all right.

15

A 'Clean' Wehrmacht?

To do evil a human being must first believe that what he's doing is good, or else that it's a well-considered act in conformity with natural law. Fortunately, it is in the nature of the human being to seek a justification for his actions.

Aleksandr Solzhenitsyn, *The Gulag Archipelago*

'I DON'T THINK I CAN make art about "my grandfather, the murderer"', I told two fellow art students on the first of many car journeys during the final year of our fine art degree, for which we were now based in Bristol. I had hoped going to Russia would provide me with a rich seam of material. But I had returned even more unsettled than before.

I was wary of exposing my story to the new art tutors. I felt I could no longer defend my grandfather or protect his image because I didn't know for sure what he had, or hadn't, done. There were too many gaps in his story. Nor did I want to subject myself to the judgement of people for whom the Second World War was a clear-cut binary narrative of good triumphing over evil. Just as I had done in my prison work, I was seeking insight into the natures of those considered guilty in order to try to understand not whether they were guilty but *how* people become capable of evil. And how – if ever – they can redeem themselves, or be redeemed. Who was I, anyway, to put my grandfather's spirit and memory through the inevitable condemnation and retribution? He had already been judged enough in his lifetime.

I felt like giving up.

The first tutorial did nothing to assuage my fears. The students had laid out their work in the small, low-ceilinged, windowless room and the tutor casually went round asking questions and offering advice. When it came to my turn, he barely looked at the sketched ideas and images from my Russia trip before launching into an aggressive interrogation of the motives for my line of inquiry.

Questions ricocheted around me as he dismissed my concepts as 'clichés' without even bothering to find out what they were. Winded by his antagonistic criticisms, I could only splutter about 'exploring nuance' and 'challenging black-and-white stereotypes'.

The approach to fine art here was as different from the fine art in Stroud as football is from rugby. As well as my grandfather, I was told to forget meaning, content and subject matter: all elements that had become part of my approach. The tutor's instructions left me floundering in a creative vacuum and heading for a big fail.

It was the German philosopher Theodor Adorno who declared, in his much-cited and oft-misunderstood conclusion to an essay in 1949: 'To write a poem after Auschwitz is barbaric.' Creating art after witnessing the scale of devastation on the Eastern Front felt similarly undoable to me. I resorted to a familiar friend: destruction.

I started dropping things from a height like bombs. First I climbed a stepladder and let a large rock smash down on to a china plate of neatly arranged slices of Battenberg cake. I deliberately chose this quintessential element of an English afternoon tea because of the German heritage that lay beneath its marzipan casing. The pink and yellow squares of its design are a homage to the wedding cake celebrating the marriage of the German Prince Louis von Battenberg to one of Queen Victoria's granddaughters.

I progressed to greater heights, dropping a series of larger rocks from a footbridge into the silted riverbed of the Avon that ebbed and flowed just outside the building and recording the event on film. Choosing everyday materials as a medium for the expression of my ideas, I experimented with mud, dragging it into the studio in buckets, and cut up and assembled laminated birch floorboards to reconstruct the devastated birch forests of the Volkhov swamplands. I took two foods typical of each of my nationalities – a fried English pork sausage and a boiled German frankfurter – and tied them together in a white bun with blood-red ketchup oozing between them. Bound enemies. That was how I felt inside.

I created a diorama in the vaulted cellar beneath my house. Headless men seated at a tabletop in white shirts and ties, up to their waists in a sea of mud that appeared to have risen around them, catching them unawares and freezing

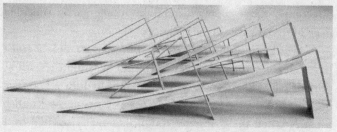

Kaputt/Broken *(2009)*.

them in time as they plotted the deadly fate of the world over a champagne lunch.

For the rest of the year, I ignored my tutor's advice to 'forget my grandfather' and focused on my final piece: a quiet slide projection of words that typed themselves into the questions I was constantly asking him in my mind. What did you feel? What did you know? What did you do?

In some places, they typed over themselves to become dense, illegible black lines conveying censorship or that which is unspeakable. In others, the words faded and emerged like silenced secrets. The tutor declared it an elegant, understated piece when it appeared in the final show. But its whispered pleas for answers got lost in the vast white halls that hummed with excited graduates. It was an excitement I felt completely unable to share.

I hurt on all levels. 'They were all murderers.' 'They were all involved.' 'They all knew.' These words still rang in my ears. I remembered my mother once telling me that when she had first come to England in the sixties and heard people claiming that surely the Germans 'must have known', she had secretly agreed with them. These quiet confessions escaped from her psyche like prisoners of war in films. They would slip under the fence when a change in the guard detail and the direction of the sweeping searchlights momentarily coincided to create a dark gap in the defences.

I was beginning to understand how impossible it must have felt for some of her generation to question the actions of their parents. As an Anglo-German, I had the advantage of being able to retreat into the safe harbours of my English identity when the going got tough. If I really wanted to, I could even have waved the flag of victory or joined in the taunting chants of 'Two world wars and one World Cup!' at football matches. Since belonging to the third generation put a greater distance between me and the grandfather I never met, I was altogether better placed to poke at the possibility of culpability for atrocities within the family than my mother was.

If all German soldiers sent to fight in the battlefield are seen as murderers, as culpable for the Holocaust because they are deemed part of the Nazi machine, surely this had implications for their descendants? Was it this sense of unfinished business that was driving me? Was I looking to justify what he did or seeking some kind of forgiveness or a way of atoning? Had I been carrying around with me an unprocessed pile of shit he may have felt but not dealt with after the war and instead, by a strange mechanism I had yet to uncover, passed on to me to resolve?

I could not answer any of these questions until I could establish whether my grandfather was guilty of murder.

Murder is defined as the unlawful, premeditated killing of one human being by another. Murderers are people who have killed with intent. Their motives may range from revenge to a belief that the death of a particular person is going to make their own life better in some way and may be catalyzed by drink, drugs or psychotic episodes.

By contrast, soldiers are trained and ordered to carry out 'premeditated killings' of the soldiers of a perceived enemy. Hitler, however, extended this to include the premeditated killings of civilians, above all, Jews. He legitimized murder.

As a prisoner of war awaiting the judgement of the enemy, my grandfather, along with fellow captured generals, defined – and defended – the roles and duties of the Wehrmacht soldier: 'We German generals are not politicians. Contrary to what the propaganda said, we never tried to influence politics. The soldier serves and swears an oath to the state, not to a particular party.'

He describes how the army protected the Weimar Republic in the same way as it had protected the empire before it and the Nazi state afterwards; how the army, officers included, had no right to vote and no cause to interfere with the will of the people; how, even under National Socialism, the army was allowed to maintain its apolitical position and the Hitler salute became obligatory only after the von Stauffenberg assassination attempt. And how even Hitler couldn't break this apolitical attitude, which was why he set up a second, political army – the Waffen SS, the military branch of the Nazi party.

After the war, the international narrative by and large supported this account of a 'clean' Wehrmacht. While the Allies scooped up identified Nazis and ordinary civilians alike in nets of culpability, they tended to look on members of the armed forces as having simply done their duty. The International Military Tribunal, which conducted the Nuremberg trials, ruled that the Wehrmacht was not a criminal organization and that the German General Staff and High Command could not be found collectively guilty. Dr Hans Laternser, an expert in Anglo-Saxon law who represented the General Staff at Nuremberg, drew on the classics, modern thinkers and Allied commanders of the Second World War to make his case, including the British field marshals Alexander and Montgomery. The former concurred that the German troops fought decently and like 'gentlemen' and, in a speech on 26 July 1946, Field Marshal Montgomery reflected my grandfather's attitude that a national army is above politics and dedicated to the state: 'The army is not a union of individuals but a fighting body, welded together through discipline and controlled by its leader. Freedom is the basis of democracy; discipline is the basis of the army.'

Among my grandfather's letters was a 1946 newsletter for German POWs, produced and circulated with the permission of the British, in which a German translation of a quote attributed to Thomas Carlyle appeared to support this statement: 'When a man enlists in the army, his soul as well as his body belong to his commanding officer. He is to be no judge of the cause for which he has to fight . . . His enemies are chosen for him and not by himself. His duty is to obey orders and to ask no questions.'

These were, after all, the same principles on which armies around the world were founded and still are today. Duty and obedience was the line I believe my grandfather took. 'Don't worry about me,' he had written confidently to my grandmother in December 1945. 'As a higher artillery commander, I couldn't commit any crimes.'

However, there were various reasons why the Allies consciously exempted the Wehrmacht from indictment at Nuremberg. Unlike the Waffen-SS, which had been predominantly comprised of volunteers (augmented by the increasing numbers of *Volksdeutsche*, ethnic Germans from eastern Europe, who were recruited as the war progressed), the Wehrmacht had drafted millions, leaving German men with few options to avoid conscription other than by offering to serve in something even worse, like a concentration camp. The Allies didn't want, either, to indiscriminately punish entire peoples in any way reminiscent of Germany's pogroms. And by this time, as the tensions of the Cold War began to mount, it was in the interests of the UK and USA to strengthen Germany as an ally and an important buffer against the Communist eastern states. To enable West Germany's rearmament, foreign public opinion of the Wehrmacht as Nazis had to be transformed.

For decades, then, the Wehrmacht was widely seen, and saw itself, as 'decent' and 'unblemished', a solid rock of honourableness within the ocean of horrors. Until the opening of an exhibition in 1995 demonstrated beyond all doubt that it absolutely was not. And especially not in the East.

Crimes of the Wehrmacht, organized by the Hamburg Institute for Social Research, presented the consensus of historians on the Wehrmacht's war of annihilation on the Eastern Front to a shocked or enraged public in cities across Germany and Austria.

In documents and photographic evidence, much of it drawn from family albums, Wehrmacht soldiers could be seen watching, even taking part in mass executions of rounded-up Jews and Russian civilians. They were pictured forcing Soviet captives on long marches, which hundreds of thousands did not survive. Those prisoners who did were subsequently starved to death or shot. Over 3 million died. A large proportion of Holocaust victims were not murdered in concentration camps but gunned down, many of them in mass killings in the Ukraine.

It wasn't, either, simply the dictum *Befehl ist Befehl* – an order is an order – that drove some soldiers to kill women and children. The perception of themselves as *Übermenschen*, ideal, superior people, instilled a hatred of *Untermenschen* so pronounced that it engendered a willingness to kill Jews,

even women and children, out of nothing more than ideological fanaticism.

Here, then, was indisputable proof of the Wehrmacht's
knowledge of and complicity in war crimes previously attributed only to the SS.

Massive criticism, controversy and debate ensued. People
demonstrated in the streets against what they saw as the betrayal
and unjust smearing of the good names of their fathers and
grandfathers. They wanted a distinction made between those
who had committed crimes and those who hadn't, arguing that
otherwise the exhibition branded Germans as genetically criminal. Authority over your actions as a soldier is impossible, they
claimed. Other nations have committed war crimes. The executions were awful for the German soldiers, too. What about
the slaughter of innocents committed by Allied soldiers in their
bombing raids?

Despite the removal of certain images due to errors of attri-
bution, inaccurate captions or misleading emotional manipulation, the organizers maintained that the key statement of the
exhibition was correct: the Wehrmacht had been involved in
planning and implementing a war of aggression and extermination against Jews, Soviet prisoners of war and civilians.

Given that I was living in Cologne at the time of the exhibition, it seems incredible to me now that all this passed me by.
Preoccupied as I was with my prison work and alternative
therapies, I paid little attention to the national media. Culturally, I was riding the wave of pacifism and emancipation in the
new Germany and not much interested in mainstream politics
or, at that point, the war. But I can remember what I realized,
with hindsight, must have been the news of the controversy
reaching my family. During a visit home I witnessed a flurry of

phone calls between my mother and her relatives in Germany, conducted in shocked whispers as she paced up and down the kitchen. I picked up the words 'Wehrmacht', *'Vati'* (dad) and *schrecklich* (terrible), none of which normally featured in their conversations.

I detected a quiet sense of panic fluttering like a trapped bird in the corridors of their dialogue. Though my grandfather was rarely talked about, I knew they had always trusted that the Prussian virtues of bravery, duty and unfailing 'correctness' in which he had been marinated since childhood were a guarantee of his honour. Their belief in his innocence of all wrongdoing was one of the lifebuoys on to which the family clung. In the storm of accusations surrounding the notion of a 'clean' Wehrmacht, it had been punctured. As it slowly sank, his grown-up children and wife were left paddling in barely disguised terror as they looked around for other floating debris to grab hold of. I, too, felt their panic, but back then, with no knowledge of Nazi Germany's military history or structure, I had no context, no framework for questions, no idea of what any of this really meant.

The exhibition ran until 1999 and its impact was profound. It shook carefully constructed deflections of guilt, gouged holes in benign memories of relatives and confirmed unspoken suspicions about others. Until then, war-battered families had been able to dissociate soldiers who had served in the internationally respected Wehrmacht from the atrocities by pinning the blame firmly on the already incriminated SS. That way they could place the shards of their loved ones' reputations as champions of Germany's honour on the ruined mantelpieces of their family consciences: polished, dented trophies saved from the rubble of condemnation.

They could do so no longer. Pandora's Box had been opened, and in 2001 the Hamburg Institute for Social Research mounted a revised exhibition, which was twice the size. This one toured for three years before being given a permanent home in the Deutsches Historisches museum in Berlin.

At around the same time, transcripts of secretly bugged, private conversations between senior Wehrmacht officers and generals held in POW interrogation camps such as Trent Park between 1939 and 1942 were declassified, giving unprecedented insights into what they had and had not known. They had clearly known a lot. And many had been active participants in a great deal more than had previously been supposed.

I would go on to discover that, even before Operation Barbarossa began, soldiers on the Eastern Front had been schooled in the main aims of the campaign. Hitler's (illegal) orders to the Wehrmacht were for total annihilation, above all of Bolshevik commissars and the Communist intelligentsia. In his pursuit of a pure-blooded *Volk*, an Aryan race with superior virtues and qualities, he dehumanized the enemy as 'Slavic *Untermensch*', declaring in 1941: 'The war against Russia will be such that it cannot be conducted in a knightly fashion. This struggle is one of ideologies and racial differences and will have to be conducted with unprecedented, unmerciful and unrelenting harshness.'

In May that year, the Barbarossa decree signed by the Wehrmacht chief, Wilhelm Keitel, outlined the military conduct towards Soviet citizens: ruthless elimination of partisans, executions without trial, collective punishments and the exemption from criminal responsibility of German soldiers who committed crimes against humanity, the USSR and POWs.

In June, the *Kommissarbefehl*, the Commissar Order, instructed the Wehrmacht to summarily execute any Soviet political commissar, or supervisory officer, for their role in enforcing the Judeo-Bolshevist ideology. Several commanders tried to get Hitler to soften the order but he refused. 'By fighting off the Jews, I am doing the Lord's work,' he had stated in *Mein Kampf*.

In November 1941, Generalfeldmarschall von Reichenau, one of the most extreme Nazis in High Command, extended this brief, drumming it into soldiers that they were not mere fighters but defenders of a ruthless racial ideology and avengers of all the 'bestialities' inflicted on the German nation by 'the subhuman species of Jewry'. For that reason, they would be required to carry out tasks that went beyond the conventional rules of war. There was no room for sentimentality.

Not all Wehrmacht generals acquiesced easily to these instructions. Many were horrified by what the SS and the other militia that made up the Einsatzgruppen, the death squads, were doing behind the front lines. Some, such as Johannes Blaskowitz, wrote to Hitler detailing the detrimental effects on the Wehrmacht soldiers and asking for it to be stopped. By November 1941, other senior army leaders were adding their voices to the concerns about the impact of genocidal warfare on their men. They complained that the SS operations to murder townspeople were happening too soon after the Wehrmacht successes, preying on the soldiers' consciences and hindering both their own operations and morale. They feared this could lead to a loss of inner balance and a propensity for brutalization even after the war. In the end, the Wehrmacht commanders made their own agreement with SS leaders, allowing the SS to continue but not until the army had moved on to capture the next town. That way the Wehrmacht could claim to have nothing to do with it.

I wished with my whole being that my grandfather had been too far away, both physically and morally, to be even remotely associated with these atrocities. Or that I would uncover some evidence that he had vehemently protested, not just against the negative repercussions on his men but – far more importantly – against the barbarity of murdering ordinary people.

I wondered about the language he had used to prepare his men for battle. I thought of his reference to the SS 'clearing up' behind them. He'd written it seemingly without compunction. How had he not seen this 'clear-up' as a wholly unacceptable deviation from the rules of warfare he'd been taught as a cadet? Might the brevity of his statement have been designed to convey private disgust, or disapproval, or even regretful acceptance? Whatever the case, on the face of it, his letters suggest he took the view that there was no alternative:

> *The Russian-backed partisan warfare dragged the poor*
> *local people into such an embittered war that it was met*
> *with equal embitterment. It wasn't a war between*
> *soldiers, but rather against animalistic hordes capable of*
> *every crime. No single German who fell into their hands*
> *came out alive. These beasts that didn't disdain killing*
> *and consuming their own fallen couldn't be looked on as*
> *regular troops . . . One Russian colonel prisoner told*
> *General Lindemann that in the winter famine of 1927,*
> *all Russians ate human flesh and that no liver was as tasty*
> *as a human liver. In spite of this, the German soldier*

> *fought fairly and respectably. All Allied soldiers who*
> *fought against Germans know that.*

Had he come to think this way as a result of his own experiences? The brutality of the partisan ambushes from day one of the invasion had indeed taken the soldiers wholly by surprise, disorientating them and instilling in many a desire for revenge that found expression in merciless reprisals. At the same time, the vocabulary he uses here suggests he had absorbed or at least accepted the pervasive propaganda that perpetuated the fear of the 'Red hordes' and dismissed the Bolshevists as inferior 'beasts'.

As more and more German soldiers, sworn to duty and obedience, willingly or not, became part of the nation's killing apparatus, the word 'murder' was rendered obsolete. This was an ideological war requiring 'special measures' and troops were expected to 'follow orders' and participate 'to the end'.

Violence, destruction and war are, of course, justified by politicians and rulers the world over as legitimate responses to a perceived threat or evil. For the trained soldier, death and killing are part of the job; the means of national defence, the re-establishment of order or the preservation of peace. You are part of the cure, the solution to a problem. 'Often you don't hate the enemy,' an ex-soldier friend once told me. 'They are just the "other side". All you have in mind is to fight for the task at hand and for your friends.'

In their bestselling 2011 book *Soldaten: On Fighting, Killing and Dying: The Secret Second World War Tapes of German POWs*, Sönke Neitzel, professor of international history at

the London School of Economics, and Harald Welzer cor-
roborate this idea and present a surprisingly different picture
from the black-and-white story of German soldiers to which
we have broadly become accustomed. Their work draws on
nearly 17,000 protocols made from recorded conversations,
held in the National Archives in London and Washington,
between German POWs in British and American captivity.
These conversations reveal the perceived normality – 'banality', even – of mass violence and atrocity but also how, like
soldiers engaged in conflict today, the rank and file were primarily focused on doing their duty, on the next battle, their
unit, their weapons, their colleagues. They were concerned
with demonstrating bravery, they sought acceptance among
their comrades and strove for promotions. In short, they
wanted to do their jobs as 'tough', disciplined, good soldiers
to the best of their ability.

Most Wehrmacht soldiers took little interest in the politics of National Socialism or its goals of genocide, ethnic
cleansing and global conquest. In fact, only between 5 and 10
per cent had a clear understanding of Nazi ideology. Another
5 to 10 per cent were decidedly anti-Nazi. However, though
only 0.2 per cent of the stories told in the recorded conversations of the German POWs related to the Holocaust, it is
perfectly clear that practically all German soldiers knew from
scenes they had witnessed, or suspected from hearsay, that
Jews were being murdered en masse. But the genocide was
not as central to their world as has been believed over the past
thirty years. In practice, political fanaticism and racism never
accrued the significance Hitler wished for in these soldiers.

Some do express horror, regret or shame when talking
about the extent of the exterminations, particularly the

atrocities against women and children, or criticize the inhumane methods. But they do not question the fact that it was taking place. Others had taken part in mass executions, seeing this as a chance to participate in 'unpunished inhumanity', as the sociologist Günther Anders called it, or looked on in what has been described as a grotesque display of 'execution tourism'. But they were not ordered to do so.

The soldiers didn't need to be anti-Semitic or racist to follow orders that transgressed standard boundaries. Their task, as they saw it, was to meet the military value system of obedience, duty and sacrifice and not to reflect on the rights or wrong of the actions, just the results. A still more complex question is whether the German generals were morally obliged to follow orders from Hitler, even when they knew these orders were flouting international law. Some were convinced Nazis; others held anti-Nazi views and hated Hitler and his regime but fought regardless. Disobeying orders would have had serious consequences, though ethically, that doesn't justify anything. At least 15,000 German soldiers were executed for desertion and up to 50,000 for minor acts of insubordination. Others were summarily killed by their officers or comrades when they refused to comply with commands.

When it comes to concentration camps and the mass murder of Jewish civilians in towns and villages throughout Nazi-occupied eastern Europe, the atrocities committed by the SS defy explanations of this kind. In this context, following orders is a lame excuse. And historians and German prosecutors have failed to find cases where refusal to comply was met with the threat of execution. Yet, with an understanding of the potentially deadly power of indoctrination and its ability to embed beliefs in minds that are receptive to influence, it becomes easier to follow the twisted logic by which the 'removal' of a certain group of people considered unworthy 'subhumans' or a threat to civilization could be justified as a 'good' or 'right' solution.

Is it even possible for a soldier to distinguish between one sense of duty, or following one set of orders, and another? If they shouldn't obey orders in every instance, what are the alternative ground rules for an army? In postwar Germany during the 1950s, the ethics and legality of 'doing one's duty as a soldier' were the subject of intense and urgent debate. Today military disobedience is accounted for in the regulations governing the German Bundeswehr, the armed forces. The German military manual states that a military order is not binding if it has no legitimate aim or cannot be reasonably executed. Furthermore, the order *must* not be obeyed if it violates the human dignity of others, contravenes international law or constitutes a crime.

But that is now, not then.

There was a book in my father's study that my mother sometimes mentioned in relation to my grandfather: *Die Verdammte Pflicht* (*Damned Duty*) by Alexander Stahlberg. He had been adjutant to the aforementioned Generalfeldmarschall Erich von Manstein and was recruited into the military resistance that culminated in the 1944 assassination attempt on Hitler's life led by Claus von Stauffenberg and other Wehrmacht officers. Despite failing to win von Manstein's support for the plot, Stahlberg still fell into the category of 'good German'.

I phoned my father to ask him about the book. He believed there had been some 'good Germans' and, in his beautifully fair and measured way, perhaps drawing on his experience as a naval officer, he alluded to the all-powerful sense of duty among these officers. When we had finished our conversation, he handed the receiver to my mother.

She picked up the thread. 'Your grandfather took his oath very seriously,' she said, an assertion I had heard many times. 'But when he was approached to take part in the Stauffenberg assassination attempt—'

'*What*?' I interrupted. My heart leaped, ready to hoist my grandfather's memory on to the hero's pedestal alongside those brave conspirators.

'—he declined,' she concluded.

I was bitterly disappointed. 'Why?' I asked glumly.

'He felt it was murder.'

This brief shift of perspective revealed to me just how desperately I wanted some indisputable evidence of my grandfather's 'goodness' so that he might be judged more kindly. Crushed though I was, I saw the discovery that he was even approached to join the conspiracy as a positive. It pointed to the plotters being aware, or at least very confident, of attitudes towards Hitler and the Nazis that marked him out as a potential ally. How ironic, then, that his soldier's decision not to kill another person unlawfully, even such an evil dictator, would later see him accused in the court of public opinion of complicity in mass murder. Participation in the assassination attempt would have assured him a status as one of history's heroes. And yet also as one of its martyrs, for it would no doubt have cost him his life.

I questioned my mother further but she couldn't elaborate much more. Her father, she said, had been apolitical and was against the plot because he believed it wasn't the right course of action for a soldier. My grandmother had agreed with him, seeing it as *Betrug:* a treasonous betrayal. In the light of this new nugget of information, I combed through the letters again and eventually found one in which my grandfather alludes to his decision not to take part 'because I reject all violent politics. We soldiers have to obey and not start a revolution'.

There they were again, those Prussian virtues that underpinned his career. As for rejecting 'all violent politics', this was something I could not understand in the context of this 'war of annihilation'.

'It is a travesty that those who dedicated their lives to the nation are now being called war criminals and traitors,' my grandfather had written as a prisoner of war. I can feel his heart in this sentence.

What was I, as his grandchild, meant to do with the 'guilty' verdict on the Wehrmacht fifty years after the end of the war? With the army's orders to murder? What would have been the right thing for my grandfather to have done at the time?

Were there any specific acts of which my grandfather had been found personally guilty? In an effort to find out, I wrote to the military archives in Freiburg requesting all the information they had on Karl von Graffen. Several months later, a pile of badly photocopied, barely legible documents landed with a heavy thud on my doorstep.

16

The Military Records

We used to wonder where war lived, what it was that
made it so vile. And now we realize that we know
where it lives . . . inside ourselves.

Albert Camus, *Notebooks 1935–1942*

THE BROWN ENVELOPE FROM the military archives in
Freiburg contained nearly fifty A4 photocopies of
reports and forms, some typed, some handwritten, nearly all
of them dotted with stamps and signatures. Nobody in the
family had seen these documents. Making sense of them was
going to challenge my grasp of both the German language
and Wehrmacht proceedings. But I hoped it would shed some
light on my grandfather's personal decisions and actions.

I trawled through them page by page, struggling to read
the handwriting and faded print. My mother helped me. The
reports, I learned, were largely standard performance appraisals carried out by superiors for the purposes of assessing my
grandfather's potential advancement as a career soldier.

In one, dated March 1941, just after Karl has been posted
to the Army High Command, his personality is described
as 'genuine, purposeful, extremely hard-working and con-
scientious, a brave and prudent commander in difficult
situations'.

He excelled in facing the enemy ... He distinguished himself ... by his calmness, presence of mind and personal courage ... Before the war against Russia he had brought his regiment to a very high level of operational efficiency and understood especially how to unify the newly formed officers corps and to transfer his great knowledge of artillery to his officers. He was also tirelessly trying to raise the level of operational efficiency of his regiment. Well above average as regimental commander, suitable for artillery commander.

There were other routine reports right up to 1944 that confirmed his consistency as a 'brave and prudent commander in difficult situations against the enemy, with excellent results. Very active, extremely accurate worker, good tactical person, represents his views strongly'.

All this seemed to add colour to the portrait I had been painting of my grandfather in my mind. 'Superior in all fields of artillery. Has achieved outstanding results in the organization of the artillery defence force. Mentally above average, physically very fresh and fit. Strong points: very reliable worker. Weak points: a little circumspect. Agreed, very good artillery commander.'

In what respect was circumspection viewed as a weakness in this context? Was he hesitant about following commands that went against his Wehrmacht values? In what way might he have been cautious? What risks might he have been unwilling to take?

The pinnacle of praise seemed to come in the form of a telegram recommending him for the Knight's Cross:

because of the successful attack by the 58th Infantry Division on 31.5.1942 to cut off the enemy, who had penetrated the lines west of Volkhov, and because of the heroic battles of the division in the central position under artillery 'drum' fire, making it possible to annihilate the enemy, who had been encircled. The successful ending of this annihilation battle on 26.6.1942 is primarily due to the commander of the 58th infantry division, Colonel von Graffen, because of his inspirational and outstanding leadership, his tireless personal involvement and, above all, because of his iron will to persevere, which was transmitted to all soldiers of the division.

The words 'annihilation battle' made me wince. But surely, I reasoned, these qualities were admired in any good soldier anywhere.

One particular correspondence from 1943 caught my attention. There had been a mix-up surrounding Karl's potential promotion to commanding general based on a successful stint as deputy. Karl himself evidently believed that he had demonstrated his suitability for the role, but a Generalfeldmarschall von Küchler had doubts about his ability and determination to oversee and co-ordinate the fighting of several divisions at once. He was of the opinion that my grandfather lacked the inner attitude of a commanding general because, even though he had been informed of the scale, importance and significance of a certain new task, he had rejected it, refusing to carry it out, objecting to minor discords and putting personal concerns before the wider interest of the whole.

I was intrigued. What important task had he rejected? What personal concerns had he voiced? Could it have been that the task in question went against his conscience to such a degree that he refused to order his men to carry it out? I searched online for more information about this von Küchler character. According to Wikipedia, he was 'supportive of Nazi racial policy and sentenced to twenty years' imprisonment for war crimes and crimes against humanity committed in the Soviet Union'. He had also ordered a halt to any criticism of the 'final ethnic solution' which, he declared, required unique and harsh measures.

I imagined my grandfather's conscience drawing a deep line in the sand as he sacrificed his professional ambitions on the altar of his soldier's morality. This was the kind of man I recognized in the accounts of friends and family. The 'good soldier'.

In spite of him not qualifying for that promotion, the reports continue to sing his praises.

> Valuable, thinking personality with a tendency to thoughtfulness/reflection; modest and loyal. Tactically well-fitted and trained and has planned and led in excellent ways ... Shows particular tendency and remarkable talent for organization. National Social attitude without reproach.

Oh my God, there it was. Tucked away between the layers of praise. 'National Social attitude without reproach'. And here was another one – 'good National Socialistic attitude' – and another: 'convinced National Socialist'. I felt sick. So did my mother, sitting with me in her conservatory. We looked at each other across the paper-strewn table. The late-morning sun disappeared behind the neighbour's tree, casting a shadow that turned the documents grey.

What did this mean? Had he just played along with Nazism in order to attain promotion? If not, by which aspects had he been 'convinced'?

Bloody hell, what now?

17

Lost Innocence

Destruction doesn't create a vacuum, it simply
transforms presence into absence.

Anne Michaels, *Fugitive Pieces*

I am waist-deep in the ocean, in the warmth of the sun. I feel
safe with the land behind and the clear sky above. Then
everything goes grey; the old, lead, dead, grey of destruction. I am no longer me but my mother as a little girl, looking
on as the devastation worsens. She sees soldiers marching . . .
The little girl can't take her eyes off it all. War in all its horror. A grown-up's hand tries to lead her away, but she's in
shock. Like a grey wave of ash moving from the right, it gets
closer to where she is standing in her harmonious world of
childhood, full of butterflies, summer light and laughter. As
it reaches her, the grey death swamps it. I can feel the little
girl's pain and panic as all that she thought was good in life
is gobbled up. Then I am crying for her; crying her tears as
she tries to tell the grey to go away, to leave some of her
childhood paradise behind for her to keep. But the grey
doesn't listen to her pleas and swallows it all.

I WAS DOING SOME SESSIONS with a friend whose techniques
for accessing traumatic memories held in the body interested me. My eyes were closed when this sequence of images

appeared, but I was fully conscious. It was as if my body was retrieving what had happened to my mother from a hidden cupboard in which the events and trauma had all been tightly locked.

As I released the grief, I hit a block, which I perceived as my mother's whole life until her escape from Jüterbog, squashed and crushed together like a compressed car in a scrapyard. An overwhelming sense of tragedy that her innocence was suddenly gone for ever. Then my whole body grew numb. It felt empty, like the loose cloth of an untenanted hand puppet. I could see clearly how my mother's wartime experiences had killed something inside her, leaving behind a vacuum nothing was ever going to be able to fill. I knew that now. Yet my mother couldn't see, or feel, any of the traumatic effects the war had had on her. Instead, somehow I had absorbed them, felt them and suffered them for her.

The war smouldered on in me. And, as I would find out, in more ways than I had anticipated.

Not all German children would have been traumatized by the war. Some had good memories of playing in ruins, of the excitement of stealing or scavenging for food or searching for bomb fragments. But a longer-term study of 400 patients in therapy between 1990 and 1993 revealed that the war and the postwar years had left their mark on 54 per cent of them: lasting physical harm caused by undernourishment; a lack of self-care; a reduced capacity for empathy; identity and intimacy issues.

Until Sabine Bode started collecting their stories for her 2004 book on the war children, there had been almost no public awareness of or research into their experiences. Even within families, much of the past remained undiscussed.

Bode's book revealed how the childhood memories were starting to trickle out like small confessions as the war children, born in the two decades from 1927 to 1947, began to grow old, exposing for the first time the traumas they had buried. Many had endured bombings, expulsions, flights, poverty, hunger, cold and bereavement. By the end of the war, 1.7 million women had lost their husbands and 2.5 million children had been left fatherless. A quarter of all youngsters grew up without a paternal figure. Some husbands and fathers would not return from Soviet imprisonment for a decade, and then only as shells of their former selves. Their minds and bodies broken by malnutrition, nightmares and physical incapacities, they would try, as my grandfather had, to re-establish their authority. But they were often complete strangers to their children and frequently succeeded only in terrorizing their families in violent or drunken outbursts, or becoming either impossibly strict or withdrawn and absent.

With 5.5 million children displaced from their homes, daily life revolved around survival and adaptation well into the fifties. Many stepped up to look after their exhausted mothers who – emotionally damaged by grief, loss or, towards the end of the war, rape – were unable to properly nurture their offspring or give them comfort, let alone protection. Despite being well-developed in terms of their cognitive abilities and becoming high achievers in adulthood, a significant number of these children had struggled – for decades – with their emotional skills.

While some had escaped into work and high achievement, others were deeply insecure and reluctant to be swayed by new ideas or new experiences. Their thinking tended to be black and white and their strong need for material security meant that any changes in living conditions caused enormous stress. Many struggled in their marriages, feeling unable to talk about their problems and attributing full blame to their partners for relationship breakdowns. Often they didn't budge from their position for years, revealing a distinct absence of self-reflection.

Bode was struck by the huge difference between the experiences of trauma of those who were seen as victims and those on the side of the perpetrators. The victims knew that they were victims. The children of the perpetrators, on the other hand, didn't feel that they had undergone terrible things. 'That was normal' is how they described so many aspects of their lives. In spite of their considerable suffering, they were forced by the atmosphere of silence, guilt and shame to ignore their own misfortunes and focus on others who had had it far worse: 'Don't be so self-important, make an effort, look forward!' young Germans were told if they voiced any complaint. With no acknowledgement of their psychological distress and little understanding of what had happened to them, they had no language for articulating their experiences and no emotional access to them.

Later books on this generation suggest that the trauma of war, the hardships and the devastated families were not the only shared legacy that had shaped their minds and lives, offering the sinister observation that Nazi indoctrination also played a role. 'The weak must be chiselled away,' Hitler had pronounced at a rally for the Hitler Youth in 1935. 'I want young men and women who can suffer pain. A young German must be as swift as a greyhound, as tough as leather, and as hard as Krupp's steel.'

This conditioning had started at birth with the cruel child-rearing guidelines laid down by the Nazi doctor Johanna Haarer in her book *The German Mother and Her First Child*. In order to grow their young into unwavering Nazis, mothers were instructed to destroy the will of the child, make it adherent to authority and harden it physically, mentally and emotionally. A baby was to be left in a dark room to cry for twenty-four hours after birth. Its needs should be ignored and it should be fed only at set times. Physical contact and tenderness were to be avoided and no reaction demonstrated to a child's feelings or fears.

Not all mothers would adhere to this regime – my grandmother, though strict, was already raising her own children pre-Haarer. But Haarer's influence lasted well into the 1960s: chillingly, almost half of the 1.2 million copies of her manual that were sold were bought after the war. Lack of physical contact alienated children from the messages given and received by their bodies, which resulted in them ignoring physical illnesses as adults. The absence of emotional responses to their feelings left them unable to feel. Showing emotions betrayed your failure to master them, so you buttoned it. This deliberate interference in the attachment process was designed to deprive the child of closeness to its mother and direct it into the arms of the Hitler Youth, where it would find its needs met. With the development of individuality suppressed, children feared being different. They were expected to sacrifice their self-worth and will and to function as a component of the established hierarchy of order and authority.

Born in 1934, a year after Hitler came to power, my mother would never have known a world before he was in charge. By the time she was five and war broke out, the

The von Graffen family, 1939.

Nazis were controlling all areas of German life. Hitler targeted the young, believing that 'whoever has the youth, has the future'. And his ideas on education amounted to mass brainwashing.

First all Jewish staff were sacked from the schools, then, gradually, Jewish children were barred. My mother remembered some of her friends suddenly not being in class any more. Teachers with different political views or a lukewarm attitude to the Nazi cause were suspended or retrained and nearly all were pressurized into joining the National Socialist Teachers' League.

The history, literature, and science curricula were skewed to support the ideology of a racial hierarchy with the archetypal Aryan man – blond, slim, strong-built and tough – at its pinnacle. The Romany, ethnic Poles, Serbs, and Slavs were inferior. The Jews were the lowest of the low. They were ridiculed and demonized in picture books aimed at children, where they were depicted as hook-nosed parasites interested only in money – images which eventually evolved into the characterization of Jews as evil *Untermenschen* who needed to be exterminated.

Biology texts were used to inculcate the principles of eugenics, while geopolitical atlases drew attention to Germany's vulnerability to 'encirclement' and the risk of being overrun by the prolific Slav nations. Germany's population density was shown as being much higher than that of the Eastern regions, thereby emphasizing the necessity for expanding Germany's borders. Hitler's autobiography, *Mein Kampf*, written while he was in prison in 1924, was repeatedly reissued and studied and children had to give Nazi salutes to their teachers to demonstrate their allegiance. His aim was to shape children into a compassionless, disciplined master race and fill their young minds with a fanatical devotion to the national cause and a personal loyalty to him.

By 1939, all other youth movements had been abolished and membership of the Hitler Youth, the umbrella term for a series of leagues for different age groups, was compulsory for children over ten. Each group wore uniforms with swastika armbands and was drilled in Nazi ideology and physical fitness. The boys learned what must have seemed exciting military skills like marching, rifle-shooting, grenade-throwing, trench-digging and map-reading while the girls were prepared for domestic life: nursing soldiers, making beds and surviving air raids. As well as being coached in gymnastics, children were trained to run 60 metres in fourteen seconds, to throw a ball 12 metres, complete a two-hour march and swim 100 metres.

My mother told me how much she, as a nine-year-old, had looked forward to being allowed to join the *Jungmädelbund*, the branch of the Hitler Youth for girls aged ten to fourteen. 'It looked such fun – the camping trips, big fires and outdoor activities, the songs and sense of belonging.' Children from rich and poor families alike could enjoy the same activities and a shared pride in the contribution they were making towards building Germany's great future.

My mother and her siblings would have also been exposed

My mother on her first day at school.

to the sentimental posters of Goebbels' relentless propaganda machine: smiling, blond children, just like them, gazing upwards and outwards as if upon a beautiful horizon, their faces superimposed over a God-like portrait of their Führer.

With fear, pain, vulnerability and tenderness condemned as weaknesses, the arts and religion were strictly controlled. Self-expression, personal conscience and original thought were seen to pose a potential threat. Children learned not to respect their own feelings, leaving them ill-equipped to take care of themselves.

I tried to imagine how these pumped-up German children might have dealt with Hitler's promises and lies when both their leader and his ideology vanished, almost overnight, in 1945.

After completing my degree, I was unsure how to proceed with my life. I disappeared into a makeshift studio in one of the stone vaults beneath my house and, in this small, womb-like cell, reacquainted myself with my old friend colour. I let it flow through me and on to the canvas uncensored, feeling my way forwards with a combination of photographic collage and oils. Canvas after canvas was painted and hung up to dry, but I had no idea exactly what I was painting. I couldn't even stand back very far to look at what I had produced owing to the confined space.

It was only in spring, when I emerged like a hedgehog from hibernation, that I could gain a sense of what I had been doing. I was still dropping bombs, now into the genteel interiors of family homes; creating everyday domestic scenes rudely interrupted by war. Tables of food abandoned by fleeing diners. Assorted objects, perhaps a shortlist of treasured possessions, hurriedly gathered for a hasty exit. Paint dribbled over inverted magazine images of interiors collaged on to canvases, worlds turned upside down. The safety, security, familiarity and warmth of 'home' destroyed.

With all my stone-turning in the family's past, my mother's recollections, and the emotions attached to them, had become dislodged from deep in my psyche, where I had stored them, not knowing what else to do with them. Now they were bubbling up and out of me. I was painting the fear and pain she had never shown or been able to feel herself when she recounted her childhood stories; reliving the trauma she, and perhaps the whole family, had experienced of being yanked from their world.

I was depicting the silver candlesticks my grandmother tried to send on ahead to Wildenhorst, the paintings left on their walls, the chairs whose silk seats were slashed by Soviet soldiers searching for money, the heirloom china smashed in angry revenge for the huts, villages and families destroyed thousands of miles to the east. Peeling wallpaper, like layers of time, revealed the other lives and other homes that lay beneath. It was all coming out.

Like my mud art, these paintings started to sell rapidly. Galleries wanted them faster than I could paint them. I was back in my element and flying once again, collaborating with a professional photographer to take my collaged still lives to another level. But I began to sense that something was missing from these artworks. Colour, form and paint no longer felt sufficient as a language. I needed the added dimension of time.

A painting exists only in space. Contained within the boundaries of the edges of the canvas, everything is presented at once, in the same moment. What I was striving for was less of a three-dimensional static object and more of a narrative, a journey – like a piece of music or a story. I wanted people to actively participate in a process from which they would emerge slightly changed.

An invitation to take part in a twelve-day art and culture forum in Laubach, a small town north-east of Frankfurt, gave me the perfect opportunity to experiment. Run by art enthusiasts and based in the grounds of the magical Schloss Laubach, it generously provided the eight or so artists involved with time, space and a steady flow of delicious meals and then left them to make art for an exhibition at the end.

I spent the first day wandering the grounds. I watched a man in a cherry-picker sculpting one of the mature trees that flanked the lake and another mending a streetlamp. The next morning, I had an idea for one of my pieces of work.

I scoured second-hand shops for crockery and furniture, bought edible ingredients from the supermarket and made contact with the local fire brigade. At a pre-arranged time, a large red fire engine pulled up in front of the *schloss*, where a small crowd had assembled. My performance started unceremoniously with me laying a bistro table with a pair of typical English and German breakfasts. Tea, toast and a fry-up on one side; coffee, fresh rolls, cheese and jam on the other. I then clambered into the basket of the fire engine with one of the firemen, taking with me three 10-kilo boulders. With a refreshing disregard for health and safety, we climbed the full 40-metre stretch of the high arm until I could see over the roof of the *schloss* into the park and across the surrounding town. Lifting one of the rocks, I leaned over the edge of the basket, took aim at the breakfast table and dropped it.

It crash-landed inches away from the table. Disconcerted

by how tiny my target was from my lofty perch, and shaking with a mixture of excitement and fear of another miss, I picked up my second boulder. This time the onlookers clapped as it pulverized the jar of marmalade before ripping a gaping hole through the white tablecloth and flimsy tabletop. The third rock finished the job. The table legs buckled like those of a dying animal, leaving both breakfasts mashed like guts in dark pools of spilled tea.

It was exhilarating. People had not known what was coming. Some were disturbed by the violent destruction of a cheerful domestic scene; others found it hilarious. Standing in front of the bombed table, I talked about my family history, fully aware that every member of the German audience

Making Rock Drop *(2012).*

would have stories of their own, many of them untold, and very probably worse than mine.

I want to hear these stories, I thought. I want to know what became of other ordinary Germans who, after the downfall of Hitler and Nazism, melted into the grey shadows of a broken land and the wreckage of their former lives. Who, when accused of complicity, gagged themselves and their children into silences that lasted into the twenty-first century. What became of all those people who lined the streets and waved as Hitler drove past in his open-topped Mercedes *Führerwagen*? Of those who were wholeheartedly convinced that it was right to banish and exterminate the Jews, to take their empty houses and buy, steal or sell their possessions? What became of the citizens who believed in and made personal sacrifices for the greater good of the 'glorious' Third Reich that Hitler had promised them? Of the women and children who were forced to flee their homes? Of the surviving soldiers returning from imprisonment, injured, exhausted, defeated and guilty? Of the war-torn families who felt unable, even among themselves, to articulate the horrors and losses they had endured? Of the war children whose traumas and suffering have long been deemed irrelevant, and even deserved, in the face of the atrocities Germany inflicted on others?

What became of the losers of the Second World War?

18

The History of the Losers

In war, whichever side may call itself the victor,
there are no winners, but all are losers.

Neville Chamberlain, speech at Kettering, 3 July 1938

Does the world know what is happening in Germany?
Millions of German women and children fell victim
to the bombing raids. Millions more were raped or
slaughtered, some as young as 12 years old. More than
half the German population lost all their possessions. Not
a single town of over 100,000 inhabitants was spared the
unrestrained annihilation. And the men were turned into
modern slaves under such unspeakable harassment that
thousands died of exhaustion.

Fourteen million Germans were ripped from their
beds, robbed of their belongings, chased out of their
farms and forced to trek like herds of cattle across
Germany to land in already over-populated areas. The
misery of these journeys is indescribable. With no food,
even some potato peel or a carrot from a compost heap
were delicacies. They had to sleep in open fields for weeks
on end with no protection from the winter cold. Whoever
became too tired died. Mothers, now half-mad, lugged
their dead children around for days. Those who had
property in the Russian zone, even if it had belonged to

*their families for centuries, had it expropriated without
compensation, and if they weren't instantly slaughtered,
they were brought to a concentration camp or deported
to Russia. Thousands chose suicide to avoid this inhuman
behaviour. Four million women, children and old men
never reached the resettlement camps. Nobody who
wasn't part of the war and is enjoying a life of security
and modern cultural amenities can imagine the misery
that arose . . .*

*The plundering of private property was not only
tolerated but recommended . . . We soldiers experienced it
first-hand, being plundered right down to our last shirt.
Watches, rings, cups, mirrors, cutlery, blankets, tents, even
the photos of our loved ones were taken away. All those
who had been looted, elderly women, children, helpless
cripples, the war-torn and the sick, were left exposed in
barbed-wire-fenced fields, without trees or bushes, in a
malaria-ridden area with a foreign climate. Not even the
basics you'd give an animal – straw, shelter and food –
were provided. Was that the assured 'good treatment'
promised by the supposedly honourable Field Marshal
Lord Alexander before the capitulation? Were those the
ideals of humanity and human rights for which the Allied
soldiers fought?*

THIS IS MY GRANDFATHER, writing down his thoughts as a
prisoner of war in Italy in 1946. For a long while I had
been too focused on his letters, and his own role in the war, to
do more than skim-read their sequel and, until now, none of
what he was saying here had landed.

I could feel his outrage. But was all this true? If it was,

why had I never heard anything of it? The history of almost every German family must have been affected.

Yet it was complicated. My grandfather was insisting that the German people deserved sympathy and understanding while completely overlooking the fact that his descriptions of their misery and suffering could equally be applied to all those who had suffered at their own hands. It suggests that either he was unaware of the extent of the Final Solution, the Nazis' plan for the global annihilation of the Jews, drawn up in 1942 – which seems highly implausible by this time – or that he didn't believe what had happened to the civilians on the Eastern Front was wrong.

I decided that the best place to start excavating the history of the losers was the fallout at the end of the war. Some hard facts would help me to check the solidity of the scaffolding on which my grandfather was building his case. Sitting at my cluttered desk, surrounded by open books and printed-out online articles, I crunched some numbers, many of them recognized estimates. The scale of loss, destruction and death made my jaw drop.

A total of around 60 million people were killed in the war. Within that statistic, the most notorious figure is, of course, the 11 million murdered in the Holocaust, of whom around 6 million were Jews. The other 5 million were Communists, homosexuals, the disabled or the mentally ill, Sinti and Roma Zigeuner ('gypsies', as the Roma people were then called), Polish civilians, Soviet citizens and POWS, German political dissidents and others.

Equally unimaginable is the figure of 26 million Russian dead, around a third of them military and two thirds civilians. Depending on your source, between 7 and 9 million

Germans died. Roughly 6 million were soldiers – one in eight German men were killed – and 3 million civilians. Half a million, mostly women, children and the elderly, had died in the British and American bombing raids: 42,000 in Hamburg, 25,000 in Dresden.

China lost up to 20 million people, Poland around 6 million, France and the USA just over and under half a million respectively. The real thunderbolt for me, however, was the United Kingdom's death toll. Just under 451,000. An almost identical figure to the number of German soldiers killed in January 1945 alone. That's 383,800 military, including combatants from overseas territories (Crown colonies and the Indian Empire), and 67,200 civilians, 40,000 of whom were bombed in the German air raids during the Blitz of 1940-41.

Why was I so surprised by this statistic? Every death is a tragedy for those left behind. But these figures put the scale of loss in other countries into a new perspective.

In Germany, the death and suffering took many forms, both during and after the war. Around 11 million soldiers were imprisoned, an estimated million of them dying of cold, exhaustion or illness in Soviet camps, from which few were released until the 1950s (the last 10,000 were finally returned from Siberia in 1955). Millions were missing. Suicide spread like an epidemic after Hitler and the Goebbels family killed themselves. Tens of thousands of German men and women, including fifty-three of the 554 army generals, followed suit, often taking their children with them.

Possibly the most shocking figure to me is the 2 million women and girls, aged eight to eighty, who were raped by Soviet soldiers at the end of the war, some as many as sixty or seventy times. An estimated 240,000 female deaths can be attributed to these brutal violations. At least 100,000 such attacks took place in Berlin where, according to many estimates, between 7,000 and 10,000 women killed themselves and their children as a result. The historian Antony Beevor has described it as the greatest phenomenon of mass rape in history.

Why were these facts not widely known? I thought back to the first book we had read in my book club a year or two before, the anonymously written *A Woman in Berlin*. 'It's obvious fabrication,' a couple of the members had agreed, dismissing the author's first-hand accounts of the multiple rapes of German women by the Soviets immediately after the war.

It wasn't just a question of the victors glossing over the suffering of the vanquished. Even in Germany, none of this was talked about until the Nobel Prize-winning novelist Günter Grass published *Im Krebsgang* (*Crabwalk*) in 2002, finally shattering the silence in which Germans had buried their war experiences and triggering a swell of TV programmes, articles and books exploring them for the first time. The novel revolves around the sinking of the German ship *Wilhelm Gustloff* – originally deployed as a cruising ocean liner for the masses in Hitler's Strength Through Joy programme – by a Soviet submarine in the Baltic Sea in January 1945. Over 9,000 fleeing German refugees and retreating military personnel died: the greatest loss of life in the sinking of a single ship in history, surpassing the death tolls of both the *Titanic* and the *Lusitania*.

Recalling the bustling Hamburg of my childhood, I found it staggering to think that, just thirty years earlier, in July

1943, the city had been flattened by eight days of Allied carpet-bombing. Though it's easy to view this as deserved retribution, the fact remains that, like the notorious raids on Dresden, these attacks killed tens of thousands of civilians in horrendous ways. How had the Germans managed to brush themselves down so effectively? How did they clear up all that rubble? The battle-orientated, male-centric history I'd been taught in the classroom and gleaned from films was shifting on its foundations.

I began to build a more comprehensive history for myself from a wider range of sources. After the unconditional capitulation on 8 May 1945, I learned, Germany had been in total chaos. Initially, the Nazi government had forbidden civilians to flee westwards in the face of the rapidly advancing and avenging Soviet army. But from 1944 onwards, with the gradual encirclement of Germany by the Allies, the government had sanctioned the evacuation of anyone of German ethnicity – largely old people, women and children under sixteen. Millions piled carts with all they could carry and, leaving their homes behind, started to trek hundreds of miles on foot, often through deep snow.

Those who stayed put faced the full force of Soviet rage and vengeance. As well as being robbed, beaten and enduring multiple rapes, women without children, or just one child, were hauled off to labour camps further east. Mothers with larger families ended up in other camps in formerly occupied countries where many women and children perished over the next two years. Immediately after the defeat of the Wehrmacht, many others fled, or were forcibly expelled, from Pomerania, Silesia, Prussia, the Baltic States and Posen (now part of Poland). Estimates suggest that

500,000 to 600,000 (some go as high as 2 million) of the refugees on the move, over half of them women and children, lost their lives through murder, starvation, hypothermia, drowning while crossing frozen rivers, sexual violence, suicide, disease, air raids or being deliberately crushed by tanks. More than the total number of British who died in the entire war.

At the Potsdam Conference in the summer of 1945, the USSR, USA and Britain redrew the map of Europe, denying Germany a quarter of its former territory and creating four main zones: the north-west was overseen by the British, the north-east by the Soviets, the south-west by the French and the south-east by the Americans. Berlin, though located in the Soviet zone, was also divided into four sectors, each under the control of the four victors.

To avoid an avenging wave of ethnic killings, the Allies came up with a policy of transferring all the remaining German-speaking populations in Poland, Hungary, Romania, Yugoslavia and Czechoslovakia, many of whom had lived there for hundreds of years, to the now-reduced German territory. 'A clean sweep will be made,' said Churchill, outlining how the Germans were to be 'given a brief amount of time to gather the bare necessities and leave'. Later, on seeing the devastation and atrocities that ensued in place of 'the orderly and humane manner' prescribed by the Potsdam Agreement, he described the mass expulsions as a 'tragedy on a prodigious scale'.

With sixty-one German cities in ruins, 20 per cent (8 million) of all German homes destroyed and nearly half of the roads, railways, water, gas and electricity supplies gone, food and resources were scarce. A quarter of the surviving German population – around 14 million people– was displaced and homeless with nowhere to go.

Fourteen million. There it was again, that figure quoted by my grandfather. I just couldn't get my head round it. This was the largest recorded episode of forced migration in history. And yet I had never heard of it.

On arrival in the Allied occupation zones, some of the German refugees were interned in former labour and concentration camps – even at Auschwitz, less than a fortnight after its liberation by the Russians. Here they were often subjected to further sadistic beatings, torture, sexual violence and malnutrition, as their captors, bent on exacting revenge, emulated some of the worst aspects of Nazi behaviour. Many lived in refugee camps while others simply slept rough or took shelter in the rubble of bombed buildings. Only the luckiest of the fleeing families, like my mother's, were able to move in with relatives.

Journalists from Britain and other Allied nations tried to publicize the dire situation and pronounced it a shambolic mass violation of human rights, but this cut no ice with the politicians, who were anxious not to be seen being soft on the Germans. George Orwell's warning that 'an enormous crime' was about to be committed, 'equivalent to transplanting the entire population of Australia', fell on deaf ears. So did Bertrand Russell's letter to the London *Times* on 23 October 1945, in which he wrote: 'In Eastern Europe now mass deportations are being carried out by our allies on an unprecedented scale, and an apparently deliberate attempt is being made to exterminate many millions of Germans, not by gas but by depriving them of their homes and of food, leaving them to die by slow and agonized starvation.'

Suddenly, it was the Germans who were the victims of inhumane policies of 'extermination' – at the hands of the Allies.

It was hard to conceive of my own family being among those 14 million displaced people. But, fortunate though they all were to have survived and to have a roof over their heads, my grandmother, mother, aunts and uncle were a part of those statistics.

In Schleswig-Holstein, refugees made up 45 per cent of the population – right into the 1960s, there was a housing shortage – and in 1945, every corner of my great-grandparents' house, including the stables, was full of refugees and Russian prisoners of war. Like all farms producing food for the nation, it came under regular attack by the Allies.

My mother collected seeds to send to the beloved canary she'd had to leave behind in Jüterbog in the care of her best friend. She would receive regular bulletins on his welfare until one day her friend had to confess that she had accidentally sat on him and that Hansi was no more. Reading between the lines of those childhood letters years later with my mother, after discovering them in a damp box in my parents' cellar, it was evident that, when the Soviets arrived, this eleven-year-old little girl had become one of those rape statistics.

When the war ended the Russian prisoners were free to leave. 'They biked round and round the lawn, radiating joy, their guards having disappeared overnight,' my grandmother recalled. The war may have been over but it was a turbulent, dangerous time and shooting continued everywhere. People came to the door from all over the place trying to barter whatever possessions they had for food. One, an artist called Emil Nolde, brought paintings to exchange for potatoes but my grandmother wasn't interested in owning art when they didn't even have the bare essentials themselves. I marvelled at the thought of her turning away one of the first Expressionists. Nolde's bold paintings are now worth a small fortune.

It was, my grandmother wrote, 'a far cry from the happy liberation that had been talked about for years'. Was she referring to the liberation promised by Hitler from the humiliating terms of the Treaty of Versailles? Or liberation from the clutches of Nazi regime?

> *The sponges froze in the icy bathroom as we could only heat the bath oven at weekends. I would get up at 4am to heat the washing boiler. We got beets from the field and had dumplings with beet syrup. We made flour from the potatoes and created a spread for bread from cooked semolina with onions and made sure we all said how delicious it tasted! The children helped a lot outside school – they had no books and there were many interruptions due to electricity failures or lack of coal. But we were luckier than most refugees for we had wonderful nature around us and were always so grateful for anything beautiful.*

I could now understand my German family's regular and effusive appreciation of everything deemed *schön* or *hübsch*

Adolf, aged fourteen.

and their lifelong refusal to see food go to waste. If there was bread left over they would rather eat a stale crust than throw it away and enjoy a warm, fresh loaf. I had also often heard from my mother and aunts, that, unlike many Germans, they had never once heard my grandmother complain. About anything at all.

The final weeks of the war were probably the most traumatic for my Onkel Adolf. Like most children, he had become a member of the Hitler Youth. Eleven years old when the conflict began, at fourteen, he had been taken out of school, recruited into the Reichsarbeitsdienst, the Reich labour service founded by Hitler, and, in a uniform with a badge denoting his rank, sent away for military training. By 1943, with most able-bodied German men in the armed services, Hitler Youth boys were being called up. This was when,

Adolf, on the far left, with the 88mm anti-aircraft flak gun.

despite being the youngest in his battery, he was drafted to Berlin to help operate the 88mm anti-aircraft flak guns, commonly known as eighty-eights, effectively small cannons directed at the Allied planes bombing the city in hopes of shooting them down. And that was where my grandmother had had to leave him when she locked up their house in Jüterbog.

In the postwar years, having studied agriculture in preparation for taking over the Grödersby farm, Adolf faced further disruption in his life when, following my grandfather's death, my great-grandmother upset the family apple cart by selling the property. Without the means to buy his own farm in Germany, Adolf had emigrated to Canada in the 1960s. Although he made a success of his life there, I believe he was homesick for the rest of his days.

Of all the von Graffen siblings, Onkel Adolf was the only one who hadn't immediately responded to my written request for memories, favourite stories, additional letters or just reflections on his or the family's wartime experiences. Eventually, he sent me three photographs of mementos of his father: one was a delicate pencil drawing of a stag's head, another a self-portrait as a young officer, the third a tin plate painted with the family crest, which my grandfather had made at the age of ten. I found this slightly strange: after all, as the eldest child and only son, he had possibly known his father best. But Onkel Adolf seemed to occupy the same chrysalis of silence as my grandmother, though in his case, the silence felt less settled.

Soon after the first package, a few pages of notes written in a Germanic hand arrived in the post. Dated April and May 1945, and scribbled on pieces of paper stapled together, they turned out to be copies of a diary my uncle had kept in the last days of the war. He had been serving in a unit near Berlin for over a year and, with mail no longer getting through, he had written it as a record for his parents of what had happened to him in case he got killed. He had already had one narrow escape, having travelled to Dresden for an interview to become an officer just before the city was carpet-bombed by the Allies in February 1945. A young colleague, who'd had to stay on an extra day, had not been so lucky.

As I read his notes, I tried to imagine each scene through the eyes of a fifteen-year-old boy.

> *26.4.45 We were woken at 4 and had only just left the station when 4 planes bombed it. There were over 100 dead . . .*

29.4.45 Today is Sunday and I am thinking of you all in Jüterbog. When I think of all the nice things we used to do, I really miss home. You realize then what a dump you are in now, but I always try and think that one day it will all be over . . .

3.5.45 The horrible low-flying aircraft came over every 10 minutes and we had to lie in the ditches. On the road, one car after another was burning. Hordes of people were fleeing everywhere, German soldiers were deserting en masse, shopkeepers were giving away their last reserves. From now, everybody has become selfish as each is thinking about his own life and his own advantage.

For any young teenager, these experiences would be hugely traumatic. Bombers flew over every night and the boys had to shoot at them. On one occasion, the severed hand of a pilot they had hit landed in Adolf's bunker. Another time, he saw the arm of his superior being blown off and then watched him die. He didn't get any time off from his position, not even to attend his beloved grandfather's funeral. 'Unbelievable how these children were ripped from their school benches,' my grandmother commented in her memoir.

They proudly entered the war yet were treated so harshly as they stood by their anti-aircraft guns in fear of death. On one visit to Berlin we saw Adolf doing their strict drills, and after one heavy bombing attack I tried to reach him but the devastation prevented me and I had to turn back with a heavy heart. Karl was a seasoned, grown-up

Marlen, my grandparents and Adolf at the Zwinger, Dresden, for the official ceremonial presentation of my grandfather's Knight's Cross, 1943.

soldier but these children experienced the war from the lowest rung without being able to defend themselves against their unqualified superiors, and especially not if their father was a general.

After his final diary entry, a day before the unconditional capitulation, Adolf and a young friend deserted, escaping

across 200 miles of the ruins of Germany, with British soldiers everywhere, to reach the family at Grödersby. My
grandmother wrote of his arrival:

> *One grey Sunday, as we were sitting in front of the house,*
> *my brother-in-law pulled up in his hansom cab with two*
> *little dilapidated soldiers – our Adolf with a friend. What*
> *an indescribable joy! After the dissolution of his unit, they*
> *had marched for ten days under the bombardment of the*
> *English planes. He lay for days in the deckchair in the*
> *garden, his legs so swollen from the long walk.*

Soon after my uncle sent me those pages from his diary, he
made a rare visit to England. Over mugs of tea in Caroline's
London sitting room, I tried to probe him gently about our
grandfather. Eventually I arrived at the question of whether
he considered himself to have been a Nazi. I could see it was
an uncomfortable one for him to address and fully expected
to receive an evasive answer. But suddenly it came out as he
turned my question back on me. 'What is a Nazi? Someone
who believed in fighting for their country? If that is the case,
then yes, I was a Nazi,' he said, emphasizing the personal
pronoun.

A silence filled the small room. But I felt no judgement,
none of us did. Like so many others, Onkel Adolf had been
no more than a child soldier, fighting real people and seeing
his comrades blown up and dying all around him. The boys
had been indoctrinated to view it as an honour to do their
duty to the *Volk* and defend their city. But bitter disappointment and an antipathy towards Hitler followed. What must
it have been like to have to live with such indelible memories

and then to be made to feel guilty or ashamed for what you had been forced to do?

For the first year after the war ended, the family did not know whether Karl was dead or alive.

In March 1945, my grandfather had been based in the little village of Quartesana, billeted with an Italian family in their villa. From there he was continually on the move back and forth behind the fluctuating front line as the troops battled to hold the Allied advance at bay. He tells my grandmother in his letters that he will be bringing her suspender belts and wool 'once they have happily concluded the war' and describes with appreciation the lily of the valley, forsythia and daisies that are appearing around him. His tone becomes more serious as he advises her how best to shelter from the bombs that are now falling hard and fast. He betrays no sense of an imminent bad ending to the war. In his last letter, dated 13 April 1945, he writes, 'Go well, my darling. Even if we have to remain apart, don't worry about how I am. All my love to the family and a thousand kisses for you. Your Karl.'

The last he knows of the fate of his wife is that, with the Russians closing in on Berlin, she is going to try to catch the last train out before the capital is overrun.

In March 1946, a postcard arrived at Grödersby from a friend of his who had been released with the news that Karl was being held prisoner in Rimini. He had tried repeatedly to make contact for nearly a year, but nothing had got through.

From that point on, however, the exchange of letters and parcels between Prisoner of War No. G8952 and my grandmother resumed, albeit with the frequency of their communications strictly limited and the correspondence censored and written in block capitals to enable the Allies to read it. The family had no money. Access to savings had been blocked and there was no military income because, as a POW, my grandfather was now subject to the law governing war criminals.

So far, he has continued to maintain the largely buoyant tone to which I have become accustomed. But that is all about to change.

19

My Grandfather, the Prisoner

The Germans are not divided into good and bad Germans . . .
There are only good and bad elements in the German
character, the latter of which generally predominate.

Instructions for British Servicemen in Germany, 1944

M Y BIGGEST DREAD — ASIDE FROM the obvious candidates of being chomped by a shark or shut in a room full of spiders — is of being accused of something and not being able to put across my side of the story. Of being or feeling innocent but not being able to prove it. Of disappearing without anybody knowing or, worse still, noticing I am missing. It happens to people all the time, in both serious and trivial ways. I'm beginning to wonder now if some of that dread is linked to my grandfather's experiences after the war.

Karl had been in Rimini since he received the order to surrender in La Stanga. For a couple of weeks he was detained at the American Prisoner of War camp, or Holding Centre CMF, in Rimini-Riccione. As one of the highest-ranking generals in northern Italy, he was placed in charge of 150,000 fellow German prisoners at the huge tented camp on a site I believe is now occupied by the international airport.

Under the Americans, he enjoyed relative freedom to walk and rest. He and his men were then handed over to 'the

Letter from Prisoner of War No. G 8952.

English', as he always referred to them, and given the task of setting up longer-term prison camps. His new captors immediately ripped the epaulettes from the shoulders of his uniform.

His letters reassure my grandmother that he is fine and 'enjoying the hospitality of the English'. He is optimistic. 'Generals aren't really being questioned at the moment, and I think it won't always be a sin to have fought for your fatherland . . . In one year I am sure I will be with you.'

Conditions for the prisoners of war were extremely basic but all of his requests, even for soap for his men, were denied. He had a tense relationship with the commanding officer, General Dawney, an English brigadier, who refused to confirm that the British had any obligation to adhere to the rules of the Geneva Convention.

It was only later that my grandfather learned from the

Allied declaration that it was the Germans alone who were refused any legal status or human rights as prisoners of war. The term 'unconditional capitulation' meant exactly what it said. Their recognition as POWs was at the discretion of the Allies and they were granted no rights under the Geneva Convention or any other protective power.

Declining to co-operate under such 'conditions, my grandfather flicked a verbal two fingers at the British with the notorious line my mother had sometimes repeated to her thrilled children – '*Leck mich am Arsch*' (kiss my arse) – and demanded to be relieved of his position.

He paid a heavy price for standing his ground. He was sent to Taranto, in the heel of Italy, where more prominent generals were being held in far worse conditions. A leg of ham given to him by the Italian family with whom he had lodged in Quartesana saved him from starvation. I found it bizarre, in the circumstances, that his high principles wouldn't allow him to join in the thieving of grapes from a neighbouring farmer. He lost over two stone in a matter of weeks.

Karl was eventually returned to the comparative luxury of Rimini where his relative freedom was restored, now at a new camp located right by the Adriatic. The weather was warm. No longer in command of 150,000 men, his days were spent swimming in the sea, collecting shells, eating melons, learning Russian and playing bridge and table tennis. There was a cinema and music in the evenings, fifty to seventy cigarettes a week and feasts of marmalade, tea, luncheon meat and cheese. Lights out was not until midnight.

'You can see you don't need to worry about welcoming back a broken man,' he told my grandmother.

He did worry, though: about how he would be able to earn a living, how he would feed his family, whether he would be allowed to work at all. My grandmother suggested he become a beekeeper. He wasn't convinced.

What he was convinced of was that he would not be found guilty by the Allies of war crimes. Yet the unsettling uncertainty of his future permeates his letters. He knew he was still a long way from being released. Trials of Luftwaffe and naval officers were underway and he was aware that these would be taking precedence. The leaders of the army would have to wait to learn their fate. The main wish of detainees in the meantime was not to be transferred back as prisoners to Germany, where conditions were harsher and food sparser.

In June 1946, my grandfather celebrated his fifty-third birthday with two of his former division commanders and a steady stream of visitors who filled his room with flowers and small gifts. Normal Italian family beach life was resuming around them. Karl, still in uniform, was starting to show signs of impatience and anger with the de-Nazification process being implemented by the Allies. 'Through the excellent education that we are enjoying from the English, I have shed my load and broken all bad habits,' he wrote sarcastically.

But captivity was beginning to take its toll. 'Life has become senseless,' he admitted in August. 'You can't just stuff the German people with religion and good books, even less so with nice speeches,' and then, effortlessly condensing my approach to working with prisoners half a century later, he added: 'Collective punishment alone can't bring about improvement.'

Rumours of a transfer to Canada spread through the camp but, in mid-November 1946, what they had all been dreading happened. They were sent back to Germany.

On arrival at the British POW camp at Munster Lager, each prisoner was given a long questionnaire to fill in about his activities, postings and attitudes to political and military problems. The answers would be graded from I–V according to a military de-Nazification classification system that would be used to determine his destiny, with those officers adjudged to fall into the most serious categories liable to be tried in open court. Karl told his wife that he was glad he had rejected the higher post in Russia, one of the options I'd seen discussed in the military reports, and reckoned that his reputation in Italy, and some of the decisions that had helped shape it, would count in his favour.

He genuinely hoped to be graded in Class V and exonerated or, at worst, in Class IV as a *Mitläufer*, or follower, a status punishable only by mild restrictions to freedoms plus fines. With Class I reserved for major offenders, the biggest fear hanging over them all was finding themselves just one rung down from there, in Class II, and potentially facing a sentence of up to ten years' imprisonment.

It took my grandfather a while to adjust to his new accommodation – a tiny room, 2 metres by 4 metres, with little in it. His bag and other possessions had been stolen in transit.

'We need everything,' he wrote. 'Even a broom handle would be good.'

There was some comfort to be had in being reunited with some old army friends and acquaintances he discovered at Munster Lager, including two of his oldest pals, now as emaciated as himself, who had been transferred from a Belgian internment camp. It was only when back on home soil, from this POW grapevine, that he learned what had happened to the men, women and children in Germany.

He soon created a little prison 'family' with two fellow Knight's Cross recipients. They shared everything, even a bed when it got really cold, taking it in turns to cook, clean and light the stove. His gratitude for what my grandmother sent him – potatoes, carrots, celeriac, cornflour, peas, beans, coffee substitute, cake and biscuits made with beet syrup – was always effusive and heartfelt. He described in detail when and with whom he ate these little luxuries, and even how he cooked them, sending his wife tips to try out for herself. Everything tasted good to them in comparison to their daily rations of '½ litre water with cabbage and a ¼ loaf of bread with a little fat . . . and the drain water that passes for tea'. Not even in Taranto, he declared, had he been given so little to eat.

He reproached my grandmother for tobacco that failed to materialize, or arrived mouldy, giving long-winded instructions on how to cultivate and dry the plants better. 'The psychological worries wear me out and smoking is the only thing that keeps me going,' he explained. 'So much hope and yearning have already been shattered. I daren't even allow myself to think about the future.'

When I hear this very different voice in my grandfather's letters, I am aware of a shift taking place in my relationship with him. Few would have much sympathy for a jailed Wehrmacht general, and it isn't sympathy that I feel, either.

Just a recognition of his situation. I have experienced the helplessness of incarcerated men, their lives in the hands of the guards and the courts, their futures wholly unpredictable. And I can feel, like a visceral memory, the impact of his long fall from general to prisoner without rights or power.

The winter of 1946–7 was bitter. Temperatures dropped to -20 degrees. The water pipes froze, lights went on and off randomly and there was an acute shortage of coal. The prisoners improvised hot-water bottles by placing bricks in the stove and then wrapping them in paper. 'In this cold, you don't get warm the whole day. As soon as you have washed with ice water, you have to stand around for half an hour for the 9 o'clock roll call, during which you get chilled to the bone. At lunch you get cold again until the afternoon roll call at 5p.m ... But it is a luxury lifestyle in comparison to the poor civilians in their provisional shelters.'

I can't help noticing that nowhere does he make any reference to the far worse conditions endured by the millions held captive in Nazi concentration camps.

In times of forced abstinence, he and his room-mates sat around in bed smoking tea leaves or drinking hair tonic and playing cards.

Their only clothes were the uniforms they had been wearing for the last three years. They darned them and sewed on buttons in an optimistic attempt to try to transform them into civilian clothes for their imagined imminent release.

We've just received our soap rations for one month – the size of two sugar cubes, and lavatory paper – one sheet per day! I would so love to scrub myself in your bath. The dirt we live in is unimaginable, but without cleaning

> *materials there's nothing we can do about it. Maybe the dirt also belongs to our education towards becoming a cultural nation. Or perhaps the English will give us some Zyankali [Cyanide-like poison]. That way they would be rid of us sooner.*

My grandfather was trying to make sense of the purpose of his imprisonment. On the one hand, it was for punishment; on the other, the soldiers were ostensibly there to be de-Nazified and re-educated as democrats. And yet: 'Everything that happens is more like an education in nihilism than an education towards democratic thinking. How a healthy political and economic life is meant to grow out of this is beyond me . . . History will later judge what was right and wrong.'

He tried to remain cheerful, demonstrated concern over what my grandmother was going through or the sickness of one of his children, and made an effort to offer her advice on their upbringing and other matters. But, locked in his cold, barbed-wire world, he was powerless to be a father or husband. His mind was gradually giving in to anger. 'What use are humanity, human rights, the rights of protection of a person and their possessions, freedom, equality, brotherhood, love of neighbour and all the other democratic ground rules if they are only ideals and not applied to all people? Can one still believe in humanity? I think it's difficult.'

I found these questions difficult to comprehend. How could he possibly complain about the absence of these rules without acknowledging how the Nazis had broken every one, and more, in the most monumental ways? Or did he still consider that warfare justified actions that are rightly condemned in times of freedom? I could understand his comments only in the light of how impotent he must have felt to protect the German people, the same people for whom he had spent years fighting.

By March 1947, he was sounding extremely depressed. 'We Germans can't expect much from life any more, and it would be better if everything came to a quick end . . . I would prefer to hang to a slow massacre. The real victims are not us soldiers, but our families, who have been expelled from house and farm without the means or support to fight against starvation.' In one letter, he talked openly and seriously about committing suicide. My aunt and grandmother destroyed that one.

In April, one of his two closest comrades, 'an immeasurably decent and fair man who can't be accused of anything', learned that he had been categorized in the feared Class II and would be spending at least another few years in a prison where 150 men shared a dormitory and conditions were even worse. His son had been killed in the war and his sick wife and young daughter were living in perturbing circumstances with no money. She wrote frequently, threatening to take both her daughter's life and her own if he wasn't released soon. He had nothing to send them. Access to his savings, and even to cigarettes, had been withdrawn. He did not dare tell her about his sentence.

One morning his room-mates found him hanging from the waterpipe in the cellar. He had left a small pile of notes in his tidied cell. His wife and daughter went the same way a week later. 'It is so sad,' wrote my grandfather, 'but it is the fate of millions. I just don't understand it. We are being held because we weren't shot dead or didn't hang ourselves.'

I thought about how both suicide and criminal

behaviour had become so normalized in German society during and after the war. Life and death had fluid boundaries, like doors hung from a single hinge, flapping in a wind of hopelessness and moral bankruptcy. In Britain, most Christian churches demonized suicide (some still do) with such vehemence and threats of eternal damnation that, to most people, it probably remained a locked and bolted door at the end of a long, dark corridor. Yet suicide seems to run through some families. I was aware of seven or eight within my wider German family tree, and taking your own life had never felt like a closed door to me, either. I knew the intolerable pain of depression, the power of the belief that the world and those you love would be better off without you, and that door had always stood ajar, an option, an invitation, even, for a way out. I never saw it as weak.

A surprise visit from his son was intended to raise my grandfather's morale but it backfired, leaving him feeling deeply humiliated. He had specifically asked that Adolf, now seventeen, should not visit. He hadn't wanted his son to see him in such a state. He told my grandmother that he had almost refused to receive him and that he wouldn't do so a second time. He'd rather hang himself. Now that it had been four years since they had seen each other, they could hold out a bit longer. For several weeks his letters began with a cool 'Dear Ilse'.

By the summer, he and his fellow prisoners of war seemed to have become resigned to their situation ('There isn't a single general here who finds it humiliating any more to be the rubbish-disposal man').

Eventually, after over two years as a POW, he faced a military tribunal. The navy, the air force, military staff and the major generals had all been processed and most of them had been released. Now it was the turn of the lieutenant generals.

On 21 June 1947 he wrote to my grandmother:

> *I had my hearing on Tuesday. I didn't tell you about it in my last letter because I had hoped to be released by the board. This proved to be a false hope as today I received my summons for next Tuesday. I am accused of being:*
> *1. A militarist*
> *2. In complete agreement with the NS programme*
> *3. A definite danger to peace and security*
> *Purely factually, they can't accuse me of anything at all . . . Nor can I, other than maybe that I wasn't born an Ally or a neutral citizen.*

My grandfather had always maintained he was not a Nazi. 'I am not like him,' he had said about another man who clearly was.

I wished I knew his definition of a Nazi.

The following Tuesday he appeared before the board again. The hearing lasted around an hour. He was told he would learn the outcome in about four weeks.

Among other things, the British were convinced that, back in 1928, my grandfather had christened his first-born after and in honour of Adolf Hitler. This assumption nearly cost my grandfather dear, but he must have been able to prove that Adolf was in fact a family name going back generations.

The news they had all been dreading arrived much sooner than expected. 'My dearest,' wrote my grandfather on 9 July. 'That which I was expecting has now happened. Of 24

*Great Onkel Adolf von Graffen with little
Adolf in Berlin, 1931.*

who heard their verdicts, 23 have been graded into Group II
and will be held indefinitely in a prison camp. I am one of
them.'

No grounds were given because the verdict had been
reached prior to any trial. My grandfather tried to strike a
brave note but he could not hide his encroaching despair.

> *Now that we have no rights and no defence on our side,
> we will just have to get on with it. I personally can't
> reproach myself for anything at all. I was neither a Nazi,
> nor did I operate as a militarist. Everybody with whom I
> came into contact knows that. On the contrary, I applied
> myself more to humaneness and human rights, more so
> than those who always just talked about it. I can also
> prove it through witnesses, but nobody values that.*

Tomorrow we will probably be taken to Adelheide, where we will be more or less buried alive. Criminals at least have an idea when they will be released . . . Nobody who hasn't experienced what we are going through, and might have to continue to go through, can know that this is far worse than a quick death.

I can feel the wound in my soul tugging like a hook in a fish's mouth. Like a fisherman, he is reeling me into his world. My mind thrashes between anger, frustration, sadness and terror. Not just in response to his potential guilt and his refusal – or complete inability – to grasp how his situation pales in comparison to the far worse situations created by the Nazi regime, but at his genuine belief in his innocence of what he personally is being accused of.

I feel the empathy I so often feel for people ensnared in situations, partly of their own making, but partly the product of the world in which they live. I feel the urgent need to understand his side of the story. But, at the same time, I long to turn my back on his thoughts and actions.

Is he a Nazi, or isn't he? What is a Nazi, anyway? I want to believe him. I want to be able to love him as my grandfather. But I just don't know how.

20

Diving Cups and Yo-Yos

Life did not stop, and one had to live.

Leo Tolstoy, *War and Peace*

I HADN'T BEEN ABLE TO make an appointment to visit the Adelheide international army base, so when the taxi driver pulled up outside the entrance, he wished me luck. He had been genuinely fascinated by my account of my quest and gave me his card, not so much for the business, but because he wanted to hear all about it. I was noticing how sharing my story with people seemed to help them to unlock their own.

Like my grandfather, who had been granted a few days' home leave in 1947, I had I climbed aboard a train heading south from Bremen station after visiting family in the north. And, like his, my destination was Delmenhorst Adelheide. But while I was excited and emotional, he had been stressed. He had missed a connection and couldn't find a car to get him back to the army base on time. He had tried asking for help from a colleague living nearby but had been turned away. He saw no other option but to leave his suitcase in the left-luggage department and set off on foot along 'the endless way' – the long avenue of birch trees leading to the British POW camp where he was to spend his final years of incarceration.

The soldiers at the entrance looked at me with expressionless faces. An Englishwoman in a floral summer dress and sunglasses, asking to be allowed in to see where her German grandfather had been held prisoner sixty years before. I suddenly felt vulnerable, and slightly mad. I had no idea how they would react. Surely, in these reconciliatory times, when British soldiers fought beside German ones in Afghanistan and wherever else, no one in the military still harboured the enmity of the two wars?

My grandfather's first impressions of his new jail had been positive. 'The barracks and surroundings are very nice, but that just makes you feel your imprisonment even more.'

Then he discovered why he had been sent to Adelheide.

I have now learned from an American soldiers' newsletter why we are here. We are guinea pigs in an English experiment, to see if, within a period of up to 10 years, they can educate 2,500 of 'the most dangerous Germans' into democrats ... Ten years is a long time ... I wonder if my health will hold out.

I had read about this experiment. People of all occupations and political backgrounds, from workers to heads of industry, were to be held in this camp and re-educated. Eventually, their families would be allowed to move there, too. The project was soon abandoned as unworkable. The categorization of my grandfather by the British as 'one of the most dangerous Germans' felt ludicrous to me. But during these early, chaotic years of Allied occupation, such judgements were commonplace. For some Britons, 'Nazis' would remain synonymous with 'Germans' right up to the present day. This unnuanced condemnation, which I had found so hurtful growing up, was part of what I wanted to redress. I felt the history books needed rewriting in a more informed way, to include the experiences of a broader range of Germans.

As I waited at the barrier, I thought of my grandmother's recollection of her first glimpse of her husband in four years. For her, too, it had been almost impossible to get permission to visit. When she finally did, she travelled down in trains so full that people were being shoved on board through the windows. The women arrived by truck, each terrified of missing their time slot. When, under heavy guard, a sorry troop of men approached, in brown uniforms with 'POW' painted in big white letters on their backs, the guards couldn't hold the women back. 'We rushed at the men to take them in our arms and embrace them. Later, as Karl and I sat opposite each other over a wooden table, words failed us. And then the half-hour was over.' The last time my grandmother had seen her husband, he had been setting off for Italy in his general's uniform, adorned with medals and symbols of honour. 'Now, even his voice was changed.'

I restrained myself from barging through the guards and instead flashed a photograph of my grandfather in uniform, as if it were a pass. It seemed to do the trick. The soldiers, curious now, seemed prepared to waive the usual Monday-morning protocol and, after making a few phone calls, they lifted the barrier. Within five minutes, an open-top Jeep was pulling up beside me. A friendly man in uniform introduced himself as my escort and off we went, bouncing over the dry terrain towards the original barracks.

The low-lying buildings nestling among the trees had been the *Sanitär*, he told me. The hospital where my grandfather had worked. At fifty-five years old he had suffered from painful arthritis, which spared him from hard labour. Instead he was allocated a job as a medic. One of his duties was weight control. Each day, he placed around a hundred men on the scales to chart their weight, or rather its decline. He himself had lost more than another stone and weighed just eight and a half stone.

We passed other low buildings that had been their living quarters. The well-spaced layout looked pleasant in the dappled sunlight. It reminded me of my old boarding school. I imagined each prisoner mechanically following the prescribed course of his days while his heart and mind yearned to be home. It would have been in one of these buildings that my grandfather would have written his letters – just one was permitted every two weeks. There was something else I particularly wanted to see: the swimming pool. In one of those letters, my grandfather had written: 'Today I won first prize in freestyle diving at a swimming competition.' His evident pleasure had struck a chord with me. One of the proudest moments of my own childhood had been winning the diving cup, aged eleven, when I had unexpectedly beaten the school champion. I remember beaming at my parents as I strode, my heart bursting with joy, across the wet flagstones to receive the silver cup. Apparently, I slipped and fell flat on my face but I don't remember that. To this day it remains the only occasion I have ever won anything.

In a further contravention of the army protocol that required me to stay in the Jeep, my kind soldier guide agreed to show me the site of the pool. Abandoning the vehicle, we

The swimming pool, Delmenhorst Adelheide, 1947.

waded through thick undergrowth until we reached a large, empty hole in the ground, surrounded by trees. Overgrown, but still recognizable as a swimming pool. I knew this was the place where my grandfather had once excelled.

As I stood there, sixty years on almost exactly to the day, I pictured him walking to the end of the now non-existent board, composing himself, as I had done myself so many times before, and raising his bony body up on to his toes to launch himself into the water. My own muscles tightened as he sucked himself into a neat shape, legs straight and toes pointed, tensing his core muscles to gain height before straightening out again. I could feel the cool water touch his fingertips, then his elbows; the slight impact to the crown of the head before his body slipped through the surface, creating a tiny splash as the water closed over his feet. I could hear the bubbles around his ears muffling the gentle clapping of the spectators, feel his head re-emerge into the air, his eyes opening as he swam to the edge, wondering how smooth his dive had looked. I could almost touch that moment in 1947.

The five months of internment were a monotonous waiting game interrupted only by a serious bout of food poisoning and intermittent parcels. Eventually, it was my grandfather's turn for an appointment with the review board. In October 1947, he commented despairingly to my grandmother, 'It is the tenth birthday of yours that we haven't been able to be with each other. And how many more will follow? One can't have hopes here any longer; too often they are dashed.'

I remembered what my Onkel Wulf, Tante Marlen's husband, had told me of his own long years as a prisoner during the war: how they were moved around in trucks, continually told they were going to be released that week, then that day, only for nothing to happen. He spoke of how he learned to live from moment to moment, suppressing any glimmers of hope that began to break through his defences. It was the only way he found he could survive the endless uncertainty.

'On 26 February 1948,' my grandfather calculated, 'I will be spending my 1001st night behind barbed wire. No need to congratulate me on this, though ... If you can spare a cup and a spoon, I could really do with them. And a bread knife.'

But in fact he had only one more week behind barbed wire to endure. The review board found him 'not guilty' on all counts with which he had been charged and, on 3 March 1948, he was finally released.

He arrived at the unfamiliar new family home, Grödersby, a ghost of his former self, both physically and psychologically.

My grandfather at Grödersby.

Every week he was required to report to the British military. With no work for returning generals, he was reduced to whittling wooden yo-yos and trying to sell them door-to-door. But he was a hopeless salesman, simply shuffling off apologetically when people expressed their complete lack of interest and closed their doors in his face.

I still didn't know what he himself felt in the two further decades he lived. What my grandfather had thought about as he sat in his chair on the veranda, smoking one cigarette after another. What had haunted him. He had been declared 'not guilty' but did he feel not guilty? Did he feel shame? Remorse? Or just humiliation? I was increasingly certain that what he had bequeathed to me on my birth was a collection of all his unprocessed emotions. To have any hope of resolving them, I had to steel myself to try to find out what they were.

At the end of his letters was a document containing his postwar 'reflections', which, so far, I had never been able to bring myself to read. But I knew I would have to.

21

'We Knew Nothing'

Those who flee from their past will always lose the race.
T.S. Eliot, *The Elder Statesman*

THOUGH AT TIMES IT felt like it, I am, of course, far from the only person to try to rattle and sieve the truth from the soil of the past. But the truth is not easily dislodged when it is triple-bound by trauma, guilt and accusations of complicity.

Born during the war or in its aftermath, the children of the perpetrating nation grew up in peacetime, but the spectres of war remained all too evident in their environment and within their families.

Most German adults were so consumed by trauma, moral shock, disappointment, grief, despondency or bitterness that they couldn't see beyond their own misery and suffering. In fact, almost unbelievably, many saw themselves as the worst victims of the war. They had lost their homes, possessions, territory and loved ones and raged at the misplaced trust, sacrifice and hard work it had demanded of them. The men, once inflated by visions of glory, domination and superiority, were now widely viewed as emasculated, emaciated, lice-ridden losers; the women hardened and unhealthily self-contained. The children's emotional development was curtailed by having to parent their parents.

Many adults donned blinkers and moved forward with

dogged determination, refusing to look back, to feel the guilt that was being dolloped on to their plates with the allocated food rations. The focus turned to the *Wiederaufbau*, the clearing and rebuilding of the bombed cities. Former Nazi party members took the places of former forced labourers, with teams of women aged between fifteen and fifty, ordered to help by the Allies, particularly in the Soviet sector, making up the numbers where there was a shortfall.

Later mythologized as the *Trümmerfrauen*, or 'rubble women', they stood in chains of ten to twenty, tearing down the remaining ruins, often with their bare hands, and sorting bricks, beams, rescued toilets and other household goods to be reused. The average work day was nine hours long, with one break at lunchtime of only twenty to thirty minutes, for which they might receive nine food ration cards and around 6 Reichsmarks. At the time a loaf of bread cost 80 Reichsmarks and a cigarette 10.

The discovery of concentration camps like Belsen and Dachau by the Allies in April 1945 had a huge impact, not only on Western public opinion but also on political and military decision-makers. Photographs and newsreel footage taken at these camps aroused intense revulsion towards Nazi Germany and Germans in general. They also became one of the instruments through which responsibility and culpability for the Second World War and the Holocaust were imposed on the German people as a nation. Local civilians were frogmarched to the camps and forced to look upon the heaps of human remains so that there was no chance that reports of what had been revealed could be dismissed as Allied propaganda. Some citizens were made to physically help bury the dead in mass graves. Many Germans deeply resented what they saw as 'victors' justice' and questioned why they were being confronted with horrors they themselves had known nothing about. Posters bearing photographs of piles of bodies hung in the American and British zones spelled it out: 'This is your fault.'

Still reeling from defeat, the majority of West Germans seemed willing to attribute responsibility for the crimes of the Third Reich to Hitler and 'a few at the top' and to condemn the chief culprits. But they were absolutely not prepared to accept complicity in what was gradually being acknowledged as the worst genocide in history. In a country that had seen itself as a land of poets and thinkers, these abominable accusations refused to stick. Keen to clear each other's names and to be awarded their de-Nazification clearance certificates, the population gradually united in a stubborn insistence that 'we knew nothing'.

These were confusing times for German children. Suddenly forbidden from making the Hitler salute or saying incriminating things in front of the victors, some would have witnessed the adults in their families blatantly lying and denying Nazi leanings, even while secretly continuing to believe in Hitler's supremacy.

While many of the older generation used their perception of themselves as victims to avoid examining their consciences, the children were left to grapple with the stains of their trauma and their crimes, and with their own unanswered questions. What had happened to their fathers? What had their fathers done? And what had they inherited from them? Even if they found out what it was that their fathers had done, Nazi deeds were usually justified or explained away as 'simply doing our duty'. And straightforward inquiries about the origins of inherited jewellery, silver, furniture or artworks were waved aside with a dismissive or adamant 'There were no Nazis in this family.' The idea of researching recent personal or national history would be viewed with suspicion as a threat to a family's honour for decades to come.

Children fell into emotional voids. Lies and secrets brushed under the carpet became the status quo. Silence filled conversations and what wasn't said assumed a greater significance than what was.

When the offspring bumped up against the walls of apparent collective amnesia as teenagers, some of them rebelled, smashing the silence with accusations and demanding that people start talking about what happened. West German kids took to the streets in violent gangs known as the Halbstarken – the 'half-strong' – and, emulating American idols such as Marlon Brando's 'Wild One' and James Dean's 'Rebel Without a Cause,' swept through cities in disorganized and destructive rampages. With no political motivation or clear agenda, their actions were seen as senseless aggression. Seventy years on, their protests at the misplaced values of their now broken and demoralized parents appear more understandable.

Some of the more educated young people confronted their parents intellectually and politically. But reason alone has no scouring power, and the emotions involved in admitting to historically proven wrongdoing were too frightening for most adults to engage with. Many simply adopted the older generation's approach of moving forward, content with a life that provided a job, a car and enough money for a holiday. Others rejected the complacency of their peers and poured their energy into bringing about social change. The following decades saw huge shifts in literature, music, art and design and new social movements that were against nuclear power, environmentally friendly and pacifist. This generation was determined that the new Germany was going to look nothing like the old.

For the descendants of the most prominent Nazis, attempts to come to terms with what their relatives had done were more personal and often more extreme. Some chose to completely cut themselves off from their families and escape the cycle of guilt in which they felt trapped by withdrawing from society or relocating abroad. The great-niece of Heinrich Himmler, the head of Hitler's SS, focused on writing books. Others spoke out publicly about Germany's guilt. Some hit the self-destruct button, succumbing to addictions or mental illness. A number of them decided not to procreate. The great-niece and nephew of Hermann Göring, Hitler's designated successor, even opted to be sterilized.

Foreigners, meanwhile, were both angered and upset by the apparent inability of many Germans to see beyond their own hardship and grasp the suffering their nation had inflicted on others. In a speech in 1949 denouncing the Allied military governments' de-Nazification process, Konrad Adenauer, the newly elected chancellor of the Federal Republic of Germany, made reference only to the suffering of Germans and failed to mention any of the victims of their war crimes. Criticized both at home and abroad and urged to accept Germany's guilt, the Federal Republic finally acknowledged the nation's responsibility towards the Jewish victims in 1952 and signed a reparations agreement with Moshe Sharett, the foreign minister of the recently established Jewish state of Israel.

Many Germans tried to minimize their country's crimes by claiming that the Jewish genocide was no worse than the murders of Native Americans or the lynchings of people of colour in the USA. There were those who held on to their beliefs in a glorious master race and in a war that had been justified, maintaining that Germany had taken on the task of defending the rest of Europe from Communism, that anti-Bolshevism had been the priority over anti-Semitism and that the world should be grateful to them. Some Wehrmacht soldiers questioned why foreign diplomats hadn't intervened against the Nazis, pointing out that they, too, had recognized, even admired, Hitler's government. One school of thought contended that the war had largely been waged as a hypocritical response of the UK and USA to the imperialist ambitions of a cultured nation wanting to acquire more territories. Another made a distinction between Hitler and the German nation as whole and expressed its loyalty to the latter.

In his book *The Question of German Guilt* (*Die Schuldfrage*), published in 1947, Karl Jaspers, a liberal philosophy teacher at Heidelberg University, active opponent of Nazism and returning exile, tried to address this blind and numb national conscience by going through each of the excuses one by one and producing a counter-argument. Beginning with the premise that everyone, including himself, was morally responsible for doing too little to stop the Nazis, he identified four types of guilt – criminal, political, moral and metaphysical – and discussed each one in turn. Some of the excuses, as well as his attributions of degrees of responsibility, are still heard to this day.

Well into the fifties, the resentment festering beneath the

surface of the collective silence left little room for reflection. The past was systematically buried and access to it blocked and censored. In the meantime, with very little therapy available in postwar Germany (the Nazis had viewed psychoanalysis as Jewish pseudo-science and banned it), people looked to the future while silently stewing in an indigestible brew of psychological overwhelm, war trauma and impotent guilt and unwittingly handing on the task they were incapable of accomplishing to the next generation.

It wasn't until the 1960s, with the trial of Adolf Eichmann, one of the key administrators of the 'Final Solution to the Jewish Question', in Jerusalem, and the Frankfurt Auschwitz trials, that younger Germans started to change the national mindset by refusing to allow the Holocaust to continue to be ignored. It was not only the irrefutable evidence presented in court that brought the extermination of the Jews back into the broad public consciousness and sent renewed tremors through German society but also the observations of Hannah Arendt, the Jewish political theorist and writer sent by *The New Yorker* to cover the Eichmann trial.

What Arendt detected in Eichmann was, in her words, 'not stupidity, but a curious, quite authentic inability to think'. He displayed no guilt for his actions, claiming he had simply done his job and acted obediently according to the laws. Arendt summed up this phenomenon in her series of 1963 reports in *The New Yorker* with the now familiar phrase 'the banality of evil'. 'The deeds were monstrous,' she wrote several years later, 'but the doer . . . was quite ordinary, commonplace, and neither demonic nor monstrous.' What's more, Eichmann wasn't an isolated case, the sole 'normal' person in a group of evil sadists. The world was being confronted by a bureaucratic system made up of perfectly ordinary men committing monstrous acts.

In 2011, Bettina Stangneth, author of *Eichmann Before Jerusalem,* would contest Arendt's interpretation, arguing that Eichmann's apparent 'banality' was a calculated strategy to play the dull-witted bureaucrat in an attempt to escape the hangman's noose. She posited that Arendt had failed to grasp the even worse notion that such unspeakable deeds are not just the domain of psychologically damaged people, but of intelligent, conscious people who both reflect on them and choose to carry them out.

In the wake of these trials, as more and more details came to light, the country's youth began to regard the silence of their parents' generation as a moral scandal, a second wave of guilt. In 1968, the '68ers' as they came to be called, spilled on to the streets of West Germany in huge demonstrations and student revolts. They marched against the Vietnam War and what they saw as bourgeois order: militarism, consumerism, hierarchy, capitalism. They protested against the revival of authoritarianism and hypocrisy within the government, incensed by the widely accepted *Befehlsnotstand* myth – that it had been impossible to disobey orders under Hitler – which enabled so many Nazis to get away with their crimes and enjoy successful second careers in positions of power in politics, industry, the police force, schools and universities. (A recent study commissioned by the government supplied some eye-opening statistics: in 1957, for example, 77 per cent of senior officials in the West German Justice Ministry were former members of the Nazi party – a higher percentage than during the Third Reich.) The 68ers were determined to expose the transgressions of the past, including the shortcomings of those cast in the more passive role of *Mitläu-fer,* or follower, of which many of their parents were guilty.

A minority turned to terrorism: the notorious Baader-Meinhof Group, or Red Army Faction, whose black-and-white mug shots I had sometimes stared at in the underground stations of Hamburg as a child, was in existence from 1970 to 1998. Responsible for thirty-four deaths, these people justified their actions as the necessary resistance to Fascism their parents had failed to put up.

Yet while rebellion may have been rolling through the streets and bringing about social change, within families it was far less prevalent as young people wrestled with the question of whether it can be permissible to love a parent or relative who has committed horrendous crimes.

This dilemma is brilliantly explored in the 2015 documentary *What Our Fathers Did: A Nazi Legacy.* Of the few children who have talked publicly about the sins of their fathers, Niklas Frank and Horst von Wächter are the most well known. Both are the sons of prominent Nazi war criminals and mass murderers, yet they take opposite attitudes towards their fathers. In the film the men are interviewed by Philippe Sands, the human rights lawyer and author of *East West Street* and *The Ratline*, whose own extended Jewish family perished in the Holocaust.

Niklas Frank has no qualms about denouncing Hans Frank, governor general of occupied Poland and Hitler's legal adviser, who was tried at Nuremberg and executed in 1945 for the mass murder of Jews and Poles. In his book *The Father: A Revenge,* Frank expresses unremitting disgust for his father and pictures him burning in hell. Horst von Wächter, on the other hand, refuses to condemn Otto Gustav von Wächter who, as governor of Kraków and Galicia in Nazi-occupied Poland, was directly responsible for the deportation and deaths of many thousands of Jews. Otto von Wächter was indicted for these crimes but never faced trial, having gone into hiding in 1945 and dying in Rome four years later.

In the documentary Horst explains how he wants to make peace with the memory of his father. He believes he is entitled and morally obliged to stand up for him. 'I must find the good in my father . . . My father was a good man, a liberal who did his best. Others would have been worse . . . I love him, I cannot say that my father was a criminal.' By contrast, on the question of making peace, Niklas Frank declares: 'I have.' He has taken the route of acknowledging Hans Frank's crimes and distancing himself completely from his father. '[He] was a bad man . . . I won't let my life be ruined by these parents.'

In 2014 I witnessed Philippe Sands chairing a similar conversation between the two men at the Southbank Centre in London. It was electrifying. Sands has since uncovered and published indisputable evidence of von Wächter's guilt but at the time, and in spite of the hostility of some of the questions directed at Horst, I found myself swinging between their opposing approaches. Was Horst's determination to love Otto von Wächter a worthy attempt to see the good in him as a human being, a naïve and stubborn denial of his vile deeds or the product of a deep psychopathology? Was Niklas's outright rejection of his father a successful working through of his father's heinous crimes or a failure to forgive? I was of the belief that the way to rid oneself of such a legacy lay somewhere in between. I didn't want to live with either hatred or untruth.

In East Germany, meanwhile, people were not being confronted with the same blame or guilt. The Berlin Wall isolated them not only from exposure to Western values but also from the condemnatory influence of the Allies. State policy, while completely ignoring the crimes of Stalin, had been anti-Fascist from the start. Many imperialist landmarks were torn down and the centrally located Neue Wache memorial to the fallen German soldiers of the First World War was rebuilt as a memorial to the victims of Fascism and militarism. Resistance heroes were honoured, a far higher percentage of Nazis were prosecuted as war criminals than in the West, textbooks taught the wrongs of Fascist ideology, the national anthem was rewritten and 8 May, which marked the end of the German 'war of theft and extermination', was celebrated as a day of liberation. In the fifties, the crimes of the SS and the Wehrmacht were already being talked about and criticized, anti-Semitism was openly discussed, Jewish émigrés were invited to return, peace songs were sung.

Being treated by the Soviets as co-victims of and co-victors over Fascism may have spared East Germans the accusations of complicity in the Nazi atrocities that were such a significant factor in the reforming of the West German collective psyche. But they were once again ensnared in a political system where denouncements, lies and cover-ups prevailed and violence against its own people was considered legitimate.

If the motivations of East Germany were more political than moral, the simple and consistent message was that the Nazis were bad. In both East and West Germany, then, the Nazis were not 'us', but someone else.

In the West, if the message was more ambivalent, the

68-ers had ripped the guilt genie out of the bottle and there was no stuffing it back.

Possibly the first clear demonstration of remorse came in 1970, when Willy Brandt, the Social Democratic chancellor of Germany, was on a state visit to Poland that coincided with a commemoration of the Jewish victims of the Warsaw Ghetto Uprising of 1943. He spontaneously dropped to his knees, uttering not a word. Later, in his autobiography, he said that 'on the abyss of German history, and carrying the burden of the millions who were murdered, I did what people do when words fail them'. This silent *'Kniefall'*, though distressing for West Germans, who saw not just humility but humiliation in the gesture, was perceived by the rest of the world as one of the first political steps towards healing the wounds.

Around the same time, the early works of two young artists, Anselm Kiefer (born in 1945) and Gerhard Richter (1932), provided a cultural nudge towards confronting rather than suppressing the past. Without explicitly pointing a finger, both artists suggested a national culpability that many Germans wanted to deny but could not. Kiefer did this through a series of contentious performances and photographic self-portraits in which he provocatively re-enacted the banned Nazi salute in various specific locations. Richter used his signature 'blurred' technique to create paintings from photographs of his Uncle Rudi, who had died in 1944, in his Wehrmacht uniform, and of his aunt, who had fallen victim to the Nazi euthanasia programme that oversaw the systematic murder of up to 300,000 people deemed incurably sick or 'unworthy of life' due to their physical or mental disabilities.

It was, however, the 1979 American TV series *Holocaust* I watched as a teenager in England that brought the horrors directly into the living rooms of 20 million ordinary Germans of all ages, laying guilt and complicity right at their feet. From this point onwards, any discussions or complaints relating to their own suffering had to be abandoned. Instead, debate focused on trying to understand and interpret the darkest chapter in their modern history.

The significant movement of the tectonic plates came on 8 May 1985, when President Weizsäcker, commemorating the fortieth anniversary of the end of the Second World War, became the first West German politician to break with traditional references to defeat, unconditional surrender or mourning and described the occasion as 'a day of liberation'. In an inspiring speech, he finally found a way to admit what other nations had known from the start: that many people had suffered more than the Germans, and that their suffering was the fault of Germany – both West and East.

By the end of the eighties, West Germany had arrived at a consensus: Nazi crimes were incomparable to any others, the Holocaust was an unparalleled atrocity and Germans should acknowledge a national responsibility for it.

The secret of reconciliation, President Weizsäcker had told the nation a few years earlier, 'is remembrance'. But for Germany, remembering would prove to be hugely perplexing. How do you remember what you would rather forget?

22

Lest We Forget

If memory is kept alive in order to cultivate old hatred and resentments, it is likely to culminate in vengeance, and in a repetition of violence. But if memory is kept alive in order to transcend hateful emotions, then remembering can be healing.

Pumla Gobodo-Madikizela, *Dare We Hope?*
Facing Our Past to Find a New Future

M Y GRANDFATHER WOULD BECOME one of millions of German soldiers who would be deliberately and systematically forgotten.

Virtually no new memorials were built after the war, partly because a 1945 Allied directive forbade the preservation of anything that hinted at commemorating or glorifying German military traditions, the Nazi party or any battles or incidents of war. And partly because German soldiers had been cogs in the Nazi killing machine and – though declared 'clean' at the Nuremberg trials, and again in the 1950 Himmerod Memorandum, which prepared the ground for rearmament – could no longer be associated with any sense of honour.

There's a notable scarcity even of graves. Of the nearly 5 million fallen soldiers, most died on foreign soil and were buried in mass graves. In one small cemetery in a valley in the Bavarian Alps, just outside Berchtesgaden, and near the

Eagle's Nest, where Hitler and his top Nazis would meet in secret, countless headstones mark graves empty of remains. Most are adorned with a ceramic photograph of a young man in his early twenties and engraved with the date and place where he died: Stalingrad, Russland or simply *im Osten,* 'in the East'. And in 1966, Adenauer laid the foundation stone of a huge, abstract memorial in Friedland dedicated to Wehrmacht soldiers returning from Soviet POW camps and Germans who had lost their homes in Allied bombings. But it's practically unknown today.

Collective references to the dead were gradually added to existing First World War memorials and, mainly in the south, humble monuments or gravestones acknowledging those missing were discreetly erected in villages and cemeteries. Since gaining access to Eastern Europe after the reunification of Germany in 1990, the German War Graves Commission, which now documents and looks after over 800 cemeteries in forty-five countries, has been interring bodies in new cemeteries. The remains of innumerable soldiers continue to be discovered. In 2017, German and Russian soldiers co-operated to rebury over a thousand troops south-east of St Petersburg, and young Germans and Russians still come together today, wading through the Volkhov swamps to retrieve the identity bracelets of soldiers from both sides and give their families the chance to provide them with a proper burial.

The remembrance of German soldiers was, and still is, viewed as problematic and therefore to be avoided. Most Germans accept that even those Wehrmacht relatives who were not Nazis cannot be publicly honoured because it would be impossible to do so without appearing to honour the cause for which they died. Even today, few Germans go on pilgrimages to war graves in Flanders, or even on their own doorsteps. Unlike the gleaming white, vertical headstones laid out in rows by the Commonwealth War Graves Commission, the worn grass paths between them testifying to the steady footfall of people from all around the world paying their respects, German military graveyards tend to be dark, overgrown and devoid of visitors, the final resting places of their inhabitants marked by simple black crosses or sombre grey plaques embedded in the ground. I've heard many people say how sad and moving they find these places.

I imagine that this conscious act of forgetting would have devastated my grandfather. He cared deeply about his men, even after their deaths, and had played a significant role in establishing memorial sites for the fallen in the Novgorod area. On our trip to Russia, my mother and I had visited the German cemetery there, a large empty space interrupted only by a tall wooden cross and several huddled clusters of stout stone ones. The contrast with the scene of formal sincerity captured in photographs I'd found of my grandfather saluting a row of soldiers at a wartime memorial service near Novgorod was inescapable.

His concern extended to the welfare of their families. In the summer of 1942, after the Battle of Volkhov, he organized a whip-round for the wives and dependents of men killed or badly wounded, and by Christmas around 1.5 million Reichsmarks had been collected and distributed. Letters from the recipients expressed their deep gratitude for this unexpected support from the front. Taking the initiative in this way, however, was seen as contravening the Nazi party's totalitarian ethos and several orders from higher positions

Karl saluting his troops at the memorial service for fallen German soldiers of the 58th Infantry Division near Novgorod.

forbade the collections. The soldiers ignored them. Only the heavy combat of the following months eventually brought the practice to a halt. According to Kurt von Zydowitz, author of a history of the 58th Infantry Division, my grandfather's 'concept of comradeship' and 'its execution is still perceived today as being exemplary'.

I did allow myself to feel proud of my grandfather for his warm humanity in the face of death. I admired him for maintaining an awareness of the importance of ceremony and dignity in acknowledging the loss of his men, especially in a time and place where there was precious little evidence that any value was accorded to human life. It reassured me that, even in the midst of ferocious fighting, he could not only still feel, but act on his feelings in a way that I am sure many no longer could.

Even before I learned this about my grandfather, I was

exploring ways of honouring and preserving through my art the memories of ordinary people lost to history. In partnership with a fellow student, I had created a series of site-specific interactive installations in Stroud Cemetery to redress the lack of recognition for the thousands of former 'inmates' of the neighbouring workhouse who were buried there in unmarked graves. Using information we researched in the council death registers, we acknowledged their lives and told snippets of their stories.

Standing together in silence in the Novgorod German cemetery, my mother and I had not known what to feel. Our emotions seemed blocked. As we read the rows and rows of names of mainly twenty-something German men, sadness eventually came; huge sadness, not for anything or anybody specific, just for everything.

Britain, in its view of itself as victor and former ruler of the world, has had no real incentive to question its history and our main remembrance ceremonies tend to focus on the positive principles of sacrifice and achievements of the two world wars. As Neil MacGregor, former director of the British Museum, founding director of the Humboldt Forum in Berlin and author of *Germany: Memories of a Nation*, puts it: 'What is very remarkable about German history as a whole is that the Germans use their history to think about the future, where the British tend to use their history to comfort themselves.'

I find it easy none the less to be moved by our annual commemoration of Armistice Day. By the impressive pageantry and heart-stirring music; the demonstrations of sincere pride, respect and gratitude to for those who fought and those who fell. And yet I have always sensed the risk it inadvertently runs of heroicizing or sentimentalizing the whole concept of war.

I recall listening to radio coverage of the 2013 UK Armistice Day ceremonies while planting bulbs in my garden. As my hands sifted the soil, I heard a former British soldier who had fought in Afghanistan speaking of the sanitizing effect of our language on our perception of war. Terms such as the 'Great War', 'fallen soldiers' or 'heroes' convey nothing of the savage reality of combat, or of the way soldiers die. 'They do not "fall",' he said, almost indignantly. He was right. They are usually blown to bits, often dying slow, terrified, lonely deaths while calling for their mothers.

And by elevating all veterans to the generic status of 'hero', an American contributor suggested, are we being disingenuous about those whose bravery far exceeded military duty? Are we overlooking the fact that by the end of the First World War, the British Army had seen 80,000 cases of shell shock? That during the Second World War, nearly 150,000 British and American soldiers deserted? And what about the Allied soldiers who behaved less than heroically when they looted, intimidated, stole and raped citizens under their occupation? Isn't such behaviour more, or equally characteristic, of war? There are no real winners, just countless shades of hero and loser, good soldier and bad, on all sides. Shouldn't our human response be to remember the terrible reverberations of war that endure long after the guns have stopped?

In Germany there is no real equivalent of the spectacle of Armistice Day commemorations in the UK. The signing of the Armistice on 11 November 1918 marked the end of the First World War for the Germans, too, but for them it did not bring peace. Instead it heralded the demise of the monarchy, years of political unrest, widespread poverty, hunger and national humiliation, all of which would till the ground for the rise of Nazism.

Since 1952, West Germany's official Remembrance Day, Volkstrauertag, has been observed annually two Sundays before the first day of Advent. A more general day of national grief and mourning, it commemorates the members of the armed forces and civilians killed in action but also the victims of armed conflict and violent oppression everywhere. Since reunification, at the main memorial ceremony at the Neue Wache building in central Berlin, wreaths are laid at the foot of the big, bulky, beautiful Käthe Kollwitz bronze of a mother holding her dead son, placed there in 1993. For many, the personal perspective of a mother mourning the loss of her child perfectly captures the misery, meaninglessness and familial tragedy of war and puts it at the heart of remembrance.

If memorials had already become subdued and solemn for the losers of the Great War, with the accent on grief rather than triumph, after the Second World War, it had been even more challenging for Germany to represent its history through traditional forms: monuments and statues designed to send future generations into battle with a sense of heroism and the promise that they will be remembered, and to inspire positive feelings of respect, gratitude and national or local pride. Typically consisting of a plinth elevating a symbol of glory or an important figure, usually a man, posing in a proud stance, and often cast in bronze, the grandiose craftsmanship and scale of classical memorials require you to literally 'look up' to them. They are the values of the time made visible; reassuring reminders of what a nation has succeeded in doing well.

By 1990, only a few such monuments remained in West Germany, festering, largely neglected, in dusty corners. In East Germany, concentration camps like Buchenwald, Sachsenhausen and Ravensbrück had been preserved both as crime scenes, cordoned off to protect evidence and allow documentation of what had happened there, and as grim cemeteries for the remains of millions, the only graves relatives had to visit and pay their respects. But no one in West Germany had shown interest in preserving sites of atrocity. After reunification, the government came under intense pressure from civilians to do something. From now on, the country's national commemorative culture would focus almost exclusively on the legacy of Hitler and the Holocaust.

Yoking together two words, *Vergangenheit* (the past) and *Bewältigung* (coping, overcoming or mastering) into one of its long composite nouns, Germany embarked on its difficult and ongoing process of *Vergangenheitsbewältigung*: the struggle to come to terms with its history.

From the end of the eighties and over the next decades, artists, sculptors and architects rose to the challenge and developed the country's unique culture of 'counter-memorials', a term coined by James E. Young, which turn all the usual notions of monuments on their heads. In the absence of an appetite to commemorate the nation's own dead, the attention had to be on its victims. Artists needed to find forms that would express guilt, shame, apology and atonement. They wanted to deter people from looking away; to force them to play a dynamic part in the remembrance of the past as a way of counteracting the danger that the more we allow a memorial to do the remembering for us, the more forgetful we become.

Chancellor Helmut Kohl embraced Germany's task and turned it into a political programme. In 1994 he dedicated 19,000 square metres of prime real estate in the heart of Berlin to the winning proposal of a competition to create a memorial to the murdered Jews of Europe.

This ultimately resulted in the now famous Holocaust memorial conceived by the Jewish American architect Peter Eisenman, consisting of 2,711 concrete slabs of different heights arranged in a grid pattern to evoke an uneasy, confusing atmosphere of a supposedly ordered system that has lost touch with humanity.Soon towns and cities across Germany were holding competitions for artists to come up with innovative ways to actively remember the victims of National Socialism. What grew out of them was a series of largely site-specific, impermanent, changing, interactive installations, projections and anti-monuments designed to keep those memories alive.

In Harburg, Hamburg, Jochen Gerz and Esther Shalev-Gerz's 12-metre tower, covered in soft lead on which people could sign their names in a stand against injustice and Fascism, was lowered 1.5 metres into the ground each year until it disappeared. In Kassel, Horst Hoheisel cast a replica of a fountain funded by a Jewish businessman and subsequently destroyed by the Nazis, turned it upside down and set it into its original sandstone base like 'a mirror image of the old one, sunk beneath the old place, in order to rescue the history of this place as a wound and as an open question'. At an unassuming sports ground in the Neukölln district of Berlin, Norbert Radermacher's slide projections revealing the site's violent history as a forced labour camp are inadvertently triggered by passersby tripping a light beam. The words travel amorphously over the foliage of the trees and a wire fence before landing, fully legible, on the pavement, remain there for a minute, then fade and disappear.

In the former Jewish quarter of Schöneberg, Renata Stih and Frieder Schnock hung eighty signs on lamp-posts, each spelling out one of the many Nazi laws that had gradually stripped Jews of their jobs, status and rights. 'We want it to be uncomfortable,' they said in response to outraged accusations of anti-Semitism. 'We don't want people to say, "We didn't know."' And across Europe, Gunter Demnig has embedded over 70,000 small, brass *Stolpersteine* into pavements, each 'stumbling stone' commemorating a Jewish individual who last lived at that spot.

Many of these counter-memorials are fraught with unforeseen conflicts of interest and frequently meet with strong objections. The construction of Eisenman's Holocaust Memorial nearly ground to a halt when it was discovered that some of the companies involved had been active in Nazi times, not least one with a subsidiary that had produced the Zyklon B gas used in the gas chambers. Despite the public outcry, with 25 million euros already invested in the project, it was considered cost-prohibitive to replace the many stelae already covered in the anti-graffiti chemical supplied by the firm. This decision was heavily criticized. As was the fact that the monument commemorated only the 6 million Jewish victims and not the 5 million others – the Roma and Sinti, homosexuals, Communists, political dissidents, Polish citizens and euthanasia victims – also massacred. This omission has since been rectified with additional memorials.

For many Jewish people, the more understated memorial at the Grunewald railway station, from which 50,000 of

Berlin's Jews were transported, has become the city's most powerful site of remembrance and an example of the significance of location. Just beyond Karol Broniatowski's concrete wall, with its hollowed-out silhouettes of deportees, is the 1998 *Gleis 17* memorial: 186 steel sheets, arranged in chronological order along both sides of the platform, each quoting the date of a departure, the number of Jewish deportees and their destination.

Berlin alone has now created over 400 monuments, as well as preserving locations where crimes took place. Many include extensive information centres or tableaux, and great care is taken to prevent them from becoming shrines for Neo-Nazis and other anti-Semites, or 'dark tourism' sites, or indeed from running any risk of being seen as condoning or

Karol Broniatowski's memorial for the deported Jews of Europe (1991) at Grunewald station.

glamorizing cruelty. Hitler's bunker, for example, lies buried under an ordinary, featureless car park and is marked only by a mundane information board.

While many memorials serve as warnings from the past, others aim to inspire courage and point to the possibility of a different future. In Munich, as you casually bump into the hefty pillars that supported the rise of Nazism – the scene of the 1923 Beer Hall Putsch; the *Führerbau*, where Chamberlain's 1938 Munich Treaty of appeasement was signed – you'll also come upon memorials to the brave members of the resistance, from Georg Elser, who singlehandedly tried but failed to blow up Hitler and other high-ranking Nazis in 1939, to Sophie Scholl, a twenty-one-year-old student, and her White Rose comrades, arrested and executed for distributing anti-war leaflets.

For me, in all their different forms, these memorials reflect a sincere desire on the part of the Germans to apologize unreservedly to their victims, without presuming forgiveness, respite or reconciliation. And they urge us all to remain vigilant. The rallying cries of 'Never again' and 'Never forget' have become the fundamental principle shaping German politics, culture and international relations. The leaders and other representatives of the country have repeatedly held up their hands in the most unconditional admission of culpability and display of penitence any nation has ever shown towards its own misdeeds.

Germany's efforts are neither perfect nor complete but by focusing on those who were destroyed, they shine a spotlight on the fallout of war; the ordinary people, the victims of murder, discrimination and violence; women, children, the elderly and infirm. They glorify nothing and nobody. Like a dig in the ribs from a sharp elbow, they prod you to wake up and pay attention.

All nations create mental images of their history. These range from triumphal events to episodes of collective trauma or loss. Only certain national traumas will be remembered through decades and centuries, potentially unifying or dividing the descendants of those who once lived through them. Like traumas within the body, these communal memories and their associated heroes or humiliations can be deliberately reactivated at any point for political or territorial gain or as grounds for wreaking revenge. Or even genocide. Slobodan Milošević, for example, recalled the 1389 Battle of Kosovo and the Serbian martyrs to stoke the desire for vengeance that led to the annihilation of over 10,000 Albanians 600 years later. Many other contemporary ethnic conflicts are fuelled by historic societal trauma.

The events through which our ancestors lived, their experiences of them, their beliefs, attitudes, actions, loyalties and dreams can influence our internal worlds. If unexamined, they can perpetuate trauma for their victims and carve the way for future perpetrators. Until a country faces the wrongdoings of its past, these legacies will continue to shape the lives and responses of descendants, often forcing their way into the present like a splinter pushed out by an infection.

We saw this all too clearly in 2020 with the murder of the African American George Floyd by a police officer in Minneapolis and the backlash as the Black Lives Matter movement and other protesters erupted on to streets around the world demanding that countries look at the atrocities of their colonial pasts and take down statues that glorify those who grew rich on the back of slavery. Not surprisingly, these demands were, and continue to be, met with massive resistance: no country wants to admit its guilt or highlight its shame.

In the UK, our heroic two world war victories are used to anchor us firmly in the moral high ground, conveniently obfuscating the concentration camps and massacres of our own increasingly contentious colonial past. But is it OK to disregard the crimes in one's own national history simply because, in comparison, they are less bad than the Holocaust? Is it OK for countries to appeal to patriotic pride on every anniversary without acknowledging any national shame of their own? Many of our monuments reveal the lopsidedness and selective memory of histories written by the victors and those holding the power and influence. In London, there is a statue of Gandhi in front of the Houses of Parliament, yet no monument to the victims of colonial brutalities. It took fifty years and a ten-year legal battle for the UK to admit guilt, apologize and pay compensation for the savage suppression of the Mau Mau insurgency in colonial Kenya. In 2015, a UK-funded memorial to the Kenyans killed and tortured was finally erected. In Nairobi. The London Imperial War Museum catalogues the violence of the Germans in the Holocaust but, until recently, did not record Britain's wartime knowledge of Nazi atrocities, of which it is now accepted that the country was aware from 1942. It was not until two new permanent galleries were opened to the public in October 2021, one dedicated to the Holocaust and the other focusing on the Second World War more generally, that the museum addressed this matter. And there are – or in some cases were until the last few years – statues and halls dedicated to the magnates enriched by colonialism, but none to the slaves on whose backs their fortunes were made.

Possibly one of Britain's most contentious monuments to the Second World War – and, until 2012, one of its most notable omissions – commemorates the bombing of Dresden, the German city considered one of the cultural jewels of Europe. Over the course of two days in February 1945, British and US bombers dropped 2,700 tons of high explosives and 200,000 incendiary devices on the historic centre in a deliberate attempt to cause as devastating a firestorm as possible. Up to 25,000 people, mainly civilians and refugees, were killed in ways that still haunt memories and imaginations today. British reactions to the carnage of Dresden were immediately divided and the magnitude of the attack remain a sensitive issue to this day. While some saw, and still see, the carpet-bombing of Germans cities as a strategic necessity, deserved revenge or a tactic required to break German morale, others view it as an indefensible war crime.

The unveiling of the RAF Bomber Command Memorial in London's Green Park in 2012 was therefore extremely emotive. Few would object to the country finally honouring and remembering the 55,573 brave airmen who lost their lives. But there was strong criticism of what some considered in the context of the Dresden bombing to be the 'distasteful' form of the memorial: seven large bronze figures of aircrew elevated on a plinth with prominent inscriptions referencing salvation and victory. It was only later that a very general commemoration of 'those of all nations who lost their lives in the bombing 1939-1945' was placed at the rear.

The London memorial stands in total contrast to the clear symbol and message of peace, forgiveness and reconciliation promoted by the city of Dresden when they rebuilt – with the support of many British donations raised by the Dresden Trust, founded in 1993 – the central Frauenkirche (Church of our Lady) destroyed in the raids.

The US Congress did not formally apologize for slavery until 2008 and there is still no monument in Washington relating to that century of extreme suffering. In fact, just like the majority of Germans in the 1950s, a majority of white Americans are resistant to offering even an apology for slavery, let alone reparations. In *Learning from the Germans*, Susan Neiman describes the work of Bryan Stephenson, an African American lawyer and founder of the Equal Justice Initiative, which has saved hundreds of prisoners from death row. He believes what is missing in America is shame. While regret or remorse has been expressed by some of the descendants of slave-owners, there is no sense of disgrace on a national level. 'Without shame, you don't actually correct. You don't do things differently. You don't acknowledge.'

Other countries besides Germany are guilty of hiding their misdeeds beneath the veneer of Nazi victimhood. In the Hague, the Historical Museum displays exhibits of Dutch misery during the Nazi occupation but avoids all reference to the collaboration that resulted in a higher percentage of Jews being deported to concentration camps from Holland than from anywhere else in Europe. And Austria successfully suppressed its far from minor involvement by declaring itself 'National Socialism's first victim' while placing its more agreeable heritages of Mozart and *The Sound of Music* front of stage. This particular splinter emerged in the mid-1980s, when the past Nazi associations of the former UN secretary general and Austrian president Kurt Waldheim were brought to light. The ensuing debate was a catalyst for change, sparking the unrelenting questioning process initiated in Germany by the 68ers and forcing Austria to confront its flagrant lack of remorse.

The resulting four-part memorial against war and Fascism, erected behind Vienna's Opera House in 1988 on the spot where several hundred people had been buried alive in a bombed cellar, nevertheless met with opposition. Some didn't want to remember, some were offended by the location and others objected to its dedication to all victims of war and Fascism. To address the latter complaint, the Turner Prize-winning British artist Rachel Whiteread was commissioned to plant her library of cast-concrete books on the ruins of Vienna's former synagogue. In 2000 this became the country's first memorial to the 65,000 Austrian Jews killed in the Holocaust. Since then, Austria's culture of remembrance has moved away from largely heroic narratives to more self-critical engagements with wrongdoings of the past, most recently, in November 2021, with the creation in the centre of Vienna of the Shoah Wall of Names, a circle of stone walls listing all 64,440 Austrian Jews who died at the hands of the Nazis.

In Japan, the unprecedented atrocity of the atomic bombings of Hiroshima and Nagasaki are well deserving of the attention they receive and have to a degree defined the way Japan sees itself today. But on a visit I made to the Hiroshima Peace Memorial Park, with its moving testimonies of survivors and heartfelt messages promoting world peace and reconciliation, I found myself searching for even the tiniest reference to the ruthless cruelty perpetrated by the former allies of the Nazis. For Japan's call for peace to be truly effective, I needed 'Japan the perpetrator' to stand hand-in-hand with 'Japan the victim'.

Over the years there have been expressions of remorse, such as the 'deep repentance' voiced by prime minister Shinzō Abe in 2015 for Japan's actions during the Second World War at a joint session of the United States Congress. But cynics weren't convinced it was so much genuine remorse as a strategic move designed to emphasize Japan's reconciliation and alliance with the USA. School textbooks in Japan still focus on the suffering of its people while glossing over the country's own devastating actions as an imperial power.

As one of the Allied victors, Russia uses the defeat of Nazi Germany to revive national pride and rally support for the state. The Great Patriotic War reaches deep into Russia's collective memory, the estimated 26 million lives lost touching nearly every family. History textbooks teach a distorted and selective national narrative by concentrating almost exclusively on the heroic aspects of the Soviet war effort without addressing either the crimes perpetrated by Stalin or his initial alliance with Nazi Germany.

A nation that doesn't understand its own history will be unable to understand its present. Yet the idea of national guilt and apology is a newish one. And while true apology can be transformative for those directly involved, is it even possible to apologize on behalf of a nation decades after the event? In 2010, after a long, excruciatingly painful process and inquiry, UK prime minister David Cameron said sorry 'on behalf of the government, indeed on behalf of our country' for the Bloody Sunday shootings of civilians in Londonderry in Northern Ireland by the British army. It had taken thirty-eight years for Britain to reach this point. None the less, the admission of culpability and genuine apology was largely appreciated in Northern Ireland and perceived as contributing to the precarious peace process.

But can an apology from people who haven't themselves done anything to people to whom something hasn't been directly done have any real effect? And what role do statues and memorials and sites of remembrance play in terms of healing the wounds?

Acknowledging past crimes is a good place to start. It discourages binary, divisive and defensive discourses about perpetrators and victims, right and wrong, and stimulates dialogues that focus on the experiences of individuals now; how they have been impacted and what would help them. Acknowledgement underlay the success of South Africa's Truth and Reconciliation Commission after the end of Apartheid. It was not about asking the state to punish, but about healing relationships between perpetrators and victims through institutionally orchestrated and supervised encounters, not dissimilar to those of a restorative justice conference. It worked when perpetrators genuinely listened, provided answers, allowed the victims' outpouring of emotions and expressed their own.

Maybe the nub of the issue has less to do with apology than with what a nation can actively do to remember its past crimes and dismantle their negative legacy. In a reflective 2010 essay, *'Wozu Gedenkstätten?'*, Jan Philipp Reemtsma, co-organizer of the *Crimes of the Wehrmacht* exhibition, asks what commemoration sites are for and suggests that the ubiquitous watchword 'Never forget' needs to be unpacked. For him, the prime purpose of preserving concentration camps – now as tourist destinations and education centres for school trips – can't be simply to warn 'Look at what happens if you discriminate against people.' Nor can it be to convert, for what guarantees are there that a visitor will identify with the victims rather than the perpetrators? It's also not right to make such places instruments of morality or political manipulation, as they initially did in the East. And if they remain too specific to Nazi crimes, visitors will fail to see the bigger picture that is relevant to all of us.

For Reemtsma, places of remembrance are primarily sacred places for self-interpretation and reflection; places to search for meaning and awaken consciousness and shame. 'A shame that, detached from the question of guilt, seizes anyone who lets themselves be seized.' He wants people to regard Nazi times not as a sudden break with civilization, but as a gradual escalation of line-crossing. Each boundary was overstepped, one at a time, in full view, until you had mass murder. He sees it as our task to recognize those boundaries and feel the horror.

Neiman suggests erecting more memorials along the lines of Berlin's little-known Rosenstraße Memorial, off Alexanderplatz, which marks the successful protest by largely non-Jewish women against the proposed Nazi deportation of their Jewish men. For a week some 600 women gathered outside Rosenstraße 2-4, peacefully demanding the release of their loved ones. The men were released on 6 March 1943. Nobody was punished. Unlike other memorials to those who were executed for their efforts, the three reddish figures and tall, round column displayed here inspire the idea that resistance isn't always futile; that sometimes, even a movement as ideologically driven and brutal as the Nazis can be made to back down under pressure.

The writer and academic Bernhard Schlink questions whether Germany's efforts to come to terms with the past are made in the hope of one day being freed from it and gaining the right to forget it. There is nothing wrong in this desire, he believes, but achieving it is impossible. The past has irrevocably been done and merely fixating on it is no guarantee of liberation from it.

In his 2009 book *'Guilt About the Past'*, Schlink compares a collective history to that of an individual. Each 'is traumatic when it is not allowed to be remembered'. He defines detraumatization as a process of becoming able to both remember and forget. For victims and perpetrators alike, it is thus not a matter of getting over the past, but of consciously living with it, and with all the questions and emotions it carries into the present.

He fully acknowledges the reality of the transgenerational transmission of guilt and trauma. Yet he strongly dismisses as 'cheap' the act of asking for forgiveness for someone else's guilt. Equally, the idea that anyone can step in on behalf of a victim to offer forgiveness is 'presumptuous'. In his view, the right to withhold or grant forgiveness is the victim's alone, an element of their relationship to the perpetrator. Forgiveness can lift the burden of guilt and be deeply healing for those on either the giving or receiving end. But it is not the only response that will allow wrongdoing to be laid to rest. A process of reconciliation can overcome differences and emphasize commonalities and our shared humanity.

Genuine understanding and truth are essential to reconciliation. Both perpetrator and victim need to be acknowledged by each other as equals, and to be acknowledged they have to be understood – not a prerequisite for options such as forgiveness, condemnation or forgetting. To see the world through someone else's eyes can lead to empathizing with them on some level. A measure of equality can be restored between both parties, making it far harder to condemn and easier to forgive.

For both Reemtsma and Schlink, the most unique and persistently disturbing aspect of the Holocaust is the descent of Germany, a culturally advanced civilization, into such inhumanity. To use Schlink's metaphor, it shattered the thin ice of morality on which not just German society was built, but all bourgeois societies around the world.

The truth is that not a single one of us is immune from becoming a doer of monstrous deeds. We are all capable of sliding or falling from positions of morality and conscience into wrongdoing, crime, even barbarity, through opportunism, ambition, humiliation, fear, coercion, pride, carelessness or just by doing what may be considered to be appropriate, sensible or correct according to the standards and expectations of the situation or time.

Germany's lessons are therefore universal, as are the questions we must all ceaselessly ask ourselves: how thick or thin is the ice today, and what structures are in place to stop us falling through it again?

23

My Grandfather on Trial

*One must come to know the mechanisms that render people
capable of such deeds, must reveal these mechanisms to them,
and strive, by awakening a general awareness of those
mechanisms, to prevent people from becoming so again.*

Theodor Adorno, *Education After Auschwitz*

I HAD COME TO REALIZE that absolutely nothing I might learn
about my grandfather could harm me as much as not
knowing had. That without the truth, healing becomes much
harder, maybe impossible. Stripped down, truth is just plain
fact and can lack the muscle to hurt. What damages us most
are lies, deceit, cover ups or silence.

While I continued to pursue answers to unresolved questions, sometimes I dreaded having to descend like a miner
into the darkness of the Second World War. It always took so
long to adjust to the lack of light and air. I just wanted to put
the past to bed, to live a different life and look at a sunnier
horizon. But I didn't know how to end our family story. Nor
had I come to any firm conclusions about my grandfather.

I hadn't set out to put him through a process of judgement. And that wasn't my aim when, with some trepidation,
I dug out the postscript to his letters: his postwar reflections,
written between 1946 and 1948 while he was a prisoner of
war, which seemed to consist largely of deliberations on the

previous decade and warnings of the dangers that he, and fellow generals being held with him, saw in the world around them. Until now, I had only skimmed these pages in search of an unequivocal condemnation of the atrocities and the treatment of the Jews, evidence of his revulsion for Hitler and the Nazis and some unashamed rejection of the idealistic goals of the war. I wanted contrition. Back then, I hadn't found it.

I didn't know exactly why I was reading them properly now, except that I felt I had to. Maybe I was still clinging to the notion that somewhere there was a clear, black-and-white, objective denouement to be reached. Guilty or not. Nazi or not. Good soldier or not. That there would be something here that would enable me to clear his name. And with it, my own.

Bracing myself once more, I retreated to an old friend's weatherboard house in Rye. Wrapped in the white interiors with pictures of boats and maritime scenes bobbing on the walls, I felt warm and safe. I filled the fridge with treats and, after a sunrise run on the beach, I made a big pot of coffee and settled on the floor to read and translate his words. This time it felt like a purposeful return to a derelict building to open drawn curtains and lift dustsheets and reveal whatever might lie beneath them.

By this stage I was bringing a better-informed perspective to the task and now his words came alive, as if he was speaking them directly to me. Finally, I felt I was inside his head and touring his mind. Go on, Großvati, I urged, present me with your reasons for rejecting the British charges that you were a 'militarist', 'in complete agreement with the NS programme' and 'a definite danger to peace and security'.

He begins by addressing the accusation that the generals should have striven for peace sooner.

*We did. Hitler was also warned. Even if they now claim it
was only because the German army was insufficiently
prepared, we did warn him. In the report of Marshall, the
former American minister of war, it was clearly ascertained
that not only did the German generals not want war, but
that they strongly opposed Hitler's military strategies. This
disproves the idea that the generals were warmongers.*

He rejects the idea that Germany was pursuing world domination as 'equally absurd'.

*Even lay people are aware that you need control of the
seas to achieve world domination. Who could seriously
believe that the few German warships – you can't even
speak of a fleet – would have been in a position to take on
the fleets of England, France and America?!*

*Whatever opinion you have of Hitler, he, too, tried to
maintain peace and to come to an agreement with the
Western democracies. This, too, is illuminated in the
Marshall Report.*

Until now, I had not been aware of that. Hitler most definitely
had wanted war with Soviet Russia – his ambitions to conquer
'Lebensraum' in the east had already been clearly outlined in
Volume 1 of *Mein Kampf*, published in 1925. However, a number of history books published in recent years have supported
my grandfather's view that neither Hitler nor the Germans
actually wanted war with Britain. Not initially, at least. Hitler
admired the imperial might of the British Empire and
expressed in his *Zweites Buch* – his thoughts on foreign policy,
written in 1928 but not published in his lifetime – the hope that

Germany would emulate British 'ruthlessness' and 'absence of moral scruples' in establishing its own colonial empire in Eastern Europe. One of his primary foreign policy aims in the 1930s was to form a military alliance with both the English and the Italians. He wanted to see the British Empire preserved as a world power, not least because he believed that its dissolution would be of little benefit to Germany and of great benefit to other countries, particularly the USA and Japan.

One of his strategies for winning over Britain was an offer of German defence support, which he hoped would contribute to his ultimate goal of joining forces with Britain so that the two countries could 'march together against America'. It was only when Britain made it clear it was not interested in any such military alliance that anti-British policies were adopted. None the less, even during the war, he seems to have maintained the hope that Britain would become a reliable German ally.

My grandfather continues to list the ways in which Hitler strove for peace, among them renouncing territories from Elsaß-Lothringen to South Tyrol and North Schleswig to the Polish Corridor that divided the bulk of Germany from the province of East Prussia, giving interwar Poland access to the Baltic Sea. The Polish Corridor was untenable. Germans were being imprisoned by the Poles. Even statesmen of other nations agreed that its creation was an error of the Versailles treaty. In a reference to the Anglo-Polish treaty of August 1939, a military alliance assuring mutual assistance in the case of a German invasion, he asserts:

> Without England's interference, a peaceful solution to the Polish situation would have been found. But, strengthened

by England's promises of help and other prompts, Poland
rejected all Germany's suggestions . . . broke off its negotiations and marched its armies up to the German border.
The battle cry of the propaganda was, 'In three days we'll
be in Berlin!'

My grandfather, then, was among the majority of
Germans who saw Germany's ensuing military response,
construed by England and France as a reason to declare war,
as unavoidable. This reiterates the German propaganda of
September 1939 that war was being caused by a British policy
of encirclement, just as in 1914. But it also disregards the
planned war of conquest in Poland and the Soviet Union that
the high-ranking military were aware of, as evidenced at the
Nuremberg Trials. 'Today some statesmen might be able to
see what it means to have Slavic neighbours, and that it takes
huge patience and political skill to maintain a degree of amic-
able relationship over centuries.'

It was certainly true that Germany's relationship with
Poland and the Slavic people had always been complicated.
Until 1871, when disparate states were united into the Germany we know today, its land borders had been fluid for
centuries. Bolshevism was widely viewed – and not just by
Nazis – as a huge danger. For the British, inhabitants of an
island surrounded by a deep-sea moat, it may be hard to
imagine being separated from multiple other nations only by
porous land borders. Perhaps the threat Germany felt from
the east is not that dissimilar to the threat perceived by some
today in the numbers or otherness of immigrants. But there
is no doubt, for the Nazis and German nationalists, that this
was also about race and a 'crusade against Judeo-Bolshevism.'

Elwyn, my online expert, was able to expand on my grandfather's position. 'He was from Plön,' Elwyn explained, 'so he would just think they were retaking what rightfully belonged to Mecklenburg and West Prussia.' And thereby defending ethnic Germans against Polish aggression. Everything was seen through the lens of the First World War and the punitive Treaty of Versailles. Germany wanted its confiscated territories back and, in some ways, it was attempting to fight the First World War all over again but this time, to win it. To do that, it had to become militarized, more efficient, more ruthless; to wage war and keep battling to the end.

As he tries to comprehend the logic of the accusations being hurled at Germany and place them within a context of Britain's apparent 'annihilation' agenda, my grandfather defends the 'peacekeeping efforts' that many historians would view much more sceptically as Hitler's strategy to placate a potential enemy while pursuing expansionist aims elsewhere.

> *All offers of peace remained unsuccessful, however, due to England's insistence that Germany must be destroyed. One doesn't need to be a politician or statesman to interpret Churchill's November 1936 warning to the House of Lords, 'Germany is too strong, we must destroy her,' as anything other than an incitement to a preventative war against Germany. In Germany's breaking of the Treaty of Versailles, England saw a threat to its world domination, and it needed an excuse that would deceive the world about its real intentions.*

I have so far been able to verify all my grandfather's sources, except for one, in relation to the 'power struggle between

England and Germany' to which he so regularly refers. In the following extract he is quoting from a letter he had seen published, but which I have been unable to track down, written by an English diplomat at the Peking Embassy on 2 December 1939 and sent to a Dr Blackwell in Leeds.

> *I see in this war a massive tragedy – in the most dramatic sense of the word – in which the German people have to be sacrificed for the greater good of the whole world . . . What's clear, though, is that two such dynamic nations as England and Germany can't exist side by side. One must go. As we don't want to, it is better, in the interest of the whole world, to sacrifice Germany. It's true that the status quo is unjust, but it is better than a big war, for every generation . . . I seriously believe that England, with its long experience and development of imperialism, is best suited to dominate the world. The only serious rival to this supremacy is Germany, and for that reason it must be destroyed.*

With the benefit of twenty-first-century hindsight, many of my grandfather's theories on the causes of the war could be dismissed as ludicrous. Indeed, one or two English hobby historians I approached for opinions pronounced his arguments to be not just false but delusional, and became quite defensive at the implication that the British might have been at any fault at all. More recently, however, the roots of the Second World War have been extended back to the end of the nineteenth century and expanded from a European scale to a global one. In his new book *Blood and Ruins*, for example, Richard Overy argues that the conflict was not just about democracy but 'a great imperialist war', the violent conclusion to decades of imperial growth and territorial aspirations.

When I visited Nicholas Stargardt, a leading scholar of Nazi Germany and author of the enlightening book, *The German War: A Nation Under Arms, 1939–45*, to discuss my grandfather's 'reflections', he confirmed that the views and justifications he expressed were widespread and typical of many Germans at the time, with their mix of bellicosity towards Poles and Russians, claims that their own actions were defensive and their readiness to blame the British for strangling German ambitions.

I can't possibly know who started what, nor am I personally interested in attributing blame. The usual dynamic behind so many conflicts is all too clear: both sides believe they have legitimate grounds to start, or pursue, a defensive war. The other thing that was becoming increasingly clear was that, even as a division leader, my grandfather was not immune to the propaganda that justified each stage of the war as 'defence', 'prevention', 'retaliation', or 'reprisal'.

His tone becomes more resigned when he admits that the Germans themselves were duped: 'In the end, the American people were just as deceived as the German people. The Germans had to believe that Hitler was pursuing peaceful politics. This was strengthened by the indisputable successes he presented.' These included, according to my grandfather, the restoration of military sovereignty, the occupation of the Rhineland, the absorption of Austria into German territory, the resolution of the Czech question, the naval treaty with England, under which Hitler voluntarily reduced the German fleet to a ratio of 3:1, the 1936 Olympic games and the joint declaration by British and French foreign ministers and Hitler that England, France and Germany would never cross weapons again. At home there was his successful tackling of social issues such as unemployment, the currency problems, the care of the elderly and the development of towns, roads and transport networks.

> *All this, plus the strength of the press and radio, must have awoken the trust in the German people that the last German question, namely the Polish Corridor, would also find a peaceful solution, especially after the supposedly impossible peace pact with Russia.*
>
> *These achievements gave Hitler a halo of infallibility from which even foreign countries were not immune. Even the future later minister Churchill, whose political forecasting ability is widely recognized, wrote in 1938: 'God send England a man like Hitler in times of emergency.' If Hitler could deceive even such a renowned statesman, how can one hold it against the German people that they believed in his capabilities?*

My grandfather is clearly cherry-picking his quotes to fit his argument. For one thing, he omits to mention Hitler's breaking of the Munich Agreement on the 'Czech question' within six months. But there are historians who assert that it was the call to defend Europe from the Communists, more than the annihilation of the Jews, that fuelled the war in the East. After the defeat of France, Hitler said: 'I could have thrown myself heart and soul into the destruction of Bolshevism, which is Germany's essential task, the ambition of my life and the raison d'être of National Socialism.' That drive to destroy

Bolshevism 'would have been coupled with the conquest of vast spaces in the east . . . to ensure the future wellbeing of the German people'. And yet, as we have seen, the 1941 invasion of the Soviet Union was a premeditated and deliberately genocidal war. And the military knew it.

I'm becoming exhausted. Empty cups litter the room. I can't see the carpet for the sea of papers and coloured stickers that mark a significant point, then vanish like exotic fish in an aquarium. I am trying to follow the thread of logic running through my grandfather's arguments. I want to get behind his apparent inability to apportion blame to Germany, himself or even Hitler.

I stare out of the window at the boats bobbing on the bay at Rye, wishing he had been a fisherman.

As he rages over the horrors to which German civilians were subjected in the flights, expulsions and interments, I sense that his unidentified audience is becoming an uninterested, bustling crowd with their hands over their ears. But I'm still listening.

And yet it feels almost taboo to be trying to understand Hitler's thinking. To be giving him any voice at all.

> *Today, where the whole development of the political situation has become history, it is not difficult to judge and condemn the German people as a generation of criminals. But why weren't they made aware of the criminal politics of their government and made to break their relationship with it while there was still time? Can one expect the German people to see things that were even concealed from outsiders? Didn't foreign countries make*

> *themselves partly responsible by not only tolerating*
> *Hitler's aspirations, but even supporting them?*
> *Certainly, the persecution of the Jews . . .*

The air catches in my throat. I am desperate to find out whether he will unconditionally condemn this part of Hitler's policy. But I don't know if I can bear to read on.

> *. . . the requirement for proof of an Aryan grandmother,*
> *the compulsion for subordinates of Himmler's SS to leave*
> *the Church were seen as questionable or alarming signs*
> *in the widest circles of the public. They could have been*
> *the cause for spontaneous expressions of the people's will.*
> *But the fundamentals were missing.*

In an argument that chimes with my grandmother's memoir, and with many other eyewitness accounts I have read, he continues:

> *Only someone who has experienced a dictatorship*
> *first-hand is entitled to pass judgement. Even a*
> *thoughtless comment against National Socialism in the*
> *closest family circles could mean death or being sent to a*
> *concentration camp. And it wouldn't just be a single*
> *person . . . but all the relatives, too. This alone made*
> *disposing of the regime unbelievably difficult, something*
> *people of democratic countries would never be able to*
> *understand.*

He writes of the countless attempts to dispose of the regime, of the over 300,000 Germans who lost their lives fighting for

freedom and rights, of the millions who died in the first concentration camps, initially established in the early 1930s for
the detention of political opponents and leaders of social and
cultural movements perceived as a threat to the Nazi regime.
'If all these attempts came to nothing,' he contends, 'it shows
how the political development and the quick unfolding of
events made the requisite careful preparations impossible.'

I don't know where he has got these figures from. They
are way out. But what bothers me more is that he is ignoring
the liberal and Social Democratic German émigrés who did
raise the alarm on the criminal politics, and the role of the
more conservative-leaning people who were either compla-
cently acquiescing or actively supporting Hitler and who saw
what was happening from 1933 as a 'national revolution' and
'rebirth' rather than an evil dictatorship. Instead, he further
defends the German people for wanting easy victories over
their external enemies. And gets furious about the 'blatant
breach of people's rights' through the Allied decision not to
apply the Geneva Convention to them. 'One can excuse a lot
due to the vast number of prisoners but not abuse to this
degree. Even the atrocities committed with Hitler's knowledge by Himmler and his relatively small clique of criminals
don't give any nation the right to subject innocents to the
same.'

This is the first mention he has made of 'the atrocities'.
And, even now, the sentence is loaded with caveats. They are
the work of 'a relatively small clique of criminals'? And
Himmler, the head of the SS, is culpable, not Hitler?

Does he believe this or is he again trying to exonerate his
own position by invoking the origin of the 'good Wehrmacht,
bad SS' myth? Apparently, it was common for soldiers to

make a distinction between Hitler and the Nazi regime. Before the war, their attitude to Hitler was quite positive and, until 1944, he was seen as a kind of monarch, the father of the Fatherland. The Nazi regime, however, had fairly quickly come to be viewed in a negative light. Many Nazi leaders – of high and low rank – were widely regarded as corrupt, incompetent, philistine and to blame for everything. Was this why my grandfather seemed to be loyal to Hitler, but not to the Nazi criminals?

Whatever the case, this reference to atrocities demonstrates no real comprehension of the geographical scale, the numbers, the degree of suffering. It may have been an allusion to Himmler's speeches to senior military figures, perhaps the one he made in October 1943 in Posen to the Reich leaders and Gauleiters, in which he explicitly discussed the extermination of the Jews. Or does it demonstrate that my grandfather, like so many Wehrmacht soldiers, was not that interested in what lay beyond his day-to-day military frame of reference?

I am finding it hard to breathe. I am convinced by the authenticity of my grandfather's outrage. I believe that he believes his reaction is justified. But come on, Großvati! How can you possibly believe this? How do you reconcile your complaints about the treatment of the German people with the pre-invasion plans to starve 10 to 20 million Slavs in order to feed the Wehrmacht, the execution of all commissars and the appalling treatment of Russian prisoners in which you yourself were involved? An estimated 3.3 million of the 5.7 million Soviet POWs died in Nazi custody, most of them between June 1941 and January 1942 on death marches from the front lines, through summary execution or deliberate starvation and exposure in camps. These decisions made by the leadership were some of the gravest crimes of the Wehrmacht. 'You absolutely would have known and contributed to this!' I yell at him furiously. 'So it is *you* who has no excuse for abuse here. You can't have it both ways. You were too senior to get your hands dirty but not senior enough to know the overall plan? Or did you really believe the Eastern Front was different? That your victims were subhuman? Is that what justified your actions?'

As if sensing my exasperation, my grandfather returns swiftly to his preferred subject: the plight of the innocent Germans. The hundreds of thousands of children who were the products of the rapes; those who were not of age at the time of Hitler's seizure of power in 1933, or who were born afterwards; all the Germans who had never heard about the atrocities. 'If even the senior men were not told about the conditions and procedures in the concentration camps, as was confirmed in the Nuremberg Trials, how could a simple civilian living far away from the camps know?'

The issue of who knew what is one of the biggest questions we're left with. It still hovers in the air today. The answer, I believe, lies only in the graves and consciences of the millions of Germans who lived through that time. Historians now generally concede that this 'not knowing' could not have been universally true. Some citizens might well genuinely have known nothing of the gas chambers. Although Jews were rounded up and taken away in broad daylight, the German people were deliberately kept ignorant of details of Nazi crimes while at the same time being made accomplices to them.

Others – 33 to 50 per cent, according to the comprehensive international analysis of oral and written interviews conducted between 1993 and 2001, and published in 2005 as *What We Knew* – would either have heard or known something about the atrocities before the war's end. Although depending on the reliability of the source, they would not necessarily have believed them possible. After all, broadcasts by the BBC could easily be dismissed as Allied propaganda. People may have heard about the horrors of the Eastern Front from returning soldiers, for example, or of the existence of the concentration camps, but not of their role in systematic murder. Both survivors and perpetrators have testified that even Jews arriving at the camps often had no idea of their fate and those already detained who saw their comrades taken further east didn't believe, or didn't want to believe, the terrible rumours about what awaited them.

However, there were plenty who definitely would have known.

My grandfather is not so much defending himself as the compatriots he has been trying to defend for nearly a decade.

> *It's only now that the eyes of the German people are being opened, and if the number of known innocent victims is only a fraction of the actual figure, every German would, at the deepest level, abhor and condemn the atrocities even more than the rest of the world. If the numbers are 5.8 or 12 million; if, indeed, instead of the 1.5 million Jews – calculated by an American newspaper – it was 5 million, nothing changes the fact that egregious and abhorrent crimes against humanity were committed.*

I pause and allow myself the tiniest glimmer of relief. His numbers are so far out, I am inclined to believe his claim that, even as a senior Wehrmacht officer, he was not privy to the extent or details of the Final Solution. Himmler had only later, in January 1944, made accomplices of the generals by telling them what was happening. By then my grandfather was fighting the Allies in Italy. In any event, as I had learned, the 'Jewish actions' on the Eastern Front were usually organized well behind the advancing front lines and, according to Neitzel and Welzer, 'Troops actively engaged in battle could thus logistically not have had much to do with these acts of mass murder.'

Can I deduce from this that my grandfather, though definitely responsible for the execution of partisans, wasn't guilty of these crimes against humanity?

Or is this just me believing what I want to believe because I want so badly for him not to have been involved? He goes on:

> *One might doubt whether hundreds of prisoners were really ripped apart by dogs or, as one released prisoner said, were hung from a Christmas tree or tortured to death in another way, but it still remains that it cannot, and should not, be denied that atrocities were committed.*

And there it is. I read that line again.

And again.

And again.

At last. Both an admission that the atrocities were abhorrent crimes and an acknowledgement that they took place. It's almost as if the only reason he hasn't mentioned them before is that condemnation of the Holocaust is a no-brainer. It was unconditionally wrong, regardless of the exact figures.

For him 'the atrocities' are what happened in the concentration camps instigated by Himmler. He can be certain he was not in any way part of that. And yet he can't allow himself at this point to concede that the man to whom he was answerable was a monster.

I want him to expand. This isn't enough.

But it is all I am going to get.

What would any other nation have done? he asks. 'What did the English people, or what did other people of the world, do against the inhumane slave trade or the thousands of Boer women and children who died in concentration camps? England's empire was built through the blood and sweat of repressed nations. Neither morals nor humanity played a role in the process.'

In recent years, amid huge opposition and only as a result of extensive protests, his questions regarding accountability for the victims of slavery and colonialism have gained traction. As endless examples of British imperial atrocities begin to surface, Britain and its empire, indeed all former occupiers of colonies, are only now being held to account for the actions of the past. Until 2015, UK taxpayers were still paying off the £20 million debt incurred by the government to compensate British slave-owners – not those enslaved – for their loss of profit when slavery was abolished. I agree with my grandfather. I have long thought this way. It has been all too easy for the atrocities perpetrated by other nations to disappear in the exceptionally dense fog of Germany's smoking guns.

Yet it is almost impossible not to read his protestations as 'whataboutery'. The Holocaust plunged Germany's war into an abyss it is still hard and painful to comprehend. That is what makes contemplating the German point of view so problematic. To do so is to risk being branded an apologist for Hitler and the Nazis. Yet here I am, trying to get inside the head of a Prussian career soldier. Not to accuse him, just to understand how it was for him and other soldiers like him. And wanting to understand a person is not the same as exonerating them. Behind his diatribe lies the devastation of being lumped in with a 'small minority' facing the disgust of the entire world. 'It can only fill one with deep shame when American animal rights charities make the serious suggestion that, instead of poor animals being exploited for the atom bomb experiments, German war criminals should be used.'

As he searches for loopholes and rails against the glaring hypocrisy of his accusers, he asks why Britain homed in on Germany's faults while ignoring those of other countries, like Stalin's Russia. Why Britain hadn't supported Germany in its negotiations with Poland to secure a peaceful outcome at Danzig. How Britain could profess moral superiority over the rest of the world, justifying its defence of Poland with the claim that no big nation has the right to impose its will on a weaker power. When had imperial Britain ever taken power imbalance into consideration?

I see with sudden clarity why I have always felt such a big conflict in my dual nationality.

My grandfather has the bit between his teeth again. 'The first step to preventing future wars is to hold to account and punish anyone who incites people to violence or riot through the press ... No nation wants war, so who has interest in it? According to *The Union Jack* ...'

I look out of the window, distracted by the reddening clouds and tiny headlights on the distant road sparkling like stars in another world. My grandfather seems to notice that I have stopped listening. Out of puff himself, he climbs down from his soapbox, a defeated man trying to salvage scraps of his former honour.

'German soldiers weren't even allowed to contact relatives in the first year,' he mutters as he shuffles away. 'And a year and a half after the weapons have been put down, German generals are still left in the dark about their future. Who makes such regulations that go against all humaneness?'

I don't know, Großvati. I don't know.

I want to howl.

'War'.

Back at my own desk at home, I type the word with one finger, as if Google might give me the answers my grandfather couldn't. I have already trawled through so much war footage that all I can see is destruction. Bullets, shells, missiles, rockets. Explosions. Plumes of fire, smoke, dust. Organized violence. Death.

This is the world of Mars, not Venus. Put it to music, and it pumps the blood through your veins, fills you with awe of the bravery of soldiers. But what of its utter pointlessness? How can war be so appalling and so appealing? So noble and so devastating? I understand the exhilaration of destruction from prison, art and building sites. But in war, everybody suffers.

I look up at two aeroplanes trailing a vapour cross in the sky behind my computer screen. I wonder what 600 further pages of my grandfather's letters might have revealed had they not been lost. What he might have told me if I had been able to ask. History and hindsight will continue to challenge or confirm his words, perhaps invalidating some or revealing meaning I can't see now in others. I will never know anything for sure. But I have walked far enough in his dusty, broken boots to be able to follow his logic.

Was he guilty? Was he a Nazi?

Granted, he never joined the Nazi party and was found 'not guilty' of all charges by the review board that finally released him from prison. And I had recently discovered that the references to his 'National Socialist attitude' could easily have been the result of a simple box-ticking exercise. In the autumn of 1942 'National Social Attitudes' was introduced as a new category of officer evaluation. It is quite likely that, just like contemporary job appraisals, military performance appraisals could be completed by a supportive officer in a way that would ensure all criteria for promotion were met. Apparently, these evaluations were thrown around with such nonchalance that some National Socialist beliefs were attributed even to officers who were demonstrably sceptical of the Nazi system.

Set against this evaluation was the fact that my grandfather was clearly considered trustworthy enough by opponents of Hitler to be approached to play a part in the assassination attempt on Hitler in July 1944. But do ticks in boxes on either side count for anything in the context of Hitler's war of annihilation? What is perhaps more important is did he *feel* guilty? For waging the war, or for losing it? For following Hitler, or for not joining the plot to kill him? Did he feel guilty for not recognizing his function within the juggernaut that murdered millions of innocent Jewish, Sinti and Roma, Polish, Russian and homosexual civilians?

Does any soldier feel guilty, or good, for acting on his or her training, obeying orders and killing the people that politics or society have demonized and appointed the enemy? By projecting evil on to others, we divide the world into two-dimensional camps. Without nuance 'we' become pure 'good' and can unite in vindication of war. Or 'organized murder', as Harry Patch, the last fighting Tommy defined it. Does that make us all guilty? All responsible?

I cannot and will not excuse or condone my grandfather's actions. But I will not judge him, either.

I imagine spectres of carnage haunted his diminished self and, in his darker moments, that doubt tugged at his conscience like a whining child refusing to be brushed aside. I think that his loss of status and honour made him defensive and angry; that the three years as a prisoner humiliated and broke him. I believe that he believed he was 'innocent' of the atrocities; that he had been fulfilling his soldier's duty but, because he could see no way back to restoring either his own honour or his country's, he felt shame.

To survive, he scrunched the whole team of tormentors into a tight bundle of unutterability and shoved it in a rucksack. Out of his sight, it clung to his back as he whittled his wooden yo-yos and hawked them from door to door. As he slid his hand across the dining table to try to reconnect with his wife. As he attended his second daughter's marriage to an Englishman and sat on the sofa with her new mother-in-law, conversing in hand gestures across the ghost of her only brother, killed by German troops at El Alamein. I believe it would have accompanied him into death if he hadn't handed it to me as our paths crossed like the planes I am watching in the sky.

Was it now my place to apologize, or ask for forgiveness, or to forgive?

Was it up to me to atone for the suffering of millions?

What can anybody do with a legacy of shame?

24

When Does the Past Pass?

*I do not believe in collective guilt. The children of the killers
are not killers. We must never blame them for what the
elders did, but we can hold them responsible for what
they do with the memory of their elders' crime.*

Auschwitz survivor Sabina Wolanski, inauguration
speech for Berlin's Holocaust Memorial

SHAME IS NOT THE same as guilt. Guilt focuses on behaviour: wrongdoing; a failure to satisfy societal values or our own internal ones. The essence of guilt is 'I *did* something bad.' Guilt can cripple a person, weakening their self-esteem and leading to anxiety or depression. In combination with fear of punishment, it can evoke remorse or a wish to make amends. We might 'confess' our guilt or share it with others.

Shame, on the other hand, we are more likely to conceal. It is more self-conscious than guilt. Shame is bound up with how others see us and anticipates exclusion. It is an intensely painful feeling of internal inadequacy, a sense that the whole self is flawed and therefore not worthy of acceptance and belonging. Its essence is: 'I *am* bad.'

Shaming – a collective response to those deemed to have broken accepted rules and codes of behaviour – may result in the loss of the right to belong to a society, family or circle of colleagues or friends. It is one of the few human reactions that can be observed in other mammals living in groups. In research experiments, male baboons that were perceived by their peers as failures, possibly due to physical weakness, were shamed by other members of the group by being shunned and deprived of food and the right to choose a female mate.

Such scrutiny, judgement and rejection can be a potent driver of violence. Ostracized baboons withdrew to the edges of the group and picked on smaller, more fragile animals like birds, crushing them in their hands until their bones broke.

Shame provokes an impulse to hide – from others and from ourselves. To blame oneself. Or to do something to save face. Withdrawal, retribution, anger or taking refuge in addictive substances or behaviour are often seen as a way through it. It is manifested in a particular body posture and autonomic pattern, similar to that demonstrated by trauma: collapse, immobilization, looking away.

In 2001 I was at a dance workshop, sitting in a large circle of a hundred people or so. We'd just danced our socks off and people were now exchanging experiences. Suddenly, a woman of roughly my age broke down in tears. 'I am so . . .' she sobbed, her face crumpling into her hands, '*ashamed* to be German.'

I had never heard anyone say these words before. I swallowed hard. I felt tears spilling down my own cheeks. Her declaration unsettled me long after the circle had dispersed. It was as if it was gently shaking my shoulder, urging me to wake up and finally name my own shame.

But ultimately, the shame wasn't mine. It didn't even belong to my generation.

How, then, have young Germans today integrated their nation's atrocities into their personal spheres of reference? And how do new generations build on this process? Since the early 1980s, Nazism and the Holocaust have been embedded in the German school curriculum, and in a multitude of contexts beyond history lessons, though the range and degree have varied not only within each *Bundesland* (state) but according to the inclinations of individual teachers. By the 1990s, students were being confronted with the past to such an extent that many complained of 'overload'. Defensiveness was a common response to feeling pressurized to incriminate grandparents they loved. Like their parents, many couldn't express sorrow on hearing the stories of Holocaust victims because that seemed to equate to an admission of guilt. Instead they displayed a sullen anger, as if part of them wanted to scream: 'We didn't do it!' Some tried to diminish German atrocities by pointing to those of other countries. Others preferred to take positions of moral superiority over their relatives.

This was enough to spur Helmut Schmidt, chancellor of West Germany from 1974 to 1982, to speak out in 1995. 'I want the facts to be known and morally judged,' he said. 'But one cuts off any hope of success if one lets the children of 18 million believe that their parents are guilty and that they are now enlightened and morally correct and would have been – had they lived at that time – resistance fighters.'

In 1998, in an acceptance speech for a peace prize awarded by the German Book Traders Association, the author Harald Walser acknowledged this sense of overload and condemned the abundance of Holocaust images in the media and the 'monumentalization' and 'ceaseless presentation of our shame', noting that the effect it had on him was to make him begin to look away. He asserted his right to be relieved from his 'duty to remember'.

The German journalist Bernd Ulrich offered a different message: 'Auschwitz was a one-off, a German crime; Germany was liberated. The younger generations must assume responsibility for the Holocaust. Freedom lies for us not in suppression but in remembrance, and no one can step outside his own shadow.'

Duty to remember. Responsibility for the Holocaust. These are massive burdens for younger generations to carry, made even heavier if family members played an active role.

In 2002, Harald Welzer's *Opa war kein Nazi* had clearly shown that the old narrative of the Nazis as 'others' and the general population as ignorant of events still predominated in Germany, in spite of the otherwise successful strides made in history classes, political education and unconventional memorials. I, too, had noticed this tendency in conversations with some of my German friends. Nobody seemed to have a single relative who had been involved in any way at all. They all fitted into Welzer's categories of resisters, heroes or victims of National Socialism: the 'he was just a librarian', the 'deserter', the 'shopkeeper'. Had none of them so much as waved to Hitler or looked the other way in fear as Jews were rounded up?

This defensiveness struck me as understandable but at the same time problematic. Initially, I, too, had believed that by tracing the events of my family history I could absolve my relatives of any wrongdoing. And if the results of my research had left me unable to exonerate my grandfather of all malfeasance as a member of the Wehrmacht, equally I found it almost impossible to lump him together with the worst Nazis and condemn him as a war criminal. But I was coming to recognize the shades of guilt between extreme good and extreme evil of which we are all capable under certain circumstances. It remains a difficult question, but I don't think I believe there is such a thing as an evil person, just evil deeds of which some Germans' relatives would certainly be guilty.

In a 2010 study of school pupils, it was found that 80 per cent considered remembrance of Nazi times to be important and 67 per cent thought their generation had a duty to make sure that Nazi Germany and the Holocaust weren't forgotten. Sixty per cent said they were personally ashamed of what Germans did under the Nazis. Many young Germans put remembrance and atonement into action by volunteering to work at memorial sites such as Auschwitz or tending the war graves of soldiers of all nationalities across Europe.

I presented these figures during a lecture I was giving to some British sixth-formers. 'Why don't they all feel ashamed?' asked one pupil. I knew what he meant: shame can be seen as an expression of condemnation, apology or remorse. But another way of looking at this might be to question why any of the young Germans feel personally ashamed. They weren't even alive at the time.

In response, I asked the student whether a 'duty to remember', or to feel ashamed should, by the same token, extend to other countries. Should British children, for example, be made to actively remember and carry the shame for the sins of their forefathers' during the British Empire's colonization of large parts of the world? For the hundreds of thousands of deaths arising from the partitioning of India in 1947? Or for the civilian casualties of the invasion of Iraq in 2003? And should American children take responsibility for the slave trade or the Vietnam War?

More and more people are coming to believe that they

should. Surely, if we are happy to accept the wealth or privilege accrued by our ancestors, we must also accept liability and responsibility for the actions that led to them? Yet there remains strong opposition to what some perceive as 'rewriting' or 'censoring' history and the tarring of long-established triumphant narratives with the 'woke' brush of failure, error and shame.

German millennials have grown up in a country whose view of itself is ever-evolving, as is the way it is seen by its former enemies. Germany's staging of the 2006 World Cup provided a fascinating snapshot of its changing face. Across the land, encouraged by the team coach, Jürgen Klinsmann – a well-known figure in the UK since his days as a player with Tottenham Hotspur – the hosts flourished the black, red and gold-striped shroud of national shame in the windows of their houses, from cars and emblazoned on their clothes. Until then, any whiff of overt German nationalism had been met with opprobrium, and Germans were deeply wary of demonstrating even a semblance of pride in their country lest it be compared to the Nazi rallies of the past or exploited by far-right organizations.

The Germans may not have won the tournament, but they won the hearts of visiting fans from around the world, eliciting from England supporters unexpected enthusiasm and effusive praise for their open-hearted hospitality, delicious cold beer, efficient transport system, wonderful weather and even, on occasion, their sense of humour.

And yet national guilt and shame remain driving forces behind German politics, culture and social life in ways it is hard for most British people to understand. Hitler and the Nazis still feature prominently in television programmes and mainstream magazines today. As Günter Grass so succinctly put it in *Crabwalk*: 'History, or to be more precise, the history we Germans have repeatedly mucked up, is like a clogged toilet. We flush and flush, but the shit keeps rising.'

It is extremely important, he added in an interview, 'to work through and grieve one's own losses. Once this has been done in Germany, there might be an energy that dares to look more closely at the involvement of German families in the Holocaust'.

For the millennial generation, it took another TV dramatization to bring history to life and finally open up family conversations. *Unsere Mütter, Unsere Väter* (our mothers, our fathers), or *Generation War*, as it was called in the UK, was a three-part series, broadcast in Germany in 2013, following the lives of five twenty-something friends living in wartime Berlin. Two brothers join the Wehrmacht, one willingly, the other, a sensitive poet, reluctantly. One girl becomes a nurse on the Eastern Front and another pursues her dream to succeed as a singer. Their Jewish friend gets involved in the Polish resistance. All of them, swept along by the tide of moral degeneracy, are inadvertently tainted by guilt to some degree. Any of these characters could have been the grandparents of today's young Germans.

Despite the programme-makers' stated aim of encouraging families to talk together about their own stories, I was a little surprised that this particular drama, with its rather unconvincing plot and, to me, rather passé message, provoked the huge public debates it did, both in Germany and around the world. But, viewed by 7 million Germans and garlanded with awards, it could not be ignored. It gave young Germans permission to ask soul-searching questions of their families and themselves – What did you do? What would I have done? – and created a climate in which their older relatives needed to engage and try to answer them.

In the light of Germany's advanced and mature culture of remembrance and atonement, its ongoing payment of reparations to victims of the Nazi regime and its active reconciliation programmes, I had assumed I would be a long way behind Germans in terms of unearthing and airing personal family histories. But I wasn't. While the official silence had been broken in the 1960s, for the most part, the private silence had continued.

Remembering or forgetting events of which you have no personal memories is actually impossible, as is taking responsibility for the fact they happened in the first place. Maybe the real challenge for today's generations is not so much a matter of examining and confronting the hard facts about who did or didn't do what as having open and compassionate discussions about the Third Reich and the Holocaust and dealing with the emotions that surround them. Indeed, learning from the mistakes of previous generations and taking responsibility for making sure that they never happen again is the duty of all of us born after the war.

That was the path I was choosing to take myself: a path of reconciliation. And that, I believe, is the point of remembrance. Because how we remember, and what we remember, of the past shapes the future we create.

25

Penetrating the Fog

There is no greater agony than bearing an untold story inside you.
Maya Angelou, *I Know Why the Caged Bird Sings*

A FRIEND TOLD ME ABOUT a Jewish man she knew: a man of my age who was going through a difficult patch in his life. He was struggling with depression. A swathe of his mother's family had been wiped out in the Holocaust. He felt guilty about being depressed when he had 'so much going for him'.

'I have a duty to be happy,' he said to my friend. That mantra had become the leitmotif of his life. I have a duty to be happy, simply for being alive. Third-generation Holocaust survivor's guilt.

As if hammered out by the keys of some internal typewriter, the headline to my own life appeared in my mind in stark block capitals: I have no right to be happy. There it was at last: the identity of the elusive jailer of my soul. Third-generation German perpetrator's guilt.

The pursuit of happiness is a human right in some cultures. It was defined as such in the American Declaration of Independence and this idea is restated in the United Nations Universal Declaration of Human Rights. But for the troubled Jewish man, the descendant of victims and survivors, it was not a right but a duty. For me, the descendant of perpetrators, it was not a right, either. It was something to be earned. Maybe one day, if you work at it hard enough. In the meantime, it remained a distant hope.

We had both been born bound.

The significance of that Cologne prisoner's depiction of me hauling prisoners out of a hole now seemed obvious.

On the most conscious level, I was trying to pull perpetrators of crimes from the dark chasms into which they had fallen.

On a subconscious level, I was trying to drag the bodies of victims murdered by the Nazis out of the pits into which they had been shot or where they had been dumped.

On an unconscious level, I was trying to lift the trauma and guilt of my German roots out of the darkness and into the light in order to heal my immediate family and future generations.

It was a form of repentant restitution. Nobody had spotted the clue at the time of my breakdowns. Very few therapists had started working with transgenerational trauma by the mid-nineties. Such thinking was still in its infancy. From 2009, that all changed with the publication of Sabine Bode's *Kriegsenkel* (*War Grandchildren*).

Although I had become increasingly convinced of the strong connection between the suffocating fog that regularly descended over my world and unresolved experiences and emotions within my family, until this point I'd had no inkling that transmission of trauma or guilt between generations was a recognized phenomenon. Nor any real idea of what exactly it was that was weighing me down.

Interrogating family narratives and prodding at family myths is perilous and painful. To what degree is it your right, or even wise, to rock the boat that you, too, are sitting in? Is it cruel to expose the jagged rubble of a bombed-out childhood, or shame-filled deeds that have since been camouflaged by veneers of goodness or genuine acts of charity and kindness? Who are we to pick at the wounds of others when we don't know the full extent of the trauma behind them? And what kind of trauma are we inflicting on others, and possibly ourselves, by uncovering acts that rightly deserve condemnation, disgust and rejection? How are we going to work out the best way to live with the knowledge we uncover?

I didn't have any answers. I just knew I had felt an existential necessity to rock my own family boat and ask difficult questions. I was lucky. My relatives had never been consciously resistant. They willingly offered me the truth as they understood it. It was, however, in the pages of *Kriegsenkel* that I found many of my questions answered.

For Sabine Bode, the most surprising aspect of her research into the 'war children' was the number of 'war grandchildren' who had got in touch with her. Born between 1960 and 1975, the third generation described lives into which the war seeped like a mist, often leaving them mirroring or re-enacting their parents' experiences of homelessness and uprootedness, or the ineradicable fears that lurked behind their emotional unavailability or façades of strength. Many mentioned confusion over their identity and a constant pressure to achieve combined with a sense of having to make amends for their parents.

Like the unstopping of a dam, other authors followed suit, flooding the German market with books offering a catalogue of witness testimonies to the now widely known and accepted concept of a *Gefühlserbschaft* or *emotionales*

Erbe – an emotional inheritance, also known as the transgenerational or intergenerational transmission of unresolved emotions. I ordered one after another and devoured them. Listing the symptoms of both war children and war grandchildren, I pinned them on to an imaginary display board in my mind, like police evidence in a TV drama.

There was no doubt about it: as the fog shrouding postwar Germans lifted, it revealed the extraordinary climate in which they had been living.

And I could relate to it all.

Drawing on other sources, I gradually built up a clearer picture of the 'fog children', as the 2015 book *Nebelkinder* dubbed the afflicted members of this third generation of Germans, with whom I had so much in common, as if we were siblings separated at birth who'd never met. Their childhoods in Germany with two German parents had been more extreme than mine. They had grown up in toxic environments with no apparent history, their family roots often lying in some far-off, inaccessible land in the east from which they had fled or been expelled. By the sixties and seventies, when they were born, the recent past was fading into a new normality in which the aberration of living alongside the remains of bunkers and explosive munitions factories and concentration camps, or the oddness of trees growing out of the roofs of houses which people had been inhabiting since 1945, went unremarked upon while parents directed their attention to leading simple, quiet and easy lives.

Petit bourgeois values of little houses, gardens, pot plants on net-curtained windowsills and shiny cars had replaced the dizzying heights of the Nazi ideology and deprivations of the war years. Grandparents who had once complained endlessly among themselves about their plight had fallen silent. How could you complain about your lost farm in East Prussia when your own people were responsible for genocide? How could you give voice to your experiences of the low-flying air attacks, the rapes and the bombs, when your brother, father or grandfather had participated in similar atrocities abroad? How could you speak of your former fantasies of Germany's greatness and the right to restore its wealth and give back jobs to the German people? How could you admit to having blamed the Jews for all Germany's ills or having believed in the ideals of striving for the perfection of a superior Aryan race? How could you talk about yourself as an individual at all, having learned to ignore your own needs in favour of *das Volk*?

In contrast to the second generation, the fathers of the third generation were neither SS officers nor Nazis. They had been children in the war and were now living in a new society. No one wanted to reopen the past – there was just too much at stake. Family secrets were kept to try to protect the children from the hideousness of their own history. For many war grandchildren there was no indication at all that some things in their family narratives didn't quite add up. And in many families, there were no obvious dramas, either. Often it was only the stories of their grandfathers' times as prisoners of war that were told.

My German contemporaries existed in a nebulous atmosphere of silent lies and cover-ups. But they could *feel* the grey voids buried in their parents' psyches and the lingering insecurities caused by the destruction of their own worlds as children. They could feel their parents' vulnerability or neediness and tried to help them. And they could feel that dark, underlying forces were at play in their lives. But, unconfident in their own perceptions, they couldn't name them. It was what wasn't being said that disturbed them most.

Parents scarred by childhood memories of carts falling through ice, of low-flying Soviet planes bombing processions of human beings on the march and of dead relatives left by the roadside were focused on rebuilding the safe homes they had lost. They managed their lifelong homesickness without help but were often unable to instil a sense of trust and orientation in their offspring.

There was little scope for self-development. The children talked of feeling loved but never being encouraged to pursue their own interests or even further education. The emphasis was on establishing the same financial security and stability for themselves. The subliminal message transmitted by a father might be 'Don't make me feel even more inferior by overtaking me' and, by a mother, 'If you don't keep up the traditions of my homeland, who will?' Thus the fog children erected barriers to their own success and often failed to find for themselves the sense of home and belonging that still eluded their parents.

The zeitgeist of the seventies and eighties was all about self-realization, self-reinvention and reaching for the stars. But not really knowing who they were prevented them from reaching their potential. In their thirties, they assumed they were just late developers but, once they hit their forties, they couldn't reassure themselves with that line any longer. They often reproached themselves: 'Why are you like this? You didn't even experience anything bad. Your claims have no weight, you are just a failure!'

One war grandchild interviewed appeared to have it

all – a good job, dream apartment, a loving partner, expensive holidays – and yet a voice inside his head constantly undermined his success. 'It's too much,' it insisted. 'It's all too good. You are not entitled to it.'

I have no right to be happy.

People who were strong, motivated and capable, who seemed made for positions of leadership, succumbed to depression, addictions, failing relationships, burn-out, broken careers or life paths, identity crises, homelessness and a general sense of being lost. Some even to suicide. A number of those who'd had to parent their own parents had grown up feeling overstretched and full of self-doubt. Already as children they had achieved a huge amount, yet they were left with a sense of failure because they'd been unable to save their parents.

I thought back to my teenage days, lying on my bed staring at the photograph of my mother, longing to rescue her from herself, blaming myself that I couldn't. As for that list of symptoms: well, I could tick them off one by one.

The parents, the now grown-up war children, expected such troubles to simply disappear over time. They might brush them off with the same 'it's normal, get over it' attitude they had been brought up with, just as my mother had brushed off my eating disorder. Or they might chastise their children, reminding them of how fortunate they were to have had it so much better. Which was, of course, true, at least in terms of security, material wealth and opportunities.

Many of the war grandchildren complained of having no emotional access to their parents, experiencing their numbness as coldness and lack of empathy. Others spoke of their parents' incomprehensible behaviour: inattentiveness, inflexible opinions, extreme need for security and total lack of interest in the contemporary world. Often the parental voice became part of a negative inner dialogue, a putter-down that grew into a domineering monster: 'You couldn't do that anyway, others can do it much better, you're bound to mess it up.' Without the encouragement and confidence of their parents and with the focus on weaknesses, mistakes and failures, every aspect of life became heavier and harder.

But small children are generally reluctant to criticize their parents because of their fear of abandonment. Their loyalty and protectiveness stop them from asking difficult questions, sometimes to the detriment of their own development. Instead they find fault with themselves, just as I had done. Or they live the life their parents want for them, often the one their mothers and fathers wished they had lived for themselves. Many of the third generation felt they needed to do this in order to be loved.

Others couldn't successfully separate themselves from their parents, feeling guilty or disloyal for leaving them to their damaged lives. Or unconsciously re-enacted their experiences in desperate attempts to fix them, like a young journalist I once read about who became obsessed with telling the stories of refugee children from Afghanistan or Serbia and tirelessly drawing attention to their plight. Until she burned out. It dawned on her only years later that her inner compulsion was driven by her mother's traumatic flight from the Soviets.

I could barely believe what I was discovering. It was as if I was reading the story of my own life written by strangers.

There were also accounts of grandchildren unconsciously taking on the guilt of a Nazi grandparent who had never talked about their past, which impelled them to attempt to compensate by giving more to others, to the world, in order to earn their right to happiness. It merely left them feeling disappointed, used or exhausted, perhaps because the cause of the guilt was not a part of the world around them.

In some cases, war grandchildren were so tormented by the idea that they might have inherited a violent or cruel streak that they punished themselves for crimes their grandparents committed, or might have committed. Wasn't that exactly what I had been doing with my unhealthy eating habits, my ultimate rejection of loving relationships and my relentless need to work myself to the point of burnout?

Perhaps the most tragic manifestation was found in those who, terrified by the possibility that such a capacity for evil could in some way be hereditary or contagious, recoiled completely from their own genes. For fear of contaminating their fellow human beings or passing on those genes, they withdrew, choosing to live alone and not to have children.

Once in therapy, war grandchildren have revealed their need to separate from their parents' war stories in order to establish their own identities. And have talked about how they were learning to recognize and express their own feelings without burdening their parents.

At breakneck speed, this sudden blizzard of accounts that resonated so strongly with my own experiences was unravelling the tight knots of my psyche, emptying out the rucksack, confronting the monster, escaping the fox's dell and ripping through all the other metaphors I'd used to try to comprehend the parts of myself that felt like alien components. When it subsided and the air cleared, I saw how my whole life had assumed a new shape.

After so many years of feeling isolated in my own

madness and guilty for being so screwed up with no apparent cause, I had found a community of people with similar experiences and symptoms. Finally, I could talk openly about these facets of myself as objective phenomena rather than just in terms of personal fucked-upedness. By owning and naming them, I could at last answer peoples' baffled questions: why do *you* feel guilty? Do you always have to think so deeply about things?

My inexplicable experiences now had a substance that no one had ever previously been able to attribute to them. No relative, no therapist, philosopher or teacher. How could they have? My particular emotional inheritance was primarily a non-Jewish German war grandchild thing. And we had all reached our forties before any of our stories had been sought out and collated.

It is not surprising that clinicians today see the effects of trauma with great frequency. Trauma and guilt are ever-present in our world. They always have been and always will be. The premise that these effects can be transmitted is also gaining traction in some professions.

In their respective books *It Didn't Start With You* and *Lost in Transmission,* Mark Wolynn and M. Gerard Fromm (and his co-authors) describe the process of transgenerational transmission as one generation's psychological wound or baggage being passed to the next. The offspring are then left to wrestle with it and find ways of bringing its full, tragic story to light without either re-triggering the trauma in their parents or breaking away from the family.

This baggage may include a sense of duty to carry out a task, such as avenging a humiliation or apologizing for a crime. It is possible, I read, that the burden of both bearing and communicating the grief of a forebear will fall on one child within a family.

This was incredible. It confirmed for me everything I had suspected, or felt, had fallen on me.

It also offered an explanation as to why my siblings and cousins were not compelled in the same way as I was to try to uncover the truths of our family history. But how exactly can we carry the memory of events and traumas that happened before we were born? Where do we carry them – in our psyches, our cells, our bones?

The theory is that a traumatic memory is self-contained and ever-present, its intensity immutable and unaltered by the passage of time. Because trauma destroys the capacity to cognize, to create symbols or memories, it rips a hole in the psyche, which others, particularly those of the next generation, experience as a form of deadness, a sense that something good has been destroyed.

It is posited that there are various mechanisms by which transgenerational trauma can occur. One is known as primitive identification, whereby a child unconsciously assimilates a parent's self-image in an attempt to heal the parent.

Another is deposited representation, whereby the parent unconsciously forces aspects of themselves on to the child, presenting it with specific tasks to perform. Thus the child becomes a depository for the parent's unprocessed shame, rage and helplessness and is forced to deal with these. This is not about bad parenting but about trauma and family efforts to cope with it. Nevertheless, there is a heavy impact on the child's sense of identity: profound confusion, a sense of being completely lost, of something being held back. A terrible knowing, yet not knowing.

'I drank up her feelings with her mother's milk.' I remembered writing this in my diary years before. Now it was becoming clearer what those feelings might have been and just how pertinent the timing of my birth had been to my entanglement in my mother's psyche. While she was pregnant with me, her father was confined to his bed overlooking the lake, heaving his last rattling breaths through congested lungs. Unable to travel to visit him, she must have felt a cocktail of ambivalence, guilt, judgement, shame, sadness and love when he died. Her thoughts of the father who had been absent, heroic, humiliated, vilified and, finally, broken, might have stirred her own wartime memories and traumas which, in turn, may have blended with her joy and excitement at the impending birth of her new baby. All these conflicting emotions would have danced through her body, flavouring her milk like the chemicals released into the bodies of stressed animals. And I drank it all up.

Dr Fromm affirmed that working through transmission is indeed painful, at times seemingly unbearably so, for it demands a process of separation, a breaking of an existing emotional chain. 'Something life-defining and deeply intimate is over,' he wrote, speaking to my own agonizing disentanglement from my mother. Often this involves a form of identity crisis as the child speaks to what their parent could not and comes to recognize how their own experience has been partly and unconsciously dictated by the task of carrying their parent's (or grandparent's) injury into the future. The hope is that eventually they come to understand how, by lifting the trauma out of the darkness of unconsciousness and into the light, they will help to prevent it being passed down to future generations.

I slumped back in my chair, trying to absorb these words which so precisely summed up what appeared to have been my life's task. All this time I had been navigating a precarious terrain of family loyalties in the midst of this fog, dodging trigger points as if they were mines. Now, through the lens of this new information, I could finally see what it was I had been trying to wrestle myself free from.

I recognized that it was shame that had lurked around corners for me, seizing any opportunity to capture and envelop me in its heavy cloak. Shame was the embarrassment and humiliation I felt when my friends turned and laughed at me. Not at my funny calamine-smeared face, but at my shameful 'bloody Kraut' roots. Shame was all my former bodily self-disgust, fears of rejection and impulse to hide packaged together to sit like lead in my psyche, drip-feeding me poison: you should have done better, given more, or less; spoken less, or more; not laughed, or laughed. Shame had driven me to pursue what I saw as paths of goodness or right-ness. It had made me angry. It had fuelled a desire to destroy – my artworks, my relationships, myself – and to become invisible, to starve and disappear, leaving no trace of myself. No children to continue my lineage. It had pushed me back down into the dark, convincing me that I was not worthy of love. Or even, at times, life.

This shame couldn't be laid in its entirety at the door of what my grandfather had done in the war or the wider deeds of the Wehrmacht. It was his personal downfall that emerged for me as the prime trauma within our family: a huge, ignored wound that suppurated on somewhere in all of our psyches.

I could see how unbearable it must have been for my mother to remember her father as a broken man. That was why the picture of him she kept on her desk showed him at the peak of his military career. That was maybe why she had so little tolerance for weakness and failure in others. It reminded her of him.

I wondered about my brother. As a child, he had felt proud of his grandfather, the talented athlete and artillerist. Maybe he had admired him, or felt an affinity with him, as one of few men in a family top-heavy with females. Had Christopher withdrawn out of an unconscious loyalty to the man and soldier who had been diminished in the eyes of the rest of the family, and indeed the world? Perhaps he had used alcohol in the same way as I had used food and work to escape feelings he couldn't comprehend, control or cope with.

It was, self-evidently, not cool to have a German general as a father or grandfather in the Britain of the 1960s, 1970s or 1980s. He was the disgraced enemy. It was the humiliation he had endured at the hands of the British that had destroyed him; the shame of being a war criminal in the eyes of the world.

And it was this unprocessed sense of shame that had been passed on, like genes, to his grandchildren. To me.

But there was something else, too.

I still had a sense of having come up against something hard, strong and cold, in both my mother and myself. Was it conceivable that, as well as carrying my grandfather's shame and absorbing my mother's unprocessed trauma, I had also clashed with the remnants of her childhood Nazi indoctrination? After all, how do you unlearn what has been drummed into you in your earliest years? Is it even possible? Or would such warped lessons irrevocably remain within the foundations of your mind, informing your adult beliefs while coming into conflict with what you were now told you should be thinking? Hitler himself had said: 'These young people will learn nothing else but how to think German and act German . . . And they will never be free again, not in their whole lives.'

Could it be that the emotional void into which I had so often fallen was the result of an education that had forced children to deny their very souls? Was this behind the combination of my mother's outer strength and the inner vulnerability from which I had tried so desperately to save her? Had all her children needed to develop strong wills and defences against her strict efforts to keep us in line? And did my unconventionality clash with an ingrained fear of being different?

Maybe my messy artistic tendencies, with their emphasis on dreaming, spontaneity and play, were a dangerous deviation from the classical order and traditional aesthetic she had been taught defined 'real' art. Maybe my boyfriends were considered 'wrong' for me because they didn't measure up to the Aryan ideal. Did we fight because my choices made her feel unacceptable? Or did she fear that I would be unacceptable?

I wondered whether the wider family's attitudes to food and body shape stemmed from the strivings for physical perfection inculcated in the Hitler Youth. Whether the apparent beliefs in an objective 'right way' to be or act were born of the Nazis' demands for unquestioning adherence to what were presented as ultimate 'truths'. And whether the inability to admit mistakes came from the need to be right in order to exist.

Then there was the family penchant for unstoppable hard work and self-sacrifice – idleness was unthinkable. Were these the outcome of an indoctrination that had calcified the soft souls of the individual until they were 'hard as Krupp's steel'? My mother was the least hypochondriac person I knew, allowing symptoms of illness, like the precursors of her late-onset Type 1 diabetes, to reach life-threatening levels before even mentioning she was feeling unwell. I knew stoicism was widely typical of the older generation, but might this have been the result of having been trained as a child to suffer pain? Or was it a subconscious fear that any admission of weakness or imperfection would be frowned upon, or even dangerous?

I shuddered at the idea that I may have stumbled on the limb of something much more concerning than any transmission of trauma or guilt. Even though I didn't want to admit it, I saw traces in myself of those traits I had seen in my mother. Ghostly shadows of judgements I neither believed nor wanted inhabited my mind, too.

It would not be until 2016, on a visit to the Nazi party rally grounds in Nuremburg, where Hitler had delivered his hypnotic sermons of hate in the 1930s, that I felt the full force of this potential legacy. As I stepped on to the unassuming Führer's rostrum and gazed out over the vast parkland that had once held rapt audiences in the hundreds of thousands, my body was engulfed by terror. I felt sick. Never have I stood in such a potent place as that small platform from which Hitler had fired his poison arrows into the minds and hearts of ordinary Germans. Never had I been able to visual-ize the scale of the Nazi movement in all its ugly, popular power with such devastating clarity.

'And they will never be free again, not in their whole lives.' Maybe these were the only true words Hitler ever uttered. But if there was a way to step out of that bastard's shadow, I would find it.

In an almost trance-like state of relief mixed with exhaus-tion, I felt my fox slink off to allow me to clamber up the leafy banks of the dark dell. He had been a guardian rather than a malevolent jailer after all, deputed to keep me search-ing the undergrowth until I had finally understood what was hidden there and found a way to release it.

For a good few days after working all this out, I stag-gered around, my eyes adjusting to the bright sunlight as all that I had missed out on came into devastating focus. My soul exploded in a kaleidoscope of emotions. I cried a lot, above all for my mother and her suffering, but also for the child I had been, trying to protect and defend her while struggling with a gang of monsters I couldn't deal with alone.

A period of mourning followed for the life I had never had. I grieved for the amount of time, energy and money I'd had to spend sorting it out. For the wasted opportunities for joy or love, the long months lost to depression. 'And it wasn't even really "my" stuff!' I wrote indignantly in my diary. A part of me felt angry. Not with anybody in particular, just at how comprehensively all this family baggage had sabotaged my character and my life.

I thought of all the therapies I had tried over the years, the depths of the despair into which I had sunk. No wonder

I had fought with my mother; no wonder I hadn't been able to manifest some of my dreams or ideas in the outer world. So much of my energy and attention had been directed at dealing with these ... 'things'. For as long as I'd been unable to name them, they had survived. At times they had taken over, but always, like mute, masked kidnappers, without identifying themselves or expressing their demands.

I could not, I reasoned, ever have been accused of not trying to beat my demons. I'd spent my whole life trying to find out who they were, what they were, what they wanted. Now, my self-absorption had paid off. It now looked to me more like the dogged pursuit of a line of inquiry than self-indulgent navel-gazing. I had dug up the knotted root of the suffocating rogue plant. Finally, I could breathe.

As the weeks wore on, I came to see those demons as pale, defeated, hollow-eyed terrorists, exhumed from their hide-outs. Am I free of them just because I have looked them in the eye? Should I now just walk away, leaving them to wither? How could I prevent them from coming back to haunt me? I remembered how inmates released from the prison in Cologne had emerged from their sentences pasty-faced and disorien-tated. They may have been free of the prison walls but they were far from free of themselves or of the revolving door that lay in wait to spin them back inside. I thought of the potential I had seen in them and tried to draw out, regardless of the crimes they had committed. And how their long-term reha-bilitation depended on further authentic communication, non-judgement and encouragement. Maybe I could do the same for my motley crew of inner assassins: nurture them back to health and transform them into redemptive forces for good.

I knew that extricating them from my own internal

architecture would be like operating on a cancer, removing a foreign body that had fed off me while killing me. I wondered who I would be without them. Which aspects of my character would be left? I was reminded of the moment in the film about the life of the British politician Mo Mowlam when she realizes that much of the endearing outspokenness people had come to love her for might actually have been a product of the brain tumour that would take her life.

I found that, though there was plenty of literature on trauma recovery, there was far less on freeing oneself from traumatic inheritances. All this was such a recent field of research. But, as I would discover, I had already equipped myself with the necessary tools and been practising the relevant techniques. I was well on my way to freedom.

26

Written into the Body

*It is through Science we prove, but through
intuition that we discover.*

Henri Poincaré, *Science and Method*

IN THE SPRING OF 2015, my beloved father finally died after a protracted battle with prostate cancer. His death left a huge void. He had been a gentleman from almost every angle: calm, mild, measured, intelligent, fair, honest, generous, funny and kind. His mind, like his life, was uncluttered, his philosophy simple. He just wanted to do what was right.

Eleven months later, my mother had a massive stroke. The previous week, as if pre-empting hers, my body had displayed its own symptoms – a tingling left arm and numbness in the left side of my face – a false, stress-related alarm for me but not for her. My legs buckled in grief when I saw her lying in the hospital, bruised and broken from her fall, taped to machines and fighting for her life while her damaged brain let go of its ability to speak – in English, at least. A little German was all she had at first. My siblings and I sat with her every day as friends queued up to help.

Her recovery was painfully slow and incomplete. She became a beautiful bird with tattered feathers and a broken wing, wholly dependent on help in every aspect of her life. Her many friends rallied with flowers, visits and generous offers of support and we eventually got her home with a series of live-in carers. Seeing her so diminished and depressed, all I wanted to do was rock her in my arms and tell her it would be all right.

It was around this time that I was introduced, at a party, to a new area of genetics in which scientists have been uncovering another mechanism for potential transgenerational transmission: epigenetics. The idea is controversial and goes against scientific convention, but I found it worth exploring.

I tend to look upon science as the more serious, thorough, slightly spoilsport older brother of the more instinctive domains of emotion, faith and intuition. Yet science, with all its brilliance, at times seems to lumber behind the teachings of religion, spirituality, art and psychology, weighed down by the instruments on which it relies to measure, quantify, explain and control human beings and the world. Western society has long looked to science for guidance, trusting its more sclerotic, proof-led conclusions while sometimes missing human common sense that needs no proof because it is simply 'known'. When left-brain science converges with right-brain thinking, even what sceptics have casually dismissed as 'hippy-dippy nonsense' gains traction and a nod from science is seen as a green light for further research and action. It is a frustratingly slow process for those who have already long perceived an instinctive validation.

The idea of epigenetics, of a chemical tag attaching to our DNA and telling our genes how to behave, is not entirely new: the term was first coined in 1942. But between 2013 and 2015 a flurry of articles was reporting the results of recent research. The way I understood it initially was that an unresolved experience can piggyback on to a gene, like a little knapsack, and be passed on to the next generation to influence certain behavioural responses. The biology is, of course, more complex.

The epigenome – from the Greek *'epi'*, meaning 'above', and 'genome', or DNA, the complete set of genetic material we inherit from our ancestors – consists of a network of chemical compounds that modify, or mark, the genome in a way that basically tells it what to do and where and when to do it. With the impact of traumatic experiences, certain parts of the DNA are activated or deactivated like switches.

There are epigenetic mechanisms in every cell: in the brain, in the skin, even in the blood, says Isabelle Mansuy, professor in neuroepigenetics at the Institute for Brain Research at the Eidgenössische Technischen Hochschule in Zurich. Unlike DNA, which is fixed for life, the surrounding epigenome is flexible and, without altering the DNA sequence, plays a role in determining which genes are active in a particular cell, shaping the physical structure of the genome and regulating or programming the expression, development and suppression of specific genes.

For decades it was thought that whatever epigenetic marks we accrue over a lifetime (different cells have different epigenetic marks) were erased and that a new embryo's epigenome was completely reprogrammed from scratch in the womb, producing offspring that were human blank slates. But it turns out this isn't completely true. Epigenetic research suggests that while the fundamental genetic code remains unchanged, some features resist reprogramming. Whether this is by design or the result of faulty erasure isn't yet known.

Studies show that marks left by the life experiences of our forebears affect how cells read genes. In other words, certain experiences can cause genes to become active or dormant, thereby potentially affecting the response of a descendant to particular situations, noises, smells and so forth. Epigenetics might explain a propensity for addiction and violence, or why some people overreact or under-react to stress and fear. But epigenetic changes are not necessarily negative. They increase the range of possible biological responses and coping strategies and often serve to prepare the next generation for life in the kind of environment experienced by their parents, for example, to deal with extreme cold or hunger. Increased rates of coronary heart disease and obesity have been noted in people born during the period of the Dutch famine of 1944 and 1945 and it has been suggested that the latter condition may be due to an inherited epigenetic modification programming the person to eat as much as they can to build up fat reserves while they have access to food in readiness for times when they will not.

The notion of the instruction and regulation of the genome by the epigenome offers an interesting perspective on genetics. In recent decades, a number of research projects have produced extraordinary evidence of the potential intergenerational transference of stress and trauma.

In an oft-cited study in Atlanta in 2013, scientists exposed mice to the scent of cherry blossom and then gave them electric shocks. The mice were allowed to breed, and when their progeny were exposed to the same smell, many reacted to it, as, in turn, did a number of their offspring, even though none of these individuals had been subjected to electric shocks. Structural changes to the area of the brain used to detect odour found in the original mice were also seen in the subsequent generations. The DNA of the shocked mice also exhibited chemical changes, known as epigenetic methylation, affecting the gene responsible for detecting odour. This indicates not that fear itself is being carried down the generations, but that fear of a scent in one generation leads to a sensitivity to the same scent in the next.

Similarly, in experiments with rats in which pups were separated from their mothers, the same behavioural changes manifested as far as the grandchildren, even though they hadn't experienced any trauma. It was as if a 'memory' was being passed on to their descendants.

Neuroscientist and epigeneticist Rachel Yehuda, one of the pioneers of research into how the effects of cataclysmic events in humans can be biologically transmitted to the next generation, discovered in one study that the children of Holocaust survivors had lower levels than their peers of cortisol, a hormone that helps the body return to normal after trauma. Quite why trauma survivors produce less cortisol is not fully understood, but very similar profiles have been reported in Vietnam veterans and infants born to mothers with PTSD as a result of the 2001 terrorist attack on New York who were pregnant at the time, suggesting the presence of trauma effects transmitted via epigenetic mechanisms.

Evidence that environmental influences such as diet, toxins, stress, trauma and war leave their mark on the genes of the next generations continues to mount. Both mothers and fathers can provide mechanisms for transmission of adult trauma effects. If a boy is traumatized before puberty, for example, epigenetic changes caused by the way he responds are passed on via his sperm. A pregnant female carrying a female foetus of twenty weeks or more will pass on her epigenetic tags to the eggs of the foetus.

But while the traumas we inherit or experience can

create a legacy of distress or vulnerability, they can also forge strength and resilience. Traumatic responses are first and foremost manifestations of the survival instinct. Indeed, every emotion – even a 'negative' one like shame – is adaptable and can be harnessed to beneficial and positive effect. New environments can result in new changes and, more importantly, not all epigenetic alterations are irreversible.

Professor Yehuda has described how the recognition of PTSD led to the acknowledgement that the repercussions of trauma don't all simply go away. She believes that further exploration of epigenetics will show us just how enduring they may be, and how they can be treated in subsequent generations. 'We're just starting to understand that just because you're born with a certain set of genes, you're not in a biological prison as a result of those genes. That changes can be made to how those genes function.'

We know that none of us is controlled by our genetic make-up. And we now know that our genetic 'read-out' – which genes are turned on and off by the epigenome – is determined primarily by our thoughts, attitudes and perceptions. Professor Isabelle Mansuy takes a similarly upbeat view. She sees epigenetics as opening the door to a whole new way of thinking that could potentially give us greater control over who we are and how healthy we want to be. 'We can change ourselves considerably and the changes can make us stronger, more strategic or efficient when faced with another difficult situation.'

Whether science can prove the theories behind epigenetics will only emerge with time and further research. For me personally, knowing the exact nature of the transmission of my inherited trauma is not important. Grasping the dynamics of the psychological transmission of trauma and the basics of epigenetics has been hugely valuable in enabling me to rationalize and name some of the difficulties I experienced. But for me, it is enough to have confirmation that by some means, whether psychological, spiritual, emotional or genetic, my body or psyche received and carried a residual impact of some of the unresolved traumas or issues of my forebears.

None the less, given the enormous ramifications of world events past and present – war, oppression, slavery, displacement, genocide, ethnic cleansing, natural disasters, the global COVID-19 pandemic – it is strange that epigenetics is not taken more seriously and better researched. In our communities we are dealing with staggering levels of domestic violence, child abuse and abandonment, rapes and murders. We are well aware of how severe the results of adverse childhood experiences (ACEs), trauma and inherited trauma can be: depression, cognitive deficits, heightened stress, anxiety, addiction, aggression, suicide. We know, too, the profound effects that both trauma and healing have not just on individuals but on societal consciousness.

As Marcus Pembrey at University of Bristol declares in an article in the *New Scientist:* 'It is high time public-health researchers took human transgenerational responses seriously.'

27

Let's Talk About It

Not everything that is faced can be changed, but
nothing can be changed until it is faced.

James Baldwin, 'As Much Truth as One Can Bear',
The New York Times Book Review, 1962

THERE IS NO SINGLE way to untangle oneself from the knotted mesh of an emotional legacy of unprocessed trauma, guilt or shame. But, regardless of whether we understand it as a spiritual wound, a family or national inheritance or an epigenetic transmission, there is broad consensus both on its general features – whether individual, historical, collective or intergenerational – and the conditions that can assist in healing us.

In my experience, healing is not a linear process but a continuing journey in which certain elements appear crucial. Gaining awareness of the nature of the invisible burden you have inherited is possibly the first step, followed by finding ways to gently begin to feel and process the impact that it has had on you. Sharing the load with trusted people can help dissolve the secrecy and shame. And, when you are ready, starting to find the gifts in the wounds. For there can be many.

In early 2016, as part of the Bristol Festival of Ideas, I took part in a panel discussion about surviving intergenerational trauma. It was organized by the Forgiveness Project, a charity that shares restorative stories of both victims or survivors and perpetrators as a way of transforming lives through encouraging empathy, tolerance and hope. It is an approach I deeply admire. There were three of us, each representing a different generation: a British survivor of a Second World War Japanese POW camp, a second-generation child of Jewish Holocaust victims and survivors and me, the grandchild of a Wehrmacht general. Two 'victims,' one 'perpetrator'. I was struck by the similarities between the symptoms of the Jewish panellist's transmitted inheritance and my own. But there was one stark difference. Where I had felt the dark presence of something that wasn't mine, she had experienced darkness as an absence, a black hole in the constellation of her family.

As we have seen, trauma is trauma, however big or small. The same goes for shame. The urgent need of the brain to suppress the traumatic event through forgetting it or self-blame can lead to trapped, frozen energy; blocked or numbed bodily feelings; reactiveness, defensiveness and a loss of connection to oneself, to others, to nature, to one's spiritual side, to life itself. But the body does not forget. Emotions demand to be felt and nature's purpose is to finish cycles of experience like grief or shock. Life wants to pulse and flow again.

To allow this to happen, we need safe spaces in the 'here and now', as opposed to the 'there and then', where the trauma was: spaces where we can acknowledge the force of what has taken place and understand the personal impact of an event; to feel what was cut off in the unconscious and to approach in a new way whatever overwhelmed us, integrating and weaving it into consciousness.

Drugs have always been used to deal with traumatic

stress. Every culture and generation has its preferred option – alcohol, Valium, cannabis, opium, Temazepam – to numb or escape their pain. But recreational or prescription drugs can temporarily block, distract from or control unwanted feelings and behaviour, they can't 'cure' trauma. Pharmaceuticals and talking therapies certainly have their place, although ultimately, medication addresses symptoms and not causes. Nothing can change what was, but multiple approaches have developed to change what is.

The PTSD specialist and author of *The Body Keeps the Score,* Bessel van der Kolk describes how, after the attacks on the World Trade Center in 2001, the only two forms of trauma treatment recommended by the US National Institutes of Health and others were various types of psychoanalytic therapy and cognitive behavioural therapy (CBT). But nobody really took these up. Most turned to acupuncture, massage, yoga and eye movement desensitization and reprocessing (EMDR), in that order: all interventions that focus on relieving the physical burdens generated by trauma. For many practitioners, then, the key to healing lies in our own bodies.

Peter Levine, the founder and pioneer of Somatic Experiencing, a form of body psychotherapy developed in the 1970s, concentrates on the exact observation of the body and the internal manifestations of trauma – not least the nervous system, skin temperature, rates of breathing, pulse, blinking and head movement, positions of hands and legs, facial expressions, tone of voice, content of words.

Richard Schwartz's Internal Family Systems Therapy (IFS), developed in the 1980s, is based on the idea that the mind of each of us is like a family in which different members have different levels of maturity, excitability, wisdom and pain. As in Bert Hellinger's family constellation work, each 'family member' stands in relation to and affects each of the others. Schwartz's method seeks to revive and reintegrate parts that have been split off or frozen by trauma.

Some techniques, like yoga, focus on breathing to calm down the physiological chaos inside us by relaxing the physical tensions in the body created by persistently bracing ourselves against danger. Meditation and mindfulness exercises draw the attention to the present moment.

For those with spiritual leanings, rituals, mantras and healing visualizations can activate the same regions of the brain associated with wellbeing and positive emotion and can, with practice, also create new neural pathways.

The arts are a proven therapeutic conduit for self-expression and the externalization of inner landscapes. The possibilities offered by a blank page or empty floor space encourage the movement of frozen parts of the mind, body and soul in all directions. They bring to the surface the beauty in the full spectrum of emotional weather, even the darkest storms, and invite exploration of ways to move through and beyond fear without getting overwhelmed or stuck.

Studies around the world consistently show that writing or journalling about upsetting events improves physical and mental health. Writing can be instrumental in naming the trauma and in helping to organize thoughts, resolve conflicts and find meaning in experiences. Being able to describe a complex feeling and having our feelings listened to and understood lights up our limbic brain and changes the physiology of the brain.

The deepest pain in us is mute. The results witnessed by

artists of all disciplines working with trauma victims, and numerous other reports and observations, attest to how effective art is in counteracting verbal inarticulacy.

A slightly different approach is required when it comes to healing intergenerational trauma. The distance between the first-hand experience and the lingering ripples of transference tends to produce more subtle symptoms and often there is no perpetrator to forgive because we are not the direct victims. Thomas Hübl, author of *Healing Collective Trauma*, compares inherited or collective trauma to karma. Both are packages of past life that are unprocessed and therefore create the conditions into which we are born. Until we can integrate them into our present, they will, unbeknownst to us, run our lives. Every time a family pathology is allowed to rumble on through a generation, the inability or refusal to name it will fell individuals and destroy lives. It takes just one person to find the courage to turn round, confront it and stop it in its tracks for peace to spread, not only back to the ancestors but forwards to the children who follow.

The trauma or wrongdoing first have to be discovered. But, as Mark Wolynn says, they leave a breadcrumb trail of clues that can lead back through our family history.

I can now clearly see my own breadcrumb trail.

It began with that childhood vision of my grandfather handing me a baton, an almost literal metaphor for the delegation of an unfinished task.

Then came my recurring nightmare of being trapped in that dark dell guarded by a wily fox. The worst part – that no one had noticed I was missing – may have been an echo of the desperation felt by my grandfather, and many others, in situations where a person disappears and nobody knows what has happened to them. Being forgotten is a form of ceasing to exist. Working with the imagery and related emotions of the dream had enabled me to enter into dialogue with my unconscious and bring to light what had been held in darkness, a process Carl Jung called 'active imagination'.

The incomprehensible image that had surfaced during the Sydney workshop of the unknown soldier who had somehow harmed me; my distressed response to the film *Downfall*; the revelation of unhealthy dynamics in the family constellation exercise all pointed to the source of the trauma.

Other clues came in my unanticipated visceral reactions to certain sites where history or suffering is etched into the landscape, in Germany, in Poland, in Russia. Sites where the past broke into the present begging to be noticed, liberated, healed. My symptoms – the eating disorder and depressions – were signposts to something I couldn't see. I feel so grateful that I was able to keep alive the tiny flame of determination not to give up searching for their causes, even while contemplating the ultimate self-destruction, suicide. It wasn't strength. I put much of it down to a form of resilience derived from having been born into a loving family; to stubborn determination; to the kindness and support of special people and to a creative temperament inclined to curiosity and openness to the metaphorical language of the soul.

It was when I actively embarked on my exploration of my family history that my inheritance properly began to dissipate. And in several ways, my personal path of healing parallels Germany's process of *Vergangenheitsbewältigung*, its coming to terms with its history. From the anger and rebellions of students to artists giving expression to the unspeakable, clothing truth in ambiguity and poetry until it was ready to declare itself in spoken words and counter-memorials.

Truth demands to be told. The author and academic Brené Brown says that 'shame cannot survive being spoken ... and being met with empathy'. Talking and sharing with close friends and family helped integrate the wounds into a bigger, more complete picture of myself. I finally came to realize that my traumatic or guilty responses and imprints were not my fault. It wasn't me.

In 2011, as part of my own commitment to speaking out about the unspeakable, I gave my first public talk. It was to pupils at my old school. Telling my story in public reconnected me to the world and my community and set in motion the process of understanding the potential for reconciliation. It was the first of hundreds of illustrated talks I would give, initially in schools and then societies, universities and at a variety of other events across Britain. I speak of the role of the arts in prisons; the Second World War as experienced by an ordinary German family – my family; Germany's postwar process of apology and atonement, its memorial culture and the different ways in which many young Germans deal with their legacy. I am often in awe of how the combination of words and art induces shifts in the audience's understanding of Germans and prisoners alike.

Most people are moved. Others are humbled and shocked. Probably the most common response I receive, whatever the theme, is 'I had no idea.' Talking about difficult events and listening to painful personal stories means getting uncomfortable. It requires courage and a willingness both to speak the truth and to hear it. This can make you feel vulnerable. But not weak. And it seems to open the door to understanding, empathy and reconciliation.

After my talks about Germany, I may be presented with a muttered defence of Bomber Command's devastation of Dresden, a distrustful question on the authenticity of Germany's restitution or doubts about the efficacy of its memorials in the face of the recent big upturn in anti-Semitism. But it is far more common for retired British army officers to approach me with watery eyes and recount a little story of a poignant meeting or friendship with a former foe or a tender declaration that my grandfather would be proud of me. Or a German woman mopping away tears and thanking me for telling her story. Or German sixth-formers confiding their own experiences of shame or a traumatic inheritance. Sometimes Jewish members of societies I have been invited to address have been advised not to attend, only, I have been told, later to regret it. Those who ignore such well-intended cautions frequently seek me out, too, take both my hands in theirs and smile, the kindness in their eyes conveying a thousand unutterable words.

It is an ongoing process, but for a moment, within the duration of the talk, we are united in trying to comprehend the incomprehensible, love the unlovable or forgive the unforgivable.

28

Light in a Tunnel

*Most discoveries even today are a combination
of serendipity and of searching.*

Siddhartha Mukherjee

After a dozen years of research into my German roots
and my grandfather's life, I was ready to turn away
from the past and fully reinhabit my own. A visit from my
Tante Dörli in the late summer of 2017 sowed the seed of a
way of drawing my odyssey to a close. For years she had been
drip-feeding me new publications and relevant articles on
current debate in Germany and discussions with her were
always fascinating and informative. As the youngest child,
she had continued living with her parents at Grödersby after
the war. Now, as we sat on my mother's veranda sipping coffee in the morning sunshine, she talked to me about a trip she
had made to Italy with her parents in 1956, revisiting some of
the scenes of my grandfather's wartime days near Bologna
and Rimini. In the same understated manner in which my
mother had imparted her nuggets of information, she recalled
how her father had often said he would like to spend his last
days there.

I instantly knew this was the place I had been searching
for to lay the ghost of my grandfather to rest. I had never got
round to exploring this area in spite of its huge significance to

378

him and its rare positive associations. Although most of his letters home from between September 1943, when he was relieved of his position in Russia and sent to Italy and February 1945, after he had finished fighting the Allies at Monte Cassino, had been lost, one particular story was preserved in the family collection: the record of an occasion on which he blatantly disobeyed an order.

With the help of Tante Dörli and her diary and photographs from their 1956 holiday, I mapped out a rough

My grandfather (centre) in Italy.

itinerary. I asked Christopher if he would like to come with me. It had been ten years since the trip I'd made to Germany to visit places connected with our family and he had failed to turn up. This time his acceptance was solid and he duly flew over from Saudi Arabia, where he was now living and working, to meet me in the mediaeval town of Ferrara.

Our first port of call was the villa of the Zona family in the little village of Quartesana, a twenty-minute train ride from Ferrara. These were the people with whom my grandfather had been lodging in 1945. His letters describe happy times in their beautiful home and postwar correspondence from Erberto Zona, the patriarch, a well-to-do pharmacist, resound with effusive Italian appreciation of my grandfather

The Zonas and von Graffens (centre) are reunited in Quartesana, 1956.

as 'a man of his word and a lifelong friend'. I knew nothing more about the family than that.

Christopher and I walked down the little road running through Quartesana, less of a village than a cluster of large, derelict villas rising out of the flat landscape. In March 1945, while my grandfather had been based here, it had been badly bombed.

We had two photographs in lieu of a map. One was from my aunt's holiday diary, the other was a still from a video Christopher had found online about the village's many abandoned villas. He had recognized the Zona residence by the shutters and a fanned window above the front door.

Peering through a series of chained iron gates and rusting fences, we eventually spotted the boarded-up ruins of the once magnificent Villa Zona. It was a sad sight, hidden behind overgrown trees and littered with plastic tables, rubbish and an old car. The remnants of my rusty Italian stretched just far enough to ask an old lady pushing a bicycle what had happened to the family. She told us that the daughter had died a few years before and now there was nobody left. I inquired in the local bar as to who might have a key to the gate. Perhaps the police station in the nearby town, the barman suggested, but a phone call there yielded nothing.

I badly wanted to stand on the spot where the two families had posed for the camera during their reunion. With a surprising lack of compunction, Christopher offered to scour the fence for a gap. We found one round the back and made our way to the door, darting between trees and bushes like cartoon villains. Time had not been kind to the villa and swarms of biting midges prevented us from lingering. I quickly performed my earth-and-tobacco ritual while

Christopher smoked an R6 cigarette in his grandfather's honour. Then, our skin already peppered with bites, we clambered back over the fence and pretended to be out for a casual walk.

The following day we headed south to Bellaria, just north of Rimini on the Adriatic coast, where my grandfather had been held prisoner after the war until his transfer to Germany in November 1946. I knew from the address he sent my grandmother that the German soldiers had been housed in the Colonia Roma, a former orphanage and holiday home for the children of railway workers. Trawling through online clues, maps and forums, I discovered some images of this enormous building, right by the sea at Igea Marina. The caption to a YouTube video of a demolition informed me that, having been derelict since 2008, it had been completely torn down in 2014.

On the train to Rimini, I re-read the letters from the first months of his imprisonment, so full of optimism about his prospects and, after six years of almost incessant battle, his enjoyment of days spent playing games, swimming in the sea, collecting shells and eating fresh, delicious fruit.

Christopher and I borrowed battered bicycles from our seafront hotel and rattled our way north along miles of beachfront. I was not hopeful that we would find much. By now, I thought, a new hotel complex would probably have been erected on the site of the demolished Colonia Roma. None the less, I felt nervous and strangely emotional, conscious of a sense of place. I was glad of Christopher's company and his measured, grounded temperament.

As we rounded the final curve of the coastline before the

location, I let out a gasp. There, crouching like a sleeping dinosaur behind some trees, was a massive grey building. It was still standing! Its boarded and broken windows squinted through the foliage like blind eyes. There was no doubt that this was the Colonia Roma. A nearby plaque described its history as a holiday colony for thousands of children from all over Italy from the 1920s until the 1970s, interrupted only by its wartime role as a prison housing over 2,000 German soldiers. That YouTube video must have been a record of the demolition of a different building.

A wire fence prohibited entry but, of course, we had to get up close. Christopher, again a more than willing accomplice, found a breach. Picking our way over the rusting chicken wire we dodged through the trees to the pillared entrance, now almost subsumed in graffiti and ivy. A dark feel of neglect and evidence of the visits of junkies and vandals had destroyed any real sense of its wartime past.

My grandfather had spent his fifty-third birthday here and, by a strange coincidence, I, too, had just turned fifty-three. As I squatted outside the front door in the heat of the late October sun, digging between the shards of glass to reach the same earth my grandfather had trodden at the same age, I could feel the presence of Prisoner G8952, a man in freefall from the pinnacle of his life, defeated and powerless, all hopes of winning the war reduced to the modest aspiration of securing a book-keeping position on his release.

Christopher and I cycled back in silence. The sun was setting into a dark red sky. My heart felt heavy with empathy for my grandfather, the prisoner.

Our final destination was the tiny mountainous republic

of San Marino. Perched high on a rocky outcrop overlooking Rimini and the sea, it is the third smallest country in Europe. Despite remaining neutral in the war it was bombed in June 1944 by the RAF in the mistaken belief that the Germans were storing munitions and hiding troops there.

As the Allies advanced northwards, the retreating Germans were ordered to blow up its railway tunnels. But San Marino was seen as a safe haven by thousands of Italian women and children fleeing bombing raids on Rimini and many would take refuge in these tunnels. My grandfather knew that forty women and children were hiding in the particular tunnel he had been commanded to destroy. This was the order he had refused to carry out.

Although no letter had survived to give us his own account of this episode, we knew from the family that his action had been acknowledged by San Marino's single-chamber parliament with the esteemed Equestrian Order of Saint Agatha for outstanding civil or military services to the republic. It was an award that had been bestowed on some prominent people, including Kings Edward VII and VIII. We were also aware, from a certificate in Tante Marlen's possession, that, on 7 August 1944, my grandfather had been made an honorary citizen of the tiny microstate. And his defence of its neutrality had been further recognized by the entry of his name into their prestigious 'Golden Book', a record of important events and visits made by dignitaries from Abraham Lincoln to the Pope.

Christopher and I had come to San Marino to see if we could find out anything more about this story and to see the book, which various relations had viewed on previous visits. But on our arrival at the town hall, the splendid mini-Palazzo

With Christopher in San Marino, 2017.

Vecchio where it had been housed, the official in charge told us that it was no longer there and that the Office for Foreign Affairs, where it was now kept, was closed for the weekend. As we were leaving the following day, we would not get to see it. She could not give us any more information. We tried to hide our disappointment from each other as we explored the mediaeval town that clings alarmingly to sheer rocky drops, triggering both Christopher's vertigo and my stubborn determination to succeed in our mission.

'Let's go back and try again,' I said, feeling sure there was a chance of a more satisfactory outcome to our visit if we persisted. This time, my pleas in incomprehensible Italian and dramatic hand gestures sent the official scuttling off. She returned with a magnificent-looking policeman in full

The certificate granting my grandfather honorary citizenship of the Republic of San Marino.

uniform, complete with green jacket, matching peaked hat, black tie, red trousers and holstered pistol. He spoke excellent English and was clearly impressed by the copy of the 1944 certificate we had brought with us.

What happened next was little short of magic. The police officer suddenly did a double-take. 'Oh, look!' he said. 'It's signed by a relative of mine!' Then, suddenly catching sight through the glass entrance door of someone walking past, he frantically beckoned him inside. The man, dressed in track-suit bottoms and trainers and accompanied by a small boy, joined us. 'This is an old friend of mine,' the policeman explained. 'He will be very interested to meet you.' The man was, it turned out to our astonishment, a former San Marino secretary of state and one of the government's sixty members of congress.

He inspected the certificate and listened to our story. 'Incredible!' he said. 'Your grandfather would have been a very important man to be entered in the Golden Book. This is an amazing story that should be celebrated. I will see if there is more I can find out about it.'

He posed with us for a quick photo, handed us his card and resumed his *passeggiata* with his son.

The police officer, after giving us a personal tour of the beautiful stone town hall, sat us down in front of a video screen and showed us a short film on the history of San Marino. Pressing pause on a black-and-white picture from 1944, he urged us to look at it carefully. We could see the entrance to a railway tunnel with people milling around it. 'These are the people fleeing from the Allied bombings of Rimini,' he said. He moved on to the next frame, a close-up of the inside of the tunnel, showing women and children sitting beside the track. 'Some of these are my family,' he told us. 'And this' – he pointed excitedly to a small boy – 'is my father!'

It was extraordinary. It didn't matter that we would never know if this was the actual tunnel and these the specific people my grandfather had refused to blow up. It was enough that they could have been. It was like the ending of a Spielberg movie. The climactic scene in which the grandchildren of a vilified man learn that their grandfather saved the lives of the entire family of the person standing in front of them. Stirring music orchestrates the emotions of the audience. People well up as the redemptive message sinks in and the credits roll.

The three of us sat speechless as the serendipity of this chance meeting that had so very nearly never happened sizzled around us. Of course, life isn't a Spielberg film and in the real world an isolated commendable act proves nothing. Redemption isn't as simple as that. But for the briefest moment, I could see my grandfather as an undisputed hero: a disobeyer of orders, a saver of many lives. A man who, on this occasion at least, unquestionably did the right thing.

The emotional impact of drawing my story to a close took me by surprise. The impending departure of my grandfather from my life highlighted the extent to which he had been present: in my mind, my dreams and through my days. Like a jealous ex-lover, he had loitered in my relationships, pulling me away and escorting me to darker depths of my humanity than any living person ever had.

Maybe it was his bravery that had taught me to face down my fears and fight for the truth.

Maybe he had inspired me to channel his warrior spirit not into waging war, but into cultivating a patch of peace inside myself where heroes, villains and victims co-exist as elements of all human beings, each with the capacity to be all of those things.

Maybe it was his need for forgiveness that helped me forgive.

Now I wanted to allow my grandfather and his story to rest in peace.

As the sun came up behind a cover of grey cloud on our last morning in Italy, Christopher and I retraced our tracks along the hotel-lined seafront to the stretch of sandy beach in front of the former POW camp in Bellaria. This would be the place to symbolically bury our grandfather, fulfilling his wish for the final days of his life to be spent here.

As well as tobacco and earth, I had brought with me the last pair of slippers he owned. Onkel Adolf had been wearing them ever since his father died, until they were falling apart and would no longer stay on his feet. At my request, rather than consigning them to the bin, he had sent them to me.

My brother and I selected a spot on the beach where we knew our grandfather had walked, gathered shells and gazed out at the clear horizon, hoping for better times. He had watched the same sun rise and set to the same ebb and flow of the tide. I unpacked my bag of symbols while Christopher got to work digging a foot-deep hole, using a broken child's spade we had found conveniently abandoned. I was touched by how wholeheartedly he had embraced my strange ways throughout our trip. 'Is this all gobbledygook to you, Christopher?' I had asked him at one stage, conscious of how significantly our approaches to the more intangible aspects of life diverged at certain points. But he, too, had witnessed the glimmer of magic in San Marino, the kind of gift of fate I had so often experienced in my quest. 'No,' he said. 'No, it isn't.'

Once the hole was deep enough to constitute a mini grave, we placed the slippers at the bottom, followed by a packet of R6 cigarettes, some English soil from my garden and photographs of our grandfather, one as a proud soldier, one as a civilian sitting on his balcony, smoking and lost in thought. I had written my goodbyes on the backs of the pictures the night before.

'Meine Uhr ist abgelaufen' were my grandfather's last words before he died, on 1 November 1964, aged seventy-one. 'My time is up.' I took from my bag some of the letters of condolence sent to the family after his death, which Tante Marlen had appended to her volume of his correspondence. These voices from over fifty years before were mostly those of his contemporaries, now long dead themselves; men steeped in the same Prussian values who had fought in the war – some in both wars – perhaps still clinging to the defence of having done their duty as soldiers in the face of the enormous complexity of their feelings and the challenges of the 1960s generation. Men whose own stories may have still lain buried or whose families may have been struggling over whether to condemn or forgive.

Written '*vom Herzen*' (from the heart), many referred to my grandfather in the affectionate diminutive as 'Karlchen'. They praised his warmth, open-mindedness and trustworthiness; his light-hearted, friendly and cheerful manner; his humour, simplicity and humility; his upright form and character.

'He was the personification of loyalty, the most honest and respectable friend that life sent me,' I read aloud as Christopher sprinkled Großvati's slippers with the first fistful of sand.

'One of the bravest and most decent soldiers, loved by both comrades and subordinates.'

Behind us, small waves rhythmically broke the silence of the early morning, like short, shallow breaths.

'He embodied the highest camaraderie with the best Prussian soldier virtues. I have often been inspired by his strength of character and his demeanour in imprisonment impressed me.'

A dog trotted past with its mildly curious owner as a tiny patch of lighter grey above the horizon promised that the sun was rising.

Großvati.

'Our so highly respected General von Graffen ... We are from our hearts grateful for the exemplary way in which, after the war, he selflessly exerted himself for the old soldiers.'

I hadn't been aware that he had continued supporting soldiers after the war. There was so much I still didn't know and never would.

Christopher didn't look up as it began to drizzle. He just sprinkled more sand, watching it cover the face of the grandfather he had never known.

In the grey silence, we each threw in handfuls of the earth from my garden and then filled the grave with sand, patting it down like parents tucking their child into bed. Then, taking off our shoes, we paddled through the shallow water – it was too cold to swim as planned – and collected shells to mark the spot until the tide washed them away.

As Christopher walked back up the beach I lingered for a moment by the little cairn of shells. 'Goodbye, Großvati,' I said, as much to myself as to him. 'Goodbye and thank you. May you now rest in peace.'

As if discarding a skin, I released my ethereal empty rucksack and, in my mind's eye, watched it float into the sky like a Chinese lantern. Then, with a full heart and unfamiliar sense of weightlessness, I joined Christopher, waiting in a nearby café with two steaming cups of strong coffee.

Epilogue

Learn from yesterday, live for today, hope for tomorrow.
The important thing is not to stop questioning.

Albert Einstein

THERE CAN NEVER BE closure or resolution to this episode of history. As it recedes into a more distant past, younger generations will uncover more facts, develop different points of view, revisit and revise the narrative.

Laying my grandfather's memory to rest on that beach in Italy did however mark a gentle closing of a door on that part of my family's past, a relinquishment of my misplaced sense of personal culpability and the beginning of a new, forward-looking way of being. But while the impact of those times might lose its potency, the importance of learning the lessons does not. We need, now more than ever, to remain vigilant that the seeds of division, discrimination, political domination and war are not allowed to grow again. For, as we have seen, none of us is immune to being ensnared in their poisonous thickets.

For me, laying something to rest does not mean forgetting it and simply moving on, but allowing its essence to shape future attitudes into ethics and actions that might prevent the same mistakes being made again. During a brief spell as a restorative justice practitioner, I witnessed conflicts being resolved through talking, listening and gaining understanding of the other's point of view. I saw the promising buds of empathy, the power of genuine apology and the peace and healing that forgiveness and reconciliation can offer. It is reconciliation that lies at the heart of what I strive to achieve through my work as a public speaker, writer, artist and trustee of the Dresden Trust.

I still have many profound and joyous encounters with people of all generations and from all sides of the conflicts of the Second World War. Possibly the least expected came in 2019, when I was introduced to a Facebook group of sons and daughters of American soldiers who had fought in the 337th regiment of the 85th Infantry Division in north Italy at the end of the war. Against my grandfather and his troops.

I was once again uncertain as to how the granddaughter of the most prominent German general in the region at that time would be received. But I was met with nothing but warmth and interest. It was as if events had come full circle. The photograph of the surrender at La Stanga with which my search had begun had now brought me into contact with the granddaughter of Colonel Hughes, the American commanding officer with whom my grandfather is pictured. I was even sent transcripts of their conversation as the terms and practicalities of surrender were negotiated: the handing over of arms, horses, supplies.

Forging this connection seventy-four years on was meaningful for us all and a group of those who were able planned to meet in La Stanga and Belluno in 2020 on the seventy-fifth anniversary of the unconditional capitulation. Local Italians were involved, my German aunts and my mother, Caroline and Christopher were intending to be there and no doubt my father and uncle would have been, too, had they still been alive. The multi-national party looked forward to dining in the guesthouse, touring the region's former battlefields and exchanging the stories of our forebears.

The plans were scuppered by a new scourge: the Covid-19 pandemic. But the hope is that one day soon, the grandchildren of that American colonel and German general will stand together in harmony on the spot where their grandfathers met as adversaries in May 1945.

And so the healing continues.

Acknowledgements

On countless occasions over the years spent writing this book, I have found myself filled with gratitude towards those who would help me reach the end.

My first big thank you must go to my two aunts in Germany, Marlen and Dörli, without whom this enterprise would not have been possible. From the start, they have passed on their family stories and memories with remarkable transparency and given so generously of their time, driving me to places of significance to our family and answering every difficult question I have posed. I have benefited from Marlen's huge achievement of typing up my grandparents' extensive writings and from many fascinating exchanges with Dörli that have kept me up to date with current debates in Germany. Each of our conversations poring over family albums brought the past a little more to life.

I am also indebted to my late uncle, Adolf, for sharing some of his most challenging childhood memories. And to all of my German first cousins for allowing me to tell the story of a family that is also theirs.

I have felt blessed to be able to tap into Elwyn Wong's wealth of knowledge and understanding of two world wars and all things military. Without him, our incredible email exchanges and his contacts, I don't believe I would have figured out the course my grandfather took across Russia. My trip there was one of the most important I have ever made.

Researching aspects of Germany's Second World War from England was not always easy, which makes me all the more grateful to the experts I approached. The eminent historian Nicholas Stargardt was kind enough to read my grandfather's reflections and to help me contextualize them. The impressive knowledge of monuments and memorials shared by Bill Niven and Roger Bowdler has been invaluable. And my German friends Maria Reinke, Karen Hedley, Frederic Sering and Susanne Hakuba kept me supplied with insights or literature I might never have otherwise come across.

In My Grandfather's Shadow went through two main phases of writing. I am incredibly grateful to Susanna Rickards, my wonderful first professional editor, whose combination of sensitivity, clarity and literary skills guided me along one of the steepest learning curves of my life. Also to my carefully selected team of trusted friends and readers of preliminary drafts for all their useful feedback and ongoing interest in the book's progress. Thank you to Lucy Wayland, for bravely making it through the earliest, most raw version. To Alice Jolly, whose talent and brilliant writing often stops me in my tracks. I am indebted to her in so many ways for developing the writer in me. To Johnny Acton, another gifted wordsmith, for his amazing attention to detail, encouragement and humour. To John Heseltine for his intimate understanding of the beauty that can be found in the dark corners of the soul and his talent at putting such things into words. To Carolyn Townsend for her many acute and sensitive insights, tremendous kindness and our frequent laughs. To Caroline Knight for her professionally informed guidance and encouragement. And to Hedda Joyce, whose own academic research mixed with personal experience of Germany's legacy have inspired me and contributed enormously to my broader understanding.

The completion of the second phase of my book to this level is largely due to people in the publishing world. Thank you to my agent, Andrew Lownie, for seeing the potential in my manuscript and helping it fly. And to everybody at Penguin Transworld: Lizzy Goudsmit, then commissioning editor, for her inspired, expanded vision of my book and quiet confidence that I could achieve it. Susanna Wadeson for overseeing the realization of that vision with such openness to my input as well as remarkable speed and decisiveness. Andrea Henry for her incredible editorial efficiency; Phil Lord for bringing all the old family photos to life; Richard Ogle for his extraordinary instinct in designing such a powerful cover; Tony Maddock for so skilfully re-creating my very low-resolution original image of my grandfather and me standing on the same spot in La Stanga.

I am also deeply grateful to the author and historian Rebecca Abrams for so thoroughly and generously reading and commenting on the book from the Jewish perspective. Having her eyes on it brought great peace to my mind. And finally, an especially big thank you goes to Caroline North McIlvanney, my brilliant editor, whose skills, knowledge, patience and sheer hard work have never ceased to amaze me. Her clarity and calm came at just the right time when I could no longer see the wood for the trees.

In Germany there are support groups for third generations who find themselves wrestling with similarly dark and heavy issues. Less so in England. However, I was fortunate to be part of a few groups whose work and goals resonate closely with mine. My thanks to Marina Catacuzino, Sandra Barefoot and all those beautiful people with whom I have connected through the Forgiveness Project. Their wisdom, caring approach and remarkable stories of resilience have been invaluable. And to Adam Barley and all the wonderful participants of his Zero One movement workshops, where I could rock my socks off and dance out the contents of my world. To Mary Hykel-Hunt at IQx2 for her many multi-dimensional insights over the years that helped me find my way. And to Evelyn Eaton, Marcus Ferrar and my fellow trustees of the Dresden Trust, who know so much about putting reconciliation into practice.

Writing can be incredibly solitary and take a real toll on the body. Kristine Hagen, Carl Benton and all at Personal Best kept me moving while Amanda Hampden, Nicola and Dug Faulkner, P.J. Keeling, Peter Moseley and Jo Stafford-Michael offered regular welcome breaks in the form of long walks and delicious dinners.

Many dear friends have seen me through some challenging years. They all made positive contributions in their own unique way, but I'd like to pay tribute in particular to Epoh Beech, Shirley Margerison, Nancy Miles, Gus Stott, Sarah Orme, Penny Porter, Clare Wimperis and Penelope Anstice, who rode the highs and lows so closely with me. Knowing I could always pick up the phone and talk things through gave me the strength on numerous occasions to surmount the hurdles and carry on.

The intense process of writing a book of this nature without doubt had an impact on my family. They valiantly put up with me and it. My lovely nephews, Danny and Nico, my brother-in-law, Dante, and my English extended family form the solid, loving foundation on which I have always been able to rely, and my gratitude to them all is heartfelt.

I know my late father would have been very proud to see this book published. 'Darling, you make people think,' he'd say to me, 'and that is so important.' If I have succeeded in that, it will be largely down to his measured fairness and clever balance of rationality and emotion, all of which shaped my own mind and writing.

There is so much for which to thank my mother, above all for allowing me to rummage through her memories, emotions and cupboards in search of stories and answers. For allowing me to tell this version of life, when I know they are so many others I could have told. She has always been there for me, celebrating each milestone with such enthusiasm, even after her stroke prevented her from fully understanding their significance. She is the bravest person I know.

It is for my siblings, Caroline and Christopher, that I save my final and perhaps biggest thanks. Although Caroline appears rarely in these pages, her presence in my life has always been immense and vital. And Christopher, who plays a bigger part, displayed typical generosity in permitting me to recount a difficult episode in his. I so appreciate the multiple readings and many hours of talking to which they have both devoted their time and thoughts. Without their support, encouragement, family humour and love, I don't think I would have been able to do 'life', let alone produce this book. Having two people by my side I am able to trust as implicitly as I trust them has without question been one of the greatest gifts life has given me.

Thank you all.

Sources and Further Reading

Introduction

In some ways I have been researching for this book all my adult life. It would be impossible to list all the sources I have drawn both facts and wisdom from, but I have done my best to include here a comprehensive list for the interested reader to further explore some of the areas this book covers.

It has not just been books, articles and essays that have informed me. The visual mediums of film and TV, exhibitions, live and online lectures and conferences, as well as my many travels to sites of significance, have all fed my imagination and coloured in the contours that academic and historical texts so skilfully create.

English-language books

Anonymous, *A Woman in Berlin* (London: Virago, 2006)

Batthyány, Sacha, *A Crime in the Family* (London: Quercus, 2017)

Bielenberg, Christabel, *The Past is Myself* (London: Corgi, 1968)

Boyd, Julia, *Travellers in the Third Reich* (London: Elliott and Thompson, 2018)

Boyne, John, *The Boy in the Striped Pyjamas* (London: Definitions, 2007)

Brook, Rhydian, *The Aftermath* (London: Penguin Books, 2014)

Broughton, Vivian, *Becoming Your True Self* (West Sussex: Green Balloon Publishing, 2014)

Craigie, Emma, *Chocolate Cake with Hitler* (London: Short Books, 2010)

Dillon, Brian, *In the Dark Room* (London: Penguin, 2006)

Doerr, Anthony, *All the Light We Cannot See* (London: Fourth Estate, 2015)

Fallada, Hans, *Alone in Berlin* (London: Penguin, 2009)

Feigel, Lara, *The Bitter Taste of Victory* (London: Bloomsbury, 2016)

Ferrar, Marcus, *A Foot in Both Camps* (LBLA Digital, 2012)

Fitzherbert, Katrin, *True to Both My Selves* (London: Virago, 1998)

Frankl, Viktor E., *Man's Search for Meaning* (London: Pocket Books, 1985)

Fromm, Erich, *The Anatomy of Human Destructiveness* (London: Penguin, 1990)

Fromm, Gerard M., (ed.) *Lost in Transmission: Studies of Trauma Across Generations* (Oxfordshire: Routledge, 2019)

Froude, James Anthony, *Thomas Carlyle: A History of His Life in London, 1834–1881* (Cambridge University Press, 2011)

Goldhagen, Daniel, *Hitler's Willing Executioners* (New York: Vintage, 1997)

Gregg, Victor, *Dresden* (London: Bloomsbury, 2019)

Harding, Thomas, *The House by the Lake* (London: Windmill Books, 2015)

Harwood, Ronald, *Collaboration* and *Taking Sides* (London: Faber & Faber, 2008)

Hawes, James, *The Shortest History of Germany* (London: Old Street Publishing, 2017)

Himmler, Katrin, *The Himmler Brothers* (London: Pan Macmillan, 2008)

Huber, Florian, *Promise Me You'll Shoot Yourself* (London: Allen Lane, 2019)

Hübl, Thomas, *Healing Collective Trauma* (Colorado: Sounds True, 2020)

Johnson, Eric A., and Reuband, Karl-Heinz, *What We Knew* (New York: Basic Books, 2006)

Kampfner, John, *Why the Germans Do It Better* (London: Atlantic Books, 2020)

Krug, Nora, *Heimat* (London: Particular Books, 2018)

Lowe, Keith, *The Fear and the Freedom* (London: Penguin, 2017)

Lowe, Keith, *Prisoners of History* (London: William Collins, 2020)

Lubbeck, William, *At Leningrad's Gates* (Barnsley: Pen & Sword Books, 2007)

MacGregor, Neil, *Germany: Memories of a Nation* (London: Allen Lane, 2014)

Maté, Gabor, *When the Body Says No* (London: Vemillion, 2019)

Michaels, Anne, *Fugitive Pieces* (London: Bloomsbury, 1998)

Milton, Giles, *Wolfram: The Boy Who Went to War* (London: Sceptre, 2011)

Morris, Heather, *The Tattooist of Auschwitz* (London: Zaffre, 2018)

Morris, Heather, *Cilka's Journey* (London: Zaffre, 2019)

Neiman, Susan, *Learning from the Germans* (London: Allen Lane, 2019)

Neitzel, Sönke and Welzer, Harald, Soldaten: On Fighting, Killing and Dying: The Secret Second World War Tapes of German POWs (London: Simon & Schuster, 2012)

Némirovsky, Irène, *Suite Française* (London: Vintage, 2007)

Neumann, Ariana, *When Time Stopped* (London: Scribner, 2020)

Niemann, Derek, *A Nazi in the Family* (London: Short Books, 2015)

Parker, Harry, *Anatomy of a Soldier* (London: Faber & Faber, 2016)

Picoult, Jodi, *The Storyteller* (London: Hodder & Stoughton, 2013)

Rimbert, Philippe, *Secret* (London: Portobello Books Ltd, 2007)

Romer, Knud, *Nothing but Fear* (London: Serpent's Tail, 2012)

Rothmann, Ralf, *To Die in Spring* (London: Picador, 2017)

Sands, Philippe, *East West Street* (London: Weidenfeld & Nicholson, 2017)

Sands, Philippe, *The Ratline* (London: Weidenfeld & Nicholson, 2020)

Schlink, Bernhard, *The Reader* (London: Phoenix, 1998)

Schlink, Bernhard, *Homecoming* (London: Phoenix, 2009)

Schlink, Bernhard, *Guilt About the Past* (Toronto: House of Anansi Press, 2010)

Schneider, Helga, *Let Me Go* (London: Vintage, 2005)

Schwarz, Géraldine, *Those Who Forget* (London: Pushkin Press, 2020)

Sebald, W. G., *Austerlitz* (London: Penguin, 2002)

Sebald, W. G., *On the Natural History of Destruction* (Canada: Knopf, 2003)

Seiffert, Rachel, *A Boy in Winter* (London: Virago Press, 2018)

Seiffert, Rachel, *The Dark Room* (London: Vintage, 2002)

Sentilles, Sarah, *Draw Your Weapons* (London: The Text Publishing Company, 2017)

Sereny, Gitta, *The German Trauma: Experiences and Reflections 1938–2001* (London: Penguin, 2000)

Stahlberg, Alexander, *Bounden Duty* (London: Brasseys, 1990)

Stargardt, Nicholas, *The German War* (London: Vintage, 2015)

Sullivan, Mark, *Beneath a Scarlet Sky* (Seattle: Lake Union, 2017)

Teege, Jennifer, *My Grandfather Would Have Shot Me* (London: Hodder & Stoughton, 2015)

Ten Boom, Corrie, *The Hiding Place* (London: Hodder & Stoughton, 2004)

Timm, Uwe, *In my Brother's Shadow* (London: Bloomsbury, 2006)

Van der Kolk, Bessel, *The Body Keeps the Score* (London: Penguin, 2014)

Wolynn, Mark, *It Didn't Start With You* (London: Penguin Books, 2017)

Young, J. E., *The Texture of Memory: Holocaust Memorials and Meaning* (New Haven and London: Yale University Press, 1993)

Zusak, Marcus, *The Book Thief* (London: Doubleday, 2007)

German-language books

Alberti, Bettina, *Seelische Trümmer* (Munich: Random House, 1967)

Bode, Sabine, *Die vergessene Generation: Die Kriegskinder brechen ihr Schweigen* (Berlin: Piper Verlag GmbH, 2005)

Bode, Sabine, *Kriegsenkel: Die Erben der vergessenen Generation* (Stuttgart: Klett-Cotta, 2009)

Bode, Sabine, *Nachkriegskinder: Die 1950er Jahregänge und ihre Soldatenväter* (Stuttgart: Klett-Cotta, 2011)

Heinzel, Sebastian, *Der Krieg in mir* (Bielefeld: Kamphausen Media GmbH, 2020)

Huber, Florian, *Hinter den Türen warten die Gespenster* (Berlin: Piper Verlag GmbH, 2019)

Schneider, Michael, and Süss, Joachim (Hg.) (eds), *Nebelkinder* (Berlin: Europa Verlag GmbH, 2015)

Unger, Raymond, *Die Heimat der Wölfe* (Berlin: Europa Verlag GmbH, 2016)

Ustorf, Anne-Ev, *Wir Kinder der Kriegskinder* (Freiberg: Herder, 2013)

Von Zydowitz, Kurt, *Die Geschichte der 58. Infantrie-Division 1939–1945*, (H. H.Podzu̱n, 1952)

Welzer, Harald; Moller, Sabine and Tschggnall, Karoline, *Opa war kein Nazi* (Berlin: Fischer Taschenbuch Verlag, 2002)

English articles and essays

Aaronovitch, David, 'Every nation must face up to its dark past', *The Times*, 1 November 2018. https://www.thetimes.co.uk/article/every-nation-must-face-up-to-its-dark-past-hhh3gmhd6

Adams, Tim, 'Neil MacGregor: "Britain forgets its past. Germany confronts it"', *The Guardian*, 17 April 2016. http://www.theguardian.com/culture/2016/apr/17/neil-macgregor-britain-germany-humboldt-forum-berlin

Adorno, Theodor, 'The Meaning of Working through the Past', in *European Perspectives: A Series in Social Thought and Cultural Criticism*, Lawrence D. Kritzman (ed.), 1959. https://www.sas.upenn.edu/~cavitch/pdf-library/Adorno_MeaningOfWorking Through.pdf

Ahren, Raphael, 'At Yad Vashem, German president says Germans haven't learned lesson of Holocaust', *Times of Israel*, 3 January 2020. https://www.timesofisrael.com/at-yad-vashem-german-president-says-germans-havent-learned-lesson-of-holocaust/

Apperly, Eliza, '"Stumbling Stones": a different vision of Holocaust remembrance', *The Guardian*, 18 February 2019. https://www.theguardian.com/cities/2019/feb/18/stumbling-stones-a-different-vision-of-holocaust-remembrance

Avnery, Uri, 'Our Mothers, Our Fathers: A Review', International Policy Digest, 28 February 2014. https://intpolicydigest.org/our-mothers-our-fathers-a-review/

Berger, Joseph, 'Gen. Hans Speidel, who plotted to kill Hitler', *New York Times*, 29 November 1984. https://www.nytimes.com/1984/11/29/obituaries/gen-hans-speidel-who-plotted-to-kill-hitler.html

Bhattacharya, Shaoni, 'The lifelong cost of burying our traumatic experiences', *New Scientist*, 5 November 2014. https://www.newscientist.com/article/mg22429941-200-the-lifelong-cost-of-burying-our-traumatic-experiences/

Bhattacharya, Shaoni, 'The surprising value of viewing traumatic experiences', *New Scientist*, 26 November 2015 https://www.newscientist.com/article/dn28555-the-surprising-value-of-viewing-traumatic-experiences/

Bhattacharya, Shaoni, 'Why we need to go on talking about trauma', *New Scientist*, 2 January 2016. https://www.newscientist.com/article/dn28719-why-we-need-to-go-on-talking-about-trauma/

Bilger, Burkhard, 'Where Germans Make Peace with their Dead', *New Yorker*, 5 September 2016. https://www.newyorker.com/magazine/2016/09/12/familienaufstellung-germanys-group-therapy

Bird, Adrian, 'Epigenetics: A ubiquitous phenomenon', *New Scientist*, 2 January 2013. https://www.newscientist.com/article/mg21728971-800-epigenetics-a-ubiquitous-phenomenon/

Bird, Adrian, 'Epigenetics: Discovery', *New Scientist*, 2 January 2013. https://www.newscientist.com/article/mg21728971-700-epigenetics-discovery/

Bird, Adrian, 'Epigenetics: Far-reaching effects', *New Scientist*, 2 January 2013. https://www.newscientist.com/article/mg21728971-900-epigenetics-far-reaching-effects/

Bird, Adrian, 'Epigenetics: What's left to find out', *New Scientist*, 2 January 2013. https://www.newscientist.com/article/mg21728972-000-epigenetics-whats-left-to-find-out/

Birnbaum, Michael, 'One thing is missing from Russia's WWII remembrance – the Allies', *Washington Post*, 9 May 2015. https://www.washingtonpost.com/world/russia-saved-europe-from-hitler-and-it-wants-you-to-remember/2015/05/09/032c606e-f33c-11e4-bca5-21b51bbdf93e_story.html

Blakemore, Erin, 'Why German Soldiers Don't Have to Obey Orders', History.com, 7 November 2017. https://www.history.com/news/why-german-soldiers-dont-have-to-obey-orders

Bond, Michael, 'Trauma of war echoes down the generations', *New Scientist*, 4 February 2015. https://www.newscientist.com/article/mg22530070-200-trauma-of-war-echoes-down-the-generations/

Bowie, Laura, 'The Impact of World War Two on the Individual and Collective Memory of Germany and its Citizens', May 2015 https://www.societies.ncl.ac.uk/pgfnewcastle/files/2015/05/Bowie-The-Impact-of-World-War-Two.pdf

Callaghan, Mark, 'Invisible Past, Invisible Future: A German's alternative response to the Holocaust', Art Times Journal, October 2010. https://www.arttimesjournal.com/speakout/Nov_Dec_10_Callaghan%20/Nov_Dec_10_Callaghan.html

Callaway, Ewen, 'Fearful Memories Passed Down to Mouse Descendants. Genetic imprint from traumatic experiences carries through at least two generations', Scientific American, 1 December 2013. https://www.scientificamerican.com/article/fearful-memories-passed-down/

Carey, Benedict, 'Can We Really Inherit Trauma? Headlines suggest that the epigenetic marks of trauma can be passed from one generation to the next. But the evidence, at least in humans, is circumstantial at best', New York Times, 10 December 2018. https://www.nytimes.com/2018/12/10/health/mind-epigenetics-genes.html

Cichowlas, Ola, 'How Russian Kids Are Taught World War II. A new history curriculum is raising concern among teachers', Moscow Times, 8 May 2017. https://www.themoscowtimes.com/2017/05/08/how-russian-kids-are-taught-world-war-ii-a57930

Chotiner, Isaac, 'How to Confront a Racist National History', New Yorker, 6 July 2020. https://www.newyorker.com/news/q-and-a/how-to-confront-a-racist-national-history

Clark, Alex, 'Nazism, slavery, empire: can countries learn from national evil?', The Guardian, 13 September 2019. https://www.theguardian.com/books/2019/sep/13/susan-neiman-interview-learning-from-the-germans?CMP=Share_iOSApp_Other

Cockburn, Harry, 'Leave.EU campaign apologises over tweet calling Merkel a "kraut" and invoking world war', The Independent, 9 October 2019. https://www.independent.co.uk/news/uk/politics/leave-eu-merkel-tweet-brexit-world-war-germany-kraut-arron-banks-a9148356.html

Coghlan, Andy, 'Stress can affect future generations' genes', New Scientist, 25 January 2013. https://www.newscientist.com/article/dn23109-stress-can-affect-future-generations-genes/

Connolly, Kate, 'Bernhard Schlink: being German is a huge burden', The Guardian, 16 September 2012. https://www.theguardian.com/world/2012/sep/16/bernhard-schlink-germany-burden-euro-crisis?newsfeed=true

Curry, Andrew, 'Parents' emotional trauma may change their children's biology. Studies in mice show how', Science, 18 July 2019. https://www.sciencemag.org/news/2019/07/parents-emotional-trauma-may-change-their-children-s-biology-studies-mice-show-how

Daxinger, Lucia and Whitelaw, Emma, 'Transgenerational epigenetic inheritance: More questions than answers', US National Library of Medicine, December 2010. https://www.ncbi.nlm.nih.gov/pmc/articles/PMC2989988/

DeAngelis, Tori, 'The legacy of trauma', American Psychological Association, February 2019. https://www.apa.org/monitor/2019/02/legacy-trauma

Dempsey, Judy, 'Germans recognized as victims of WWII', New York Times, 9 May 2005. https://www.nytimes.com/2005/05/09/world/europe/germans-recognized-as-victims-of-wwii.html

Der Bundespräsident, 'Fifth World Holocaust Forum at Yad Vashem', 23 January 2020. http://www.bundespraesident.de/

SharedDocs/Reden/EN/Frank-Walter-Steinmeier/Reden/
2020/01/200123-World-Holocaust-Forum-Yad-Vashem.htm

Douglas, R.M. 'The European Atrocity You Never Heard About',
The Chronicle of Higher Education, 11 June 2012. https://www.
chronicle.com/article/the-european-atrocity-you-never-heard-about/

Duba, Ursula, 'How Do Young Germans Deal with the Legacy of
the Holocaust and the Third Reich?', PBS, 31 May 2005. http://
www.pbs.org/wgbh/pages/frontline/shows/germans/germans/
howdo.html

Evans, Richard J., 'How should we remember the Holocaust? Why
the plan for a new national memorial in Westminster is causing
such division', New Statesman, 20 January 2021. https://www.
newstatesman.com/politics/2021/01/how-should-we-remember-
holocaust

Evans, Richard J., 'The Other Horror', The New Republic, 25
June2012.https://newrepublic.com/article/102925/orderly-humane-
expulsion-germans-richard-evans

Freeman, Hadley, 'The Nazis tried to kill kindness. We fight
against that', *The Guardian*, 29 January 2019. https://www.
theguardian.com/news/2019/jan/29/nazis-tried-to-kill-kindness-
holocaust-survivors-grandson-ss-officer?CMP=Share_iOSApp_
Other

Gallagher, James, 'Memories' pass between generations', BBC
News, 1 December 2013. https://www.bbc.co.uk/news/health-
25156510

Geddes, Linda, 'Fear of a smell can be passed down several
generations', *New Scientist*, 1 December 2013. https://www.
newscientist.com/article/dn24677-fear-of-a-smell-can-be-passed-down-
several-generations/

Georgiou, George, 'Hellinger's Soul Healing', Da Vinci Natural
Health Center. https://www.naturaltherapycenter.com/
hellingers-soul-healing/

Gillespie, Claire, 'What Is Generational Trauma? Here's How
Experts Explain It', Health.com, 27 October 2020. https://www.
health.com/condition/ptsd/generational-trauma

Gilligan, James, 'Shame, Guilt, and Violence', 2003. Social Research, vol. 70, no. 4, The New School, pp. 1149–80. http://www.jstor.org/stable/40971965

Görtz, Birgit, 'Austria debates its role in the Nazi era', DW.com, 11 March 2013. https://www.dw.com/en/austria-debates-its-role-in-the-nazi-era/a-16664190

Gray, Richard, 'Phobias may be memories passed down in genes from ancestors', *Daily Telegraph*, 1 December 2013. https://www.telegraph.co.uk/news/science/science-news/10486479/Phobias-may-be-memories-passed-down-in-genes-from-ancestors.html

Habbe, Christian, 'A Time of Retribution: Paying with Life and Limb for the Crimes of Nazi Germany', *Der Spiegel*, 27 May 2011. https://www.spiegel.de/international/germany/a-time-of-retribution-paying-with-life-and-limb-for-the-crimes-of-nazi-germany-a-759737.html

Habermas, Jürgen, 'On How Postwar Germany Has Faced Its Recent Past', *Common Knowledge*, 1 April 2019. https://read.dukeupress.edu/common-knowledge/article-abstract/25/1-3/364/140025/On-How-Postwar-Germany-Has-Faced-Its-Recent-Past?redirectedFrom=fulltext

Hammond, Claudia, 'What we get wrong about time', BBC.com, 3 December 2019. https://www.bbc.com/future/article/20191203-what-we-get-wrong-about-time

Hamzelou, Jessica, 'Trauma leaves its mark on immune system genes', *New Scientist*, 6 May 2010. https://www.newscientist.com/article/dn18865-trauma-leaves-its-mark-on-immune-system-genes/

Henriques, Martha, 'Can the legacy of trauma be passed down the generations?', BBC.com, 26 March 2019. https://www.bbc.com/future/article/20190326-what-is-epigenetics

Hirsch, Afua, 'Britain's colonial crimes deserve a lasting memorial. Here's why', *The Guardian*, 22 November 2017. https://www.theguardian.com/commentisfree/2017/nov/22/british-empire-museum-colonial-crimes-memorial

'How Germany Remembers the World Wars', BBC.com, 15
    November 2020. https://www.bbc.co.uk/news/world-54924973

Huggler, Justin, 'German president asks for forgiveness on 80th
    anniversary of start of Second World War', *Daily Telegraph*, 1
    September 2019. https://www.telegraph.co.uk/news/2019/09/01/
    german-president-asks-forgiveness-80th-anniversary-start-
    second/?WT.mc_id=tmg_share_em

Hurley, Dan, 'Grandma's Experiences Leave a Mark on Your
    Genes', *Discover*, 25 Jun 2015. https://www.discovermagazine.
    com/health/grandmas-experiences-leave-a-mark-on-your-genes

Invernizzi-Accetti, Carlo, 'A small Italian town can teach the
    world how to defuse controversial monuments', *The Guardian*, 6
    December 2017. https://www.theguardian.com/commentisfree/
    2017/dec/06/bolzano-italian-town-defuse-controversial-
    monuments

Iyengar, Udita et al. 'Unresolved trauma in mothers:
    intergenerational effects and the role of reorganization", US
    National Library of Medicine, 1 Sept. 2014. https://www.ncbi.
    nlm.nih.gov/pmc/articles/PMC4150444/#B47

Jeffries, Stuart, 'Fanning the flames', *The Guardian*, 23 December
    2006. https://www.theguardian.com/world/2006/dec/23/germany.
    secondworldwar

Jenkins, Simon, 'It's time to move on from these overblown
    commemorations of war', *The Guardian*, 6 June 2019. https://
    www.theguardian.com/commentisfree/2019/jun/06/
    commemorations-war-d-day-europe

Jenkins, Simon, 'Germany, I apologise for this sickening avalanche
    of first world war worship', *The Guardian*, 30 January 2014.
    https://www.theguardian.com/commentisfree/2014/jan/30/
    first-world-war-worship-sickening-avalanche

Jones, Jonathan, 'Why Germany would win the World Cup of
    modern art too', *The Guardian*, 14 July 2014. https://www.
    theguardian.com/artanddesign/jonathanjonesblog/2014/jul/14/
    why-germany-wins-modern-art-world-cup

Kellermann, Nathan Pf, 'Epigenetic transmission of Holocaust
    trauma: can nightmares be inherited?', 2013. https://doctorsonly.

co.il/wp-content/uploads/2013/07/08_Epigenetic-Transmission.
pdf

Kleiner, Kurt, 'Battle scars take years to surface', *New Scientist*,
19 August 1995. https://www.newscientist.com/article/
mg14719911-100-battle-scars-take-years-to-surface/

Knight, Ben and Brown, Mark, 'Appointment of Neil MacGregor
as head of Humboldt Forum silences critics', *The Guardian*, 10
April 2015. https://www.theguardian.com/world/2015/apr/10/
appointment-of-neil-macgregor-as-head-of-humboldt-forum-
silences-critics

Lamia, Mary C., 'Shame: A concealed, Contagious, and Dangerous
Emotion', *Psychology Today*, 4 April 2011. https://www.
psychologytoday.com/gb/blog/intense-emotions-and-strong-
feelings/201104/
shame-concealed-contagious-and-dangerous-emotion

Le Faucheur, Christelle, review of Welzer, Harald; Moller, Sabine;
Tschuggnall, Karoline, '"Opa war kein Nazi":
Nazionalsozialismus und Holocaust im Familiengedächtnis',
Humanities and Social Sciences Net Online, April 2004. https://
www.h-net.org/reviews/showrev.php?id=9159

Leick, Romain, '"Our Mothers, Our Fathers": Next-Generation
WWII Atonement', *Der Spiegel*, 28 March 2013. https://www.
spiegel.de/international/germany/zdf-tv-miniseries-reopens-
german-wounds-of-wwii-past-a-891332.html

Lowe, Keith, 'A City Tried to Move a Monument. The Fight That
Ensued Shows the Power of History', *Time*, 8 December 2020.
https://time.com/5912853/katyn-monument/

Lowe, Keith, 'A Monumental Controversy', Monuments,
December 2020. https://stichting-liberation-route-europe.
instantmagazine.com/libre-magazine-1/libre-9-copy-1/
monuments-keith-lowe/

Lowe, Keith, 'Not a laughing Matter: Different Cultures of the
Second World War Remembrance Across Europe', ENRS, 14
February 2014. https://enrs.eu/article/not-a-laughing-matter-
different-cultures-of-the-second-world-war-remembrance-
across-europe

Mackenzie, Debora, 'Trauma of war hits troops years later', *New Scientist*, 24 August 2005. https://www.newscientist.com/article/mg18725143-800-trauma-of-war-hits-troops-years-later/

Manjapra, Kris, 'When will Britain face up to its crimes against humanity?', *The Guardian*, 29 March 2018. https://www.theguardian.com/news/2018/mar/29/slavery-abolition-compensation-when-will-britain-face-up-to-its-crimes-against-humanity?fbclid=IwAR37RPsfluWKWW_Ig0E19OqsTsgI7mR1BzXj7YjeOFRbB37yRTC72OzefRo

Manning, Sanchez, 'Britain's colonial shame: Slave-owners given huge payouts after abolition', *The Independent*, 24 February 2013. https://www.independent.co.uk/news/uk/home-news/britains-colonial-shame-slave-owners-given-huge-payouts-after-abolition-8508358.html

Mauss-Hanke, Angela, ' "You feel it, but you don't want to believe it": Traces of National Socialism in Germans of the 21st century', Psychoanalysis and Politics, 14 April 2021. https://www.psa-pol.org/crises/you-feel-it-but-you-dont-want-to-believe-it/

McGreal, Chris, 'Britain blocks EU apology for slave trade', *The Guardian*, 3 September 2001. https://www.theguardian.com/world/2001/sep/03/race.uk

McInnes, Himali, 'We don't live in isolation. Our ancestors' trauma can affect our health generations later', *The Guardian*, 13 September 2021. https://www.theguardian.com/world/2021/sep/14/we-dont-live-in-isolation-our-ancestors-trauma-can-affect-our-health-generations-later?CMP=Share_iOSApp_Other&fbclid=IwAR3PNvorWCiFHaZ7_TEujaxgIHAzib2K2OsRE0WNW9d0TVP9F6L_vOy5YRQ

Melber, Henning and Kössler, Reinhart, 'Colonial amnesia and Germany's efforts to achieve "internal liberation"', 19 May 2020. https://theconversation.com/colonial-amnesia-and-germanys-efforts-to-achieve-internal-liberation-138840

Miles, Malcolm, 'Remembering the Unrememberable – The Harburg Monument Against Fascism (Jochen and Esther Shalev Gerz, 2009)', 12 May 2010. http://vddb.elaba.lt/fedora/get/

LT-eLABa-0001:J.04~2010~ISSN_1822-4555.N_6.PG_63-71/
DS.002.1.01.ARTIC

Neiman, Susan, 'History and Guilt: Can America face up to the terrible reality of slavery in the way that Germany has faced up to the Holocaust?', Aeon, 12 August 2013. https://aeon.co/essays/dare-we-compare-american-slavery-to-the-holocaust

Neiman, Susan, 'There Are No Nostalgic Nazi Memorials: Americans could learn from how drastically German society has moved away from the nadir of its history', *The Atlantic*, 14 September 2019. https://www.theatlantic.com/ideas/archive/2019/09/germany-has-no-nazi-memorials/597937/

Neitzel, Sönke, 'Understanding World War II through the eyes of German soldiers', LSE, 2016. https://www.lse.ac.uk/Research/research-impact-case-studies/understanding-world-war-two-through-eyes-german-soldiers

Niven, Bill, 'The Legacy of Second German Empire Memorials after 1945', Academia, 1 September 2009. https://www.academia.edu/11320657/The_Legacy_of_Second_German_Empire_Memorials_after_1945

Nolte, Ernst, 'The Past That Will Not Pass: A Speech That Could Be Written but Not Delivered', German History in Documents and Images, 1986. https://ghdi.ghi-dc.org/pdf/eng/Chapter14Doc11Intro.pdf

Olusoga, David, 'Statues are not the issue. These are "history wars", a battle over the past', *The Guardian*, 27 August 2017. https://www.theguardian.com/commentisfree/2017/aug/26/statues-were-not-erected-to-teach-us-history-but-to-exert-power

Press Association, 'Don't celebrate first world war, says minister in charge of centenary', *The Guardian*, 7 February 2014. http://www.theguardian.com/world/2014/feb/07/dont-celebrate-first-world-war-says-minister-in-charge-of-centenary

Quinn, Robin, 'The day that Deutschland died: Retracing the fate of captured Axis soldiers at the end of WW2', *The Independent*, 1 May 2015. https://www.independent.co.uk/news/world/europe/the-day-that-deutschland-died-retracing-the-fate-of-captured-axis-soldiers-at-the-end-of-ww2-10216869.html

Rawnsley, Andrew, 'Easy to blame the Germans. Smarter to learn from them', *The Guardian*, 20 May 2012. https://www. theguardian.com/commentisfree/2012/may/20/andrew-rawnsley-dont-blame-the-germans

Reuters, '65 years after WW2 – should Germans still feel guilty?', The Way, 7 May 2010. https://atvsat.com/en/articles/culture/1080-65-years-after-ww2--should-germans-still-feel-guilty.html

Riley, Charlotte Lydia, 'Don't worry about 're-writing history': it's literally what we historians do', *The Guardian*, 10 June 2020. https://www.theguardian.com/commentisfree/2020/jun/10/rewriting-history-historians-statue-past

Riva, Maria Grazia, 'The role of the traumatic "Transgenerational unsaid" Historical, social, educational, psychological in life histories', Department of Human Sciences for Education University of Milan-Bicocca, 2 March 2013. https://www.siped.it/wp-content/uploads/2013/12/Pagine-da-pedagogia_oggi_2-2013-26092013-3.pdf

Saini, Angela, 'Epigenetics: genes, environment and the generation game', *The Guardian*, 7 September 2014. https://www. theguardian.com/science/2014/sep/07/epigenetics-heredity-diabetes-obesity-increased-cancer-risk

Sands, Philippe, 'On the trail of a Nazi war criminal: 'It's my duty as a son to find the good in my father', *The Guardian*, 18 April 2020. https://www.theguardian.com/books/2020/apr/18/on-the-trail-of-a-nazi-war-criminal-its-my-duty-as-a-son-to-find-the-good-in-my-father?CMP=Share_iOSApp_Other

Schwarz, Géraldine, 'Germans know that toppling a few statues isn't enough to confront the past', *The Guardian*, 23 June 2020. https://www.theguardian.com/commentisfree/2020/jun/23/germans-know-toppling-statues-confront-past-britain-empire-nazism

Shattuck, Jessica, 'I Loved My Grandmother. But She Was a Nazi', *New York Times*, 24 March 2017. https://nytimes/2nO4vlc

Steward, Fred, 'The UK needs to build a memorial for the people we enslaved', OpenDemocracy.net, 3 April 2021. https://www.

opendemocracy.net/en/opendemocracyuk/britain-needs-build-memorial-people-we-enslaved/

Tharoor, Ishaan, 'How the Soviet Union helped save the world from Hitler during World War II. 'It was the Western Allies' extreme good fortune that the Russians, and not themselves, paid almost the entire 'butcher's bill' for defeating Nazi Germany', *The Independent*, 9 May 2016. https://www.independent.co.uk/news/world/the-soviet-union-helped-save-the-world-from-hitler-a7020926.html

'Hitler and the Generals', Weapons and Warfare, 27 October 2015. https://weaponsandwarfare.com/2015/10/27/hitler-and-the-generals/

'"This Country Is At War With Germany": When Britain Entered WWII in 1939', Forces Net, 3 September 2020. https://www.forces.net/news/world-prepares-remember-outbreak-wwii

Thomson, Helen, 'First evidence of how parents' lives could change children's DNA', *New Scientist*, 4 June 2015. https://www.newscientist.com/article/dn27658-first-evidence-of-how-parents-lives-could-change-childrens-dna/

Thompson, Helen, 'Study of Holocaust survivors finds trauma passed on to children's genes', *The Guardian*, 21 August 2105. https://www.theguardian.com/science/2015/aug/21/study-of-holocaust-survivors-finds-trauma-passed-on-to-childrens-genes

Tooze, Adam, 'We Remember World War II Wrong. In the middle of the biggest international crisis ever since, it's time to admit what the war was—and wasn't', 7 May 2020. https://foreignpolicy.com/2020/05/07/world-war-2-victory-day-russia-75th-anniversary/

Trilling, Daniel, 'Until we reckon with our imperial history, Britain's toxic culture war will burn', *The Guardian*, 10 June 2020. https://www.theguardian.com/commentisfree/2020/jun/10/britain-imperial-past-culture-war-toxic-crimes-empire

'Understanding the Impact of Trauma', *Trauma-Informed Care in Behavioral Health Services*, Chapter 3, Treatment Improvement Protocol (TIP) Series, No. 57, 2014. Center for Substance Abuse

Treatment, Rockville (MD). https://www.ncbi.nlm.nih.gov/books/NBK207191/

Walker, Shaun, 'WW2 commemorations expose differences at heart of Europe', *The Guardian*, 30 August 2019. https://www.theguardian.com/world/2019/aug/30/truth-is-a-casualty-80-years-after-start-of-second-world-war

Walser, Martin, 'Experiences while Composing a Sunday Speech', 11 October 1998. https://germanhistorydocs.ghi-dc.org/pdf/eng/Chapter5_doc10-English.pdf

West, Jean, 'Holocaust survivors' grandchildren call for action over inherited trauma', *The Guardian*, 3 August 2015. https://www.theguardian.com/world/2015/aug/03/holocaust-survivors-grandchildren-inherited-trauma

White, Thomas, 'What did Hannah Arendt really mean by the banality of evil', Britannica.com, 23 April 2018. https://www.britannica.com/story/what-did-hannah-arendt-really-mean-by-the-banality-of-evil

Widdicombe, Lizzie, 'What Can We Learn From The Germans About Confronting Our History?' *New Yorker*, 21 October 2019. https://www.newyorker.com/culture/cultural-comment/what-can-we-learn-from-the-germans-about-confronting-our-history

Williams, Zoe, 'Trauma, trust and triumph: psychiatrist Bessel van der Kolk on how to recover from our deepest pain', *The Guardian*, 20 September 2021. https://www.theguardian.com/society/2021/sep/20/trauma-trust-and-triumph-psychiatrist-bessel-van-der-kolk-on-how-to-recover-from-our-deepest-pain

Wishart, Ruth, 'Why I'll be a VE Day Dodger', 5 May 2020. http://ruthwishart.scot/blog/why-ill-be-a-ve-day-dodger

Wollaston, Sam, 'Generation War review: gripping drama with the confidence to confront the past', *The Guardian*, 28 April 2014. https://www.theguardian.com/tv-and-radio/2014/apr/28/generation-war-tv-review

Woody, Christopher, 'Germany's post-World War II government was riddled with former Nazis', 10 October 2016. https://www.

businessinsider.com/former-nazi-officials-in-germany-post-world-war-ii-government-2016-10?r=US&IR=T

Yalom, Victor and Marie-Helene, 'Peter Levine on Somatic Experiencing', psychotherapy.net, April 2010. https://www.psychotherapy.net/interview/interview-peter-levine

Yehuda, Rachel and Lehmer, Amy, 'Intergenerational transmission of trauma effects: putative role of epigenetic mechanisms', 7 September 2018. https://www.ncbi.nlm.nih.gov/pmc/articles/PMC6127768/

Young, James E, 'The Counter-Monument: Memory against Itself in Germany Today.' Critical Inquiry, vol. 18, no. 2, The University of Chicago Press, 1992, pp. 267–96. http://www.jstor.org/stable/1343784

Zeitz, Joshua, 'Why There Are No Nazi Statues in Germany', *Politico*, 20 August 2017. https://www.politico.com/magazine/story/2017/08/20/why-there-are-no-nazi-statues-in-germany-215510

German articles and essays

Abé, Nicola, 'Lammert will gemeinsame Erinnerungskultur', *Der Spiegel*, 27 January 2014. https://www.spiegel.de/politik/deutschland/gedenkjahr-2014-lammert-will-gemeinsame-erinnerungskultur-a-945693.html

Bundespräsidialamt, 'Speech by Federal President Richard von Weizsäcker during the Ceremony Commemorating the 40th Anniversary of the End of War in Europe and of National-Socialist Tyranny on 8 May 1985 at the Bundestag, Bonn', 8 May 1985. https://www.bundespraesident.de/SharedDocs/Downloads/DE/Reden/2015/02/150202-RvW-Rede-8-Mai-1985-englisch.pdf?__blob=publicationFile

Bundespräsidialamt, 'Speech by Federal President Frank-Walter Steinmeier on the 75th anniversary of the liberation from National Socialism and the end of the Second World War in Europe at the Central Memorial of the Federal Republic of Germany to the Victims of War and Tyranny (Neue Wache) in Berlin on 8 May 2020'. https://www.bundespraesident.de/

SharedDocs/Downloads/DE/Reden/2020/05/200508-75-Jahre-Ende-WKII-Englisch.pdf?__blob=publicationFile

Buse, U., Gutsch, J-M., Polonyi, M., Ramsel, Y, Smoltczyk, A., 'Die Holzschachtel, in die mein Großvater den Horror ritzte', 30 August 2019.
https://www.spiegel.de/panorama/zweiter-weltkrieg-die-holzschachtel-in-die-mein-grossvater-den-horror-ritzte-a-00000000-0002-0001-0000-000165695584

'Gauk warnt vor Schulssstrich. "Es gibt keine deutsche Identität ohne Auschwitz": Am 70. Jahrestag der Befreiung des Konzentrationslagers mahnte Bundespräsident Gauck, die Erinnerung wach zu halten', Zeit Online, 27 January 2015.
https://www.zeit.de/politik/deutschland/2015-01/holocaust-gedenken-berlin-auschwitz-gauck-lammert

Janker, Karin, 'Spätfolgen des Zweiten Weltkriegs. Die Kinder der Traumatisierten', *Süddeutsche Zeitung*, 12 September 2015.
https://www.sueddeutsche.de/politik/spaetfolgen-des-zweiten-weltkriegs-die-kinder-der-traumatisierten-1.2632536

Kade, Claudia, 'Es gibt keine Deutsche Identität ohne Auschwitz', Welt, 27 January 2015. https://www.welt.de/politik/deutschland/article136817561/Es-gibt-keine-Deutsche-Identitaet-ohne-Auschwitz.html

Lohre, Mathias, 'Das zähe Seelenerbe des Zweiten Weltkrieges', Zeit Online, 13 April 2016. https://www.zeit.de/gesellschaft/zeitgeschehen/2016-04/kriegsenkel-2-weltkrieg-folgen-erbe-schuld-trauma

Miller, Alice, 'Wie kommt das Böse in die Welt?', 1 June 2002.
https://www.alice-miller.com/de/wie-kommt-das-bose-in-die-welt/

Nolte, Ernst, 'Vergangenheit, die nicht vergehen will: Eine Rede, die geschrieben, aber nicht mehr gehalten werden konnte', [Historikerstreit], 100(0) Schlüssel Dokumente, 6 June 1986.
https://www.1000dokumente.de/index.html?c=dokument_de&dokument=0080_nol&object=translation&l=de

Reemtsma, Jan Philipp, 'Wozu Gedenkstätten?', BPB, 10 June 2010. https://www.bpb.de/apuz/32663/wozu-gedenkstaetten

Seidler, Christoph, 'Lange Schatten – Die Kinder der Kriegskinder kommen in die Psychoanalyse', Psychosozial Verlag, 2003. https://www.psychosozial-verlag.de/catalog/product_info.php/products_id/25905

Staas, Christian, 'Was geht mich das noch an?', Zeit Online, 4 November 2010. https://www.zeit.de/2010/45/Erinnern-NS-Zeit-Jugendliche

Süselbeck, Jan, 'Traumatisierte Nazis, aus der Ferne betrachtet: Der deutschsprachige Familienroman krankte lange Jahre an zu großer Nähe der Schreibenden zu Täterinnen und Tätern. Eine neue Generation wagt nun den distanzierten Blick', Zeit Online, 22 October 2020. https://www.zeit.de/kultur/literatur/2020-10/familienromane-literatur-ns-geschichte-generationen

Teller, Janne, 'Wie das deutsche Schuldgefühl die europäische Ehre rettet', *Frankfurter Allgemeine*, 9 May 2015. https://www.faz.net/aktuell/feuilleton/debatten/janne-teller-zur-last-der-deutschen-geschichte-14221785.html

Ulrich, Bernd, 'Nie wieder. Immer wieder: Wen die Beschäftigung mit Auschwitz nicht mehr verstört, der macht etwas falsch', Zeit Online, 27 January 2005. https://www.zeit.de/2005/05/01____1__Leiter

Visual Media

The arts, films, documentaries and TV series informed me every bit as much as the written word.

YouTube

'A Defeated People' (16 April 2010) YouTube video, added by PublicResourceOrg [online]. Available on https://www.youtube.com/watch?v=dcnDJRLszoM

'Afua Hirsch: Don't glorify controversial "heroes"' (25 May 2018) YouTube video, added by Sky News [online]. Available at https://www.youtube.com/watch?v=OnswK-vfOSA

'Berlin unter den Alliierten (1945–1949)' Ganzer Film in HD (15 June 2017) YouTube video, added by Berlin Channel [online]. Available at https://www.youtube.com/watch?v=KS_Vw5DMlEI

'Biology's Second Law – The Weismann Barrier, the Barrier that Wasn't' (9 April 2012) YouTube video, added by ESFTV [online]. Available at https://www.youtube.com/watch?v=dlcg8QuKSDk

'Confronting Histories of Violence and Populism – Roundtable Discussion' (7 May 2021) YouTube video, added by GoetheUK [online]. Available at https://www.youtube.com/watch?v=eLbgL1KpUwo

"Death Mills" US Government "Denazification" film, 1946 (23 July 2018) YouTube video, added by Hardcore History [online]. Available on https://www.youtube.com/watch?v=sv4MXdFKfi4

'Deutschland Stunde Null' (20 November 2016) YouTube video, added by François NEIS [online]. Available at https://www.youtube.com/watch?v=Aux3Rgis8u4

'Germany After WW2 | A Defeated People | Documentary on Germany in the Immediate Aftermath of WW2' (24 July 2014) YouTube video, added by The Best Film Archives [online]. Available at https://www.youtube.com/watch?v=tpTZ4531XS0

'General Vlasov and the massacre of Russian Army in WWII' (1 June 2011) YouTube video, added by DocsOnline [online]. Available on https://www.youtube.com/watch?v=R0Wn HEMOzk4

'Germany 1945: Sensationally restored film footage by George Stevens' (6 May 2020) YouTube video, added by CHRONOS-MEDIA History [online]. Available on https://www.youtube.com/watch?v=Hwy8SzVmWGc

'James E. Young – The Stages of Memory: Reflections on Memorialisation and Global Commemoration' (23 September 2020) YouTube video, added by British Association for Holocaust Studies [online]. Available at https://www.youtube.com/watch?v=6VEbNkt_DTs

'Our Trauma as Heritage'. Thomas Hübl & Prof. Isabelle Mansuy (9 September 2017) YouTube video, added by The Pocket

Project [online]. Available at https://www.youtube.com/watch?v=kJHkNwRnt1M

'Sönke Neitzel: What are soldiers fighting for? The German case from Kaiserreich to Berlin Republic' (25 February 2021) YouTube video, added by history hub [online]. Available on https://www.youtube.com/watch?v=phhmXyrRQb8

'Sönke Neitzel: Mindset of WWII German Soldiers' (13 November 2012) YouTube video, added by The Agenda with Steve Paikin [online]. Available on https://www.youtube.com/watch?v=4eIn0IBsnBE

'Stalingrad – The Unconquerable (1942)' (13 April 2014) YouTube video, added by British Pathé [online]. Available at https://www.youtube.com/watch?v=IOFQvk6muvw

'Top Signs of Inherited Family Trauma & How to Break Free! | MARK WOLYNN | It Didn't Start with You' (17 October 2016), YouTube video, added by Michael Sandler's Inspire Nation [online]. Available at https://www.youtube.com/watch?v=50otm7C1UFA

'Why Did the German Army Fight to the End? (?), added by Center for Strategic & International Studies [Online]. Available at https://www.youtube.com/watch?v=UI72BLrwqR0

'World War II In Colour: Episodes 1–13' (23 September 2018) YouTube video, added by World at War [online]. Available at https://www.youtube.com/watch?v=LC6_NNjZENU

'Your Job in Germany, 1945' (5 March 2014) YouTube video, added by US National Archives [online]. Available on https://www.youtube.com/watch?v=821R0lGUL6A

TED Talks

Brown, Brené, Listening to shame, March 2012 https://www.ted.com/talks/brene_brown_listening_to_shame?language=en

Brown, Brené, The power of vulnerability, June 2010 https://www.ted.com/talks/brene_brown_the_power_of_vulnerability?language=en

Szyf, Moshe, 'How early life experience is written into DNA', July 2016. https://www.ted.com/talks/moshe_szyf_how_early_life_ experience_is_written_into_dna?utm_source=newsletter_ weekly_2017-04-01&utm_campaign=newsletter_weekly&utm_ medium=email&utm_content=top_right_image#t-249655

TV and Online Documentaries

Apocalypse: The Second World War, Episodes 1–6, 2009. https:// www.imdb.com/title/tt1508238/

Berlin 1945 Episodes 1–3 (November 2020) BBC Four https://www. bbc.co.uk/programmes/m000p9tc

Berlin – Schicksalsjahre einer Stadt (2018–2021) https://www. rbb-online.de/berlin-schicksalsjahre/themen/berlin--- schicksalsjahre-einer-stadt.html

Children Saved from the Nazis: The Story of Sir Nicholas Winton (February 2016) BBC One https://www.bbc.co.uk/programmes/ b06z95s1

The Dark Side of British History You Weren't Taught in School, George Monbiot, 13 June 2020. https://www.doubledown.news/ watch/2020/13/june/the-dark-side-of-british-history-you- werent-taught-in-school-george-monbiot

Deutschland 83 (2015) Deutschland 86 (2018) Deutschland 89 (2018) [TV series] https://www.channel4.com/programmes/ deutschland-83

Die Wehrmacht – Eine Bilanz. 2007. [TV series. Documentary]

Generation War: Our Mothers, Our Fathers. 2013. [TV series] written by Stefan Kolditz

Hitler's Children (23 May 2012) BBC Two https://www.bbc.co.uk/ iplayer/episode/b01j10j3/hitlers-children

Hitler's Hidden Drug Habit [documentary], 19 October 2014 https:// www.imdb.com/title/tt4130388/

Hitler: The Rise and Fall (2016) History Channel https://www. amazon.co.uk/Hitler-Rise-Fall-1/dp/B01LY0VNG5

I Was There: The Great War Interviews Episodes 1–13 (1960s) BBC Two https://www.bbc.co.uk/iplayer/group/p01tbj6p

Lost Home Movies of Nazi Germany, Series 1 (December 2019) BBC Four https://www.bbc.co.uk/programmes/m000crdh

My Family, the Holocaust and Me (November 2020) BBC One https://www.bbc.co.uk/programmes/m000pbwk

My Father was a Nazi Commandant (19 September 2012) BBC Four https://www.bbc.co.uk/programmes/b013ffkx

Nazis: A Warning from History (September 1997, 1998, 2000) BBC Two https://www.bbc.co.uk/programmes/b01kkxvd/episodes/guide

Return to Belsen with Jonathan Dimbleby (November 2020) ITV1 https://holocausteducation.org.uk/return-belsen-jonathan-dimbleby/

Spying on Hitler's Army: The Secret Recordings (May 2013) Channel 4 https://www.channel4.com/press/news/spying-hitlers-army-secret-recordings

Storyville: My Nazi Legacy (27 December 2016) BBC Four https://www.bbc.co.uk/programmes/b075f0n4

The Girl Who Forgave the Nazis [documentary], 2016 https://www.imdb.com/title/tt8270656/

The Last Survivors (27 January 2021) BBC Two https://www.bbc.co.uk/programmes/b0c1ngrx

The Same Sky, October 2020 https://www.channel4.com/programmes/the-same-sky

Unsere wunderbaren Jahren. 2020. [TV mini-series]

The Wisdom of Trauma (2021) Zaya Benazzo and Maurizio Benazzo (& Caroline Campbell), director. https://thewisdomoftrauma.com

World on Fire. 2019. [TV series]. Peter Bowker, creator

Radio

As Others See Us, Poland, Neil MacGregor, 6 September 2019, BBC Radio 4 https://www.bbc.co.uk/programmes/m0008432

Crossing Continents – Russia: Digging up the Dead, January 2014, BBC Radio 4 https://www.bbc.co.uk/programmes/b03nt864

Four Thought: How to Remember – Sam Edwards, 6 November 2013, BBC Radio 4 http://www.bbc.co.uk/programmes/b03gg7nk

Germany: Memories of a Nation, Neil Macgregor, 2014, BBC Radio 4 https://www.bbc.co.uk/programmes/b04dwbwz

Grossman's War, December 2019, BBC Radio 4 https://www.bbc.co.uk/programmes/m000btvz/episodes/player

Guilty Architecture, 26 April 2018, BBC Radio 4 https://www.bbc.co.uk/programmes/b0b01rvh

Moral Maze: 6 November 2013, BBC Radio 4 https://www.bbc.co.uk/programmes/b03gg7nh

Nuremberg: The Trial of the Nazi War Criminals Episodes 1–16, August 2021, BBC Radio 4 https://www.bbc.co.uk/sounds/brand/p09sgpfw

Race and our Public Space, 8 July 2020, BBC Radio 4 https://www.bbc.co.uk/programmes/m000kvmd

The Reith Lectures: Margaret MacMillan – The Mark of Cain, 2020, BBC Radio 4 https://www.bbc.co.uk/programmes/b0b8d340/episodes/player

This Thing of Darkness, 2020, BBC Radio 4 https://www.bbc.co.uk/sounds/play/brand:m000fpnb/p083nt4p

Tunnel 29, November 2019, BBC Radio 4 https://www.bbc.co.uk/programmes/m000b0rr

Unspeakable: History is another family member – Alice Musabende, 4 August 2021, BBC Radio 4 https://www.bbc.co.uk/programmes/m000ydls

Podcasts

Germany: Justice and Memory (12 January 2020) BBC The Documentary Podcast https://www.bbc.co.uk/programmes/p07zy24g

Germany's World War Two, Professor Nicholas Stargardt (18 July 2017) History Extra podcast https://play.acast.com/s/historyextra/germany-sworldwartwo

gestern ist jetzt – Der Podcast für Familiengeschichte im Nazionalsocialismus http://gesternistjetzt.de

How to heal inherited family trauma and not pass it on, with Mark Wolynn (14 November 2019) The Motherkind Podcast https://podcasts.apple.com/gb/podcast/how-to-heal-inherited-family-trauma-not-pass-it-on/id1295306961?i=1000456802834

Intrigue: The Ratline (December 2019) BBC Podcast https://www.bbc.co.uk/programmes/m0000phy

Legacies of the Holocaust, Interview with Mary Fulbook and Richard J. Evans (24 January 2019) History Extra podcast https://www.historyextra.com/period/second-world-war/mary-fulbrook-wolfson-prize-holocaust-trial-nazi-germany-hitler-crimes/

Living with the past: the Second World War (2 March 2019) Monocle 24: The Foreign Desk https://monocle.com/radio/shows/the-foreign-desk/269/

On Being with Krista Tippett, 'Rachel Yehuda: How Trauma and Resilience Cross Generations', 30 July 2015. https://onbeing.org/programs/rachel-yehuda-how-trauma-and-resilience-cross-generations-nov2017/

Poland, 1939: World War Two begins (5 September 2019) History Extra podcast https://podcasts.apple.com/gb/podcast/history-extra-podcast/id256580326?i=1000448688780

Rethink: Tom Rivett-Carnac – Re-thinking History (30 June 2020) BBC Podcast https://www.bbc.co.uk/programmes/p08jd8vv

Should I stay or I should go? The problem with historical monuments in 2020 (10 October 2020) History Extra podcast https://play.acast.com/s/historyextra/shouldistayorishouldgo-theproblemwith historicalmonumentsin2020

To Berlin and Beyond, Episodes 1–7 (2020) https://75jahrekrieg sende.berlin/en/podcast/#

War: What is it good for? (19 November 2021) Monocle 24: The Foreign Desk https://omny.fm/shows/monocle-24-the-foreign-desk-2/war-what-is-it-good-for-1

Films

A Defeated People. 1946. [Film]. Humphrey Jennings. dir.

A Hidden Life. 2020. [Film]. Terrence Malick. dir.

All Quiet on the Western Front. 1930. [Film]. Lewis Milestone. dir.

Anthropoid. 2016. [Film]. Sean Ellis. dir.

Before the Fall (Napola – Elite für den Führer). 2004. [Film]. Dennis Gansel. dir.

Beyond the Wall (Jenseits der Mauer). 2009. [Film]. Friedemann Fromm. dir.

Bornholmer Straße. 2014. [Film] Christian Schwochow. dir.

Cold War (Zimna wojna). 2018. [Film]. Pawel Pawlikowski. dir.

Das Boot. 1981. [Film]. Wolfgang Petersen. dir.

Doctor Faustus. 1982. [Film]. Franz Seitz. dir.

Dunkirk. 2017. [Film]. Christopher Nolan. dir.

Enemies (Feinde). 1940. [Film]. Victor Tourjansky. dir.

Escape from Warsaw (Lauf Junge Lauf). 2013. [Film] Pepe Danquart. dir.

Final Account. 2021. [Film]. Luke Holland. dir.

Flucht und Vertreibung. 2005. [Film]. Eva Berthold und Jost von Mor. dir.

Frantz. 2016. [Film]. François Ozon. dir.

Germany Year Zero (Germania anno zero). 1948. [Film]. Roberto Rossellini. dir.

Homecoming (Heimkehr). 1941. [Film] Gustav Ucicky. dir.

Ivan's Childhood. 1962. [Film] Andrei Tarkovsky. dir.

JoJo Rabbit. 2019. [Film]. Taika Waititi. dir.

Lou Andreas-Salomé, The Audacity To Be Free. 2016. [Film]. Cordula Kablitz-Post. dir.

March of Millions (Die Flucht). 2007. [Film]. Kai Wessel. dir.

Mephisto. 1981. [Film]. István Szabó. dir.

Mr Jones. 2019. [Film]. Agnieszka Holland. dir.

Murderers Among Us (Die Mörder sind unter uns). 1946. [Film]. Wolfgang Staudte. dir.

Never Look Away (Werk ohne Autor). 2018. [Film]. Florian Henckel von Donnersmarck. dir.

Night will Fall. 2014. [Documentary Film]. Andre Singer. dir.

Phoenix. 2014. [Film]. Christian Petzoid. dir.

Resistance. 2020. [Film]. Jonathan Jakubowicz. dir.

Saviours in the night (Unter Bauern). 2009. [Film]. Ludi Boeken. dir.

Somewhere in Berlin (Irgendwo in Berlin). 1946. [Film]. Gerhard
  Lamprecht. dir.

Son of Saul (Saul Fia). 2015. [Film]. László Nemes. dir.

The Aftermath. 2019. [Film]. James Kent. dir.

The Desert Fox: The Story of Rommel. 1951. [Film]. Henry
  Hathaway. dir. USA: 20th Century Fox

The Flat. 2011. [Film]. Arnon Goldfinger. dir.

The Baader Meinhof Complex (Der Baader Meinhof Komplex). 2008.
  [Film]. Uli Edel. dir.

The Nasty Girl (Das schreckliche Mädchen). 1990. [Film]. Michael
  Verhoeven. dir.

The White Ribbon (Das weiße Band). 2009. [Film]. Michael
  Haneke. dir.

The Reader. 2008. [Film]. Stephen Daldry. dir.

The Devil's General (Des Teufels General). 1955. [Film]. Helmut
  Käutner. dir.

The General Case (Die Akte General). 2016. [Film]. Stephan
  Wagner. dir.

The Lives of Others (Das Leben der Anderen). 2006. [Film]. Florian
  Henckel von Donnersmarck. dir.

The Last Days. 1998. [Documentary]. James Moll. dir.

The People vs. Fritz Bauer (Der Staat gegen Fritz Bauer). 2015.
  [Film] Lars Kraume. dir.

The Unknown Soldier (Der unbekannte Soldat). 2006 [Documentary].
  Michael Verhoeven. dir.

The Windemere Children. 2020. [Film]. Michael Samuels. dir.

Transit. 2018. [Film]. Christian Petzold. dir.

Triumph of the Will (Triumph des Willens). 1935. [Film]. Leni
  Riefenstahl. dir.

What Our Fathers Did: A Nazi Legacy. 2015. [Documentary] David
  Evans. dir.

Winterkinder: Die Schweigende Generation. 2005. [Documentary
  Film]. Jens Schanze. dir.

1917. 2019. [Film]. Sam Mendes. dir.

1945. 2017. [Film]. Ferenc Török. dir.

Live or Online Lectures and Conferences

I was grateful to have attended (and in some cases contributed to) the following lectures, conferences and courses, and would like to acknowledge their contributors.

'A Bystander Society? Passivity and Complicity in Nazi Germany', Professor Mary Fulbrook, UCL, Pears Institute for the Study of Antisemitism in collaboration with the Institute of Historical Research, 18 February 2020

Advanced Master Program on the Treatment of Trauma, The National Institute for the Clinical Application of Behavioural Medicine, 2 November 2020. https://www.nicabm.com

'Children of the Third Reich – Moral debate with Horst von Wächter, Niklas Frank and Philippe Sands', Southbank, London, 13 February 2014

Collective Trauma Summit 2020: The Power of Collective Healing, October 2020 https://collectivetraumasummit.com

'*Deutscher Traum und deutsches Trauma*', Hamburg, 29 September – 3 October 2011

Intergenerational Trauma Conference, 19–20 January 2021 https:// inheritedtrauma.org

'My Nazi Legacy – in conversation with Philippe Sands', Institute of Group Analysis, London NW3 5BY, 28 October 2016.

National Army Museum online lectures https://www.nam.ac.uk

'Those Who Forget: A conversation with Géraldine Schwarz and Philippe Sands', Goethe Institut, 29 September 2020. https:// www.artrabbit.com/events/discussion-those-who-forget-a-conversation-with-géraldine-schwarz

Transgenerational Trauma Conference: Recognising and transforming legacies of pain, 7–8 October 2021 https://catalog. pesi.co.uk/sales/uk_s_001504_transgenerationaltrauma_therapy-organic-233992

Working with stories of lived experience, The Forgiveness Project, February/March 2021 https://www.theforgivenesspro ject.com

Useful Websites

Axis History Forum: https://forum.axishistory.com

Forum Kriegsenkel: http://www.forumkriegsenkel.de

Historical War Militaria Forum: http://www.
 historicalwarmilitariaforum.com

Kriegsenkel e.V.: http://www.kriegsenkel.de/

Militaria Forums: Wehrmacht-Awards.com

Stiftung Denkal für die ermordeten Juden Europas: https://www.
 stiftung-denkmal.de

The Dresden Trust: https://dresdentrust.org

The Forgiveness Project: https://www.theforgivenessproject.com

Picture Acknowledgements

Nearly all the photographs in this book are from the author's personal collection or family albums. The publisher would like to thank IG Modell & Dioramenbau i.d. Bundeswehr for their kind permission to reproduce the image of the swimming pool at Delmenhorst-Adelheide POW camp. While every effort has been made to trace the owners of copyright material reproduced herein, the publishers would like to apologize for any omissions and will be pleased to incorporate missing acknowledgements at the earliest opportunity.

Index

10 pg TK

Index

434

Index

Index

Index

Index